D1266933

D1266933

FARRAR
STRAUS
GIROUX

GLORY IN A LINE

GLORY IN A LINE

A LIFE OF FOUJITA—THE ARTIST

CAUGHT BETWEEN EAST & WEST

PHYLLIS BIRNBAUM

FABER AND FABER, INC.

AN AFFILIATE OF FARRAR, STRAUS AND GIROUX

NEW YORK

Faber and Faber, Inc.
An affiliate of Farrar, Straus and Giroux
19 Union Square West, New York 10003

Copyright © 2006 by Phyllis Birnbaum
All rights reserved
Distributed in Canada by Douglas & McIntyre Ltd.
Printed in the United States of America
First edition, 2006

Grateful acknowledgment is made for permission to reprint the following previously published material: Translations of "J'ai tant rêvé de toi," "Fortunes," and "No Pasaran" are from *Robert Desnos, Surrealism, and the Marvelous in Everyday Life* by Katharine Conley, by permission of the University of Nebraska Press, copyright © 2003 by the Board of Regents of the University of Nebraska. These translations, and other translations from the works of Robert Desnos, are based on the original French versions found in his *Oeuvres*, ed. Marie-Claire Dumas, copyright © 1999, by permission of Éditions Gallimard, Paris. Excerpt on page 160 copyright 1930 by Condé Nast Publications. All rights reserved. Originally published in *The New Yorker*. Reprinted by permission. Foujita's artwork copyright © 2004 by Artists Rights Society (ARS), New York / ADAGP, Paris. All rights reserved.

Library of Congress Cataloging-in-Publication Data
Birnbaum, Phyllis.
    Glory in a line : a life of Foujita : the artist caught between East and West / Phyllis Birnbaum.— 1st ed.
        p.   cm.
    Includes bibliographical references and index.
    ISBN-13: 978-0-571-21179-1 (hardcover : alk. paper)
    ISBN-10: 0-571-21179-8 (hardcover : alk. paper)
    1. Foujita, Tsugouharu, 1886–1968.   2. Painters—Japan—Biography.
3. Expatriate painters—France—Biography.   I. Title.

ND1059.F6B57 2006
759.952—dc22

                                                              2006007000

Designed by Jonathan D. Lippincott

www.fsgbooks.com

1   3   5   7   9   10   8   6   4   2

Frontispiece: Foujita in Paris, 1927. (Berenice Abbott/Commerce Graphics Ltd., Inc.)

3 4015 06926 5146

FOR ASHOK

CONTENTS

PREFACE

When we think of the famous expatriates in Paris during the early decades of the twentieth century, certain names immediately come to mind. We remember the American expatriate Hemingway, who strolled through the Jardin du Luxembourg in the evenings, frequented Harry's Bar, and wrote fiction in his Left Bank apartment. The Italian Modigliani must appear on this list of notables, since it was in Paris that he painted immortal works and drank too much. Picasso, a Spaniard, not only changed the course of modern art while he was in Paris, but also performed toreador dances in neighborhood cafés.

And then there was Foujita. This Japanese artist also became famous for his distinctive paintings, and his wild behavior ensured that his name was known throughout the city and beyond. While his artistic works stirred the French critics to rapture, patrons assured him of immense wealth.

In the years that followed, however, Foujita's reputation diminished as prolonged scuffles battered him and his legacy. In his heyday in the 1920s, he seemed to be destined for an enviable posthumous niche, but the arguments that started over his cooperation with the Japanese military regime during the Second World War did not stop even with his death in 1968. There was too much rancor on both sides, and decades had to pass before the ill feeling abated.

Nowadays, Foujita seems to be struggling to his feet again, with the help of researchers in various countries. In Japan, the interest is strongest, for the Japanese have not tired of reviewing Foujita's life story, seeking not only to gather information about this Japanese celebrity but also to gain insights into their own national character. What should be said about an artist who traveled extensively and was at his ease in many world capitals but who finally embraced a most parochial brand of chauvinism? And what should be said about a country that had also cheered on its military during the war but afterward could not accommodate the contradictions in that same man? In addition to the sometimes soul-searching Japanese works, there have been new studies of Foujita in France, Latin America, and the United States, ranging widely in their exploration of his achievements and psychology.

It is not difficult to understand the reasons behind this enthusiasm, and I, too, have got caught up in the search for an understanding of Foujita. While writing this biography, I not only visited museums, archives, and individuals who knew him in Paris, Tokyo, and New York City, I also tried to remain still and see him as he was. This has not been an easy task amidst the battles still being fought about his place in history. The biographical studies of Foujita are so sharply polarized that they often cannot be taken seriously. In fact, I have found some of his Japanese biographers frightening—sword-wielding assassins out to find the most wicked impulses behind his actions. Then there are the Japanese who are determined to drown out these others and cannot say a negative word about him. In France, the tone has been sweeter— perhaps because Foujita's ability to express himself in French was limited and so he was simply seen as a Japanese artist without nuances, reaching toward caricature, always effervescent and sociable, with endless silly costumes at the ready.

Such highly charged studies are now gradually giving way to more measured approaches, and with the emergence of new materials, Foujita has become more than just a particular researcher's devil or saint. For me, a collection of Foujita's letters, written from Japan just after the Second World War, has been crucial, enabling me to see him clearly for the first time. These letters, recently deposited in a Los Angeles museum, have only begun to attract attention among Foujita researchers. They were written in Tokyo after the war, when Foujita was desperate to escape from Japan and the fierce criticism of his wartime cooperation with the military. He wrote to the Japanese artist Henry Sugimoto in New York City of his anger at being judged unfairly, his patriotism as a Japanese, and his pride in his own achievements. As I read these letters, I could imagine Foujita seated cross-legged in his chair, writing furiously about his predicament. Unburdening himself, Foujita is bitter, kindhearted, angry, loyal, petty, deeply involved in his work—surely the same complicated person that he was in real life.

Apart from making my way through the partisan brawls about Foujita, I have had other new adventures, since writing a biography of a Japanese man is a departure for me. Until now, I have spent much time immersed in the lives of Japanese women, translating their works and writing their biographies. In these stories of women, Japanese men, while prominent, do not always play endearing roles. Actually, I have at times been moved to censure, implying, for example, that a certain Japanese husband was not extraordinarily considerate as his wife descended into madness. In general, I have rallied to the side of my heroines when their men proved feckless once again.

In order to write this biography of Foujita, I had to leave the women to their fates, abandon them when they were replaced by other, perhaps more elegant women, or died young, victims of their own bad luck or excesses. In the past, I would have lingered over such cases; I certainly would have taken up the cause of one woman in Foujita's life, who was pilloried as a shrew by many around her. Certainly, I would have spent time trying to figure out why she continually harangued her husband and everyone else. This time, I have had to push on in another direction and let such women forge ahead without my ministrations. I must say that as I reread this book, I found places where my transformation has been incomplete, since, from time to time, I can hear that former biographer of women trying to get a word in.

I have been greatly helped by the research of Sasaki Shigeo, who has collected an extensive compendium of documents by and about Foujita. In this meticulously compiled sheaf of papers, Foujita speaks for himself at various times of his life, in interviews or in his own journalistic essays, sharing his thoughts about both grave and trivial matters. As I have mentioned, the facts of Foujita's life have become garbled over the years, through his willful scrambling of the facts, as well as by biographical biases, and the natural distortion of information that has been transmitted between France and Japan. In sifting through these differing accounts and trying to fasten upon the truth, I have used Sasaki's documents as my standard and referred to them constantly.

And then there is Paris. In Paris, I definitely felt Foujita within my comprehension. I spent five months in Paris, in the heart of Montparnasse. While there, I puzzled over the complexity of the French libraries and walked everywhere, to track down Foujita's old hangouts and friends. Since I have spent so much time in Tokyo, Paris was a new and exotic place for me. "Ah, so this is the Western world!" I often exclaimed to myself as I took in the sights. Sometimes I found myself taken aback by French customs that were so very different from what I was used to in Japan. At such moments, I remembered Foujita, who must have also been discomfited at first. But I understood my subject best when I experienced a newcomer's pleasure at Paris's beauty, so far from the clamor and clutter of Tokyo.

Foujita, too—I told myself—must have felt this same enchantment.

P.B.

A Note on the Text

Japanese names are generally given in Japanese order, the family name followed by the given name. I usually refer to Japanese by their family names, and so Kawashima Riichirō is referred to as Kawashima.

A few of the Japanese mentioned are better known by their artistic names, and in those cases I refer to them by those names. For example, Mori Ōgai is referred to as Ōgai, though his family name is Mori.

For Japanese-Americans, or those Japanese who regularly use Western order for their names, I use Western word order—given name first, followed by family name.

To complicate matters even further, Foujita used different names for himself over the course of his life. In Japan, he started out as Fujita Tsuguharu (with his family name first). This remains one of his "official" names. When he moved to France, he sought a name less daunting to Westerners and eventually settled on "Foujita." At other times in his life, he called himself Fujita Tsuguji or Léonard Foujita, among other names. I have referred to him by the name he is usually known by in the west—Foujita—but other versions of his name turn up in the text, in quotations from the Japanese.

Japanese can count their ages using a system different from the one used in the West—a child is one on the date of birth and two the following New Year's Day—but sometimes they use the Western system. Frequently it is hard to determine whether the Japanese count or the Western count is being used. For this reason, I have left the ages as cited in the original documents.

All translations are my own, unless otherwise indicated.

GLORY IN A LINE

ONE

DETWEEN EAST AND WEST

*I love Tokyo very much, but being a foreigner in Paris provides me
with the distance I require to understand myself.*

—*Foujita*

I t seems best to think of Foujita in Paris. After all, he first attracted attention on the Left Bank, winning applause for his drawings of cats
and for the startling whiteness of his nudes. At Parisian cafés during
the 1920s, Foujita became a fixture, with his trademark bangs, round
glasses, and hoop earrings; late into the night, he could be found chat-
ting with cronies at the tables of his favorite haunts. He took pleasure
in dressing up for his appearances around Paris's Montparnasse district
and sported a slave trader's loincloth at a costume ball, but he also
went through a Neo-Grecian period. Decked out in a Greek tunic and
sandals, Foujita joined a group dancing in the woods.

Foujita liked to say that he knew everyone worth knowing in 1920s
Paris. Picasso was one of his acquaintances; Diego Rivera painted him
in his Greek outfit; his memoirs tell of the time when he lived just a
floor above Modigliani, whose untidiness was apparently monumental.
More important to his career was his friendship with the voluptuous
Kiki, the celebrated Montparnasse personality. Known as the "Queen
of Montparnasse," Kiki was the nude in a painting that brought Foujita
acclaim. The relationship between Foujita, a Japanese artist brought
up in a military family in Tokyo, and this bawdy, full-breasted woman

from Burgundy has been the source of speculation. Until he died, he felt obliged to insist to one and all that they had been only the best of friends. Foujita recalled that when Kiki arrived at his studio, "she came in slowly and timidly, her cute little finger held up to her small red mouth, swinging her behind confidently." And since this was, after all, Paris in the Roaring Twenties, he went on to concede that she was naked beneath her coat—"a small handkerchief, in lively colors, pinned to the inside of her coat gave the illusion of her latest dress."

Around 1922, when Kiki turned up in her coat, Foujita had been an expatriate in Paris for nine years. He had left Tokyo with few prospects for success, but vowed to make his mark in France. In this he was like the many artists from all over the world who flocked to Paris during that time, but Foujita stood out from the others in his exuberance, his discipline, and his expertise with a delicate Japanese paintbrush. Early in his career, Foujita established an artistic reputation when his paintings of Parisian landscapes and vivacious cats were exhibited in galleries around town. Still, Foujita was shrewd enough to recognize that cat paws, which he could draw in remarkable detail, would not get him the world-class fame he so eagerly sought. It was perhaps with this in mind that he followed the example of the masters in the Louvre whose works he studied for hours on end: Foujita also put effort into painting nude women.

Kiki proved crucial to this endeavor, but Foujita admitted that he had certain difficulties with her at first. Not the kind of model who meekly settled down, she required expert handling, and Foujita was not immediately up to the job:

> She took my place in front of the easel, told me not to move, and calmly began to draw my portrait. When the work was finished, she had sucked and bitten all my pencils and lost my small eraser, and delighted, danced, sung, and yelled, and walked all over a box of Camembert. She demanded money from me for posing and left triumphantly, carrying her drawing with her. Three minutes later at the Café du Dôme, a rich American collector bought this drawing for an outrageous price. That day I wasn't sure which of the two of us was the painter.

We can assume that Foujita gained control of the situation, for the next day Kiki returned to his studio in a more docile state of mind. He had her pose nude on a couch covered with white fabric, where she reclined in grand languor, her hand at her head. In Foujita's painting, Kiki has the look of a woman accustomed to disrobing, and we know from available evidence that the expression came naturally to her. Foujita portrayed her showing off a fleshy, lovely body without the slightest qualm. He entered this work in the Salon d'Automne and was elated by the reaction. "In the morning, all the newspapers talked about it. At noon the Minister congratulated me. In the evening, for the sum of 8,000 francs, it was sold to a famous collector. The buyer for the State arrived too late. It was an immense success." Kiki would not, of course, permit him to forget her role in this triumph. "Kiki and I were each equally pleased; for the second time I wasn't sure who was the artist."

Since others had no doubt about who was responsible for this and other creations, Foujita became the darling of the French art world. That was a big change of fortune for an artist who had, just a few years before, sold his clothing to pay for meals. The French critics were ecstatic about Foujita's originality and his combination of Eastern and Western traditions. They were impressed by Foujita's restrained use of color: in those days artists usually brought countless hues to their paintings, but Foujita made his name on white. Foujita employed a special, spectacular white in his paintings, a white that seemed to give Kiki flesh of ivory. At the Salon d'Automne, crowds jockeyed for space in front of Foujita's works to take in their magical emanations, while artists tried to determine the ingredients that had gone into producing such effects. For this reason, Foujita guarded his recipe for the white color, keeping competitors out of his studio where they might steal his secrets.

Not only did his white bring a splendid shimmer to Kiki's skin, that same white also allowed Foujita to introduce Japanese elements into his creation. His white oil paint had been concocted so that he could draw upon it with what looked like *sumi*, the ink the Japanese used in ink paintings and calligraphy. This may not seem like an earthshaking achievement, but for Foujita, the look of black sumi on white made all the difference. In his version of sumi, he could outline Kiki's body with a thin line of amazing flexibility and grace. The line seemed to flow with impossible fluidity as it followed her legs, her hips, her whole torso. Foujita's lines, which harked back to traditional art forms, gave his oil paintings just the Japanese touch that he sought. Though many contemporaries tried to imitate Foujita—"That's a line which never stops," according to one admirer—none ever succeeded.

The Japanese elements introduced into his Western-style oil painting served Foujita well, since things Japanese were still venerated in France during that period. Decades before, the Impressionist Monet had painted his wife in a gaudy Japanese kimono; Toulouse-Lautrec tried out the techniques he had learned from Japanese woodblock-print artists like Hokusai and Hiroshige; van Gogh, another enthusiast, went one step further in creating oil paintings that closely resembled actual Japanese works. In this atmosphere of lingering *japonisme*, where Japanese fans, leaping carp, and vases also had a place, Foujita—in residence on rue Delambre, Paris, but lately of Tokyo—reminded the art world of his origins.

Foujita wrote later that he had trained himself over long years to create his paintings of nudes: "I suddenly realized one day that there are very few paintings of nudes in Japan. In the paintings of Harunobu or Utamaro, there are merely glimpses of part of an arm or a small area around the knee. I realized that they conveyed the sensation of skin only in those places. For the first time I decided to try to represent that most beautiful of materials: human skin. It had been eight years since I had drawn nudes, but I really attained exceptional success."

The French were captivated by Foujita's descriptions of artistic struggle, and critics clamored for the superlatives to describe this Japanese artist's achievements. He went on to paint more nudes and cats and still lifes, showing off the white color and the faultless line in many variations. "In the art of Foujita there is a little bit of the magician's art and even the illusionist's," rhapsodized the French critic André Warnod. "His paintings bloom like the Japanese paper flowers children love." Back home in Japan, Foujita's colleagues were less inclined to go in for such expressions of rapture. On the contrary, some of Foujita's countrymen saw his success as a sham. These Japanese believed that he had too keen an eye for the marketplace and too little respect for the purity of his calling. They said that in his oil paintings, Foujita was offering the French a warmed-over version of the kind of art available in Japan for centuries. "His work seemed very Japanese to the Japanese," the art historian Hayashi Yōko has written. "Many Japanese artists, indignant, couldn't figure out what this work was all about. They thought that they could do better."

Despite these dissenting voices, Foujita achieved great fame with his paintings of cats and female nudes, which became the rage of Europe. As the years went by, he continued to develop his talents for art and controversy and flamboyance. In 1927, he moved into a house in an elegant part of Paris, on a narrow cobblestone street. He made so much money that he bought a fancy car and stuck a small Rodin bust on the hood. A Basque chauffeur (who was also a jai alai champion) wore a cap and uniform as he drove Foujita and his third wife, Youki, around town. Exulting in his notoriety, Foujita tattooed a watch on his wrist and led the line of cancan dancers at the Ubu Ball. He was a publicity hound from the outset, and there were accusations that Foujita had purposely risked his life in a bicycle accident just to get his name in the papers. He became so well-known in Paris that a mannequin of his likeness (complete with bangs, hoop earrings, and round eyeglasses) was used to sell clothes in department store windows. Since Foujita personified Japan for Europeans then, Japanese tourists in Paris were often stopped on the streets and asked if they knew him.

Although some of his Japanese contemporaries considered Foujita's antics an embarrassment, a backward look makes it seem churlish to deny him these pleasures. After all, only he, among the Japanese artists who went to Paris in the early part of the twentieth century, achieved such immense success among Westerners. Along the way, Foujita conquered the language problems and the diffidence that afflicted many of his compatriots. He was the sole Japanese artist to be considered part of the international group known as the School of Paris (École de Paris), which, in addition to Modigliani and Chagall, included other important figures in twentieth-century art.

No less remarkably, Foujita avoided succumbing to the illnesses, the loneliness, and the despair that ruined many other Japanese artists in Paris. Most of these others had, sooner or later, seen the impossibility of establishing reputations in the world of Western art. When Foujita was starting out, Europeans believed that Japanese artists were best suited to creating woodblock prints of old Tokyo (preferably with Mount Fuji and cherry blossoms in the background) or screens decorated with wading cranes. French critics scoffed at the notion that any Japanese could possibly master the Western techniques of oil painting. "This was considered as bizarre as a Frenchman taking up sumo wrestling or opening a sushi shop," Hayashi likes to say. Daunted by the scorn, many Japanese artists packed up their canvases and headed back home. Foujita, in contrast to other Japanese who set up their easels in studios near the Seine, remained abroad for much of his life, making friends with the likes of the Lithuanian artist Chaim Soutine and the American Alexander Calder.

There are many wonderful photographs that tell the story of Foujita's flair and brazenness. In a playful mood, he grinned for the camera by the beach at Deauville as he cruised down the boardwalk on a child's bicycle. Again, hugging music hall star Mistinguett, he sat beneath an orange tree in a loud outfit he had sewn himself. Another photo, taken at the height of his fame, had him standing in the sitting room of his luxurious Paris house. On this occasion, he was dressed in a long woven jacket and seemed very much the lord of costly furnishings.

But Foujita's exultation did not last forever, and other, later photographs recorded grim times. His talents and ambitions brought him bitterness at the end. By 1953, he had traveled throughout the world on numerous occasions and exhibited in many capitals. He had lived in Paris for years, then gone home to Tokyo for a sojourn, then back to Paris, and so on. He had also been through scathing experiences, especially in Japan. During the Second World War, he had painted many works for the Japanese militarist government, and after the war, a number of Japanese reviled him for his contributions to the war effort. This time, the French art critics did not rise in his defense. Eventually, Foujita left Japan and never returned.

Some 1953 photographs caught him back in Paris, the last stop in his wanderings. Despite the bad times, his fame had not deserted him, and his paintings still commanded high prices. By then, he had married again, this time a Japanese woman named Kimiyo, who became his fifth wife. They had tried to settle down in a new apartment, but Japan was very much on Foujita's mind. He and his wife scoured Paris for Japanese foodstuffs, which were not easy to find. He kissed her in joy when he obtained azuki beans, to make *oshiruko*, a sweet soup.

The photographs taken for the Japanese magazine *Mizue* showed Foujita at sixty-six, in his crammed Paris studio with his paintbrush in hand, about to draw one of the lines that his rivals could never duplicate. Even in Paris he was unable to escape from gossip about him in Japan, and he responded to reports of his having turned away Japanese visitors:

I have never driven a guest away. But even so, all sorts of things are being said about me. I don't let it worry me. The more I help people, the more they criticize me. When people who work for me say such things, that's one thing, but when ugly rumors about me are spread by people I've taught to paint, it makes you think a little . . . As for my work, these days it has become more detailed. That's because I am trying to turn the problem of my nearsightedness into a special feature of my painting . . . The other day, when I met Matisse, he said to me, "It's wonderful that you can draw such a fine line." And I told him, "I'm young, so I can do it. When I grow old like you, I will draw a different kind of line." Speaking of getting old, I've come to believe that you can't do good work until you grow old.

TWO

A TOKYO INTERLUDE

Modernity starts in Paris.
—Takamura Kōtarō

I n the West, he is known as "Foujita," but the Japanese generally use the un-Frenchified versions of his name, Fujita Tsuguharu or Fujita Tsuguji. Whatever you call him, his life story will always be a riddle. Both his friends and enemies have worked hard at interpreting the facts to their own liking, and many documents have not yet been released to the public. In addition, Foujita himself had a way of analyzing events that did not always square with reality. He wrote letters (in Japanese, French, and English) by the dozen to his vast circle of friends and business associates—writing as he must have talked, with gusto, switching subjects mid-sentence, then going back, reaching out to correspondents in moments of solitude, which he found difficult to tolerate. His letters vociferously defended his view of major and minor controversies.

In addition, Foujita's Japanese widow, Kimiyo—his fifth wife—has been aggressive in protecting his name from those she believes are out to damage his reputation or exhibit paintings she considers fakes. In the latter part of his life, Foujita repeatedly complained, as he did to the *Mizue* magazine reporter mentioned in the last chapter, of being abandoned by Japanese colleagues and by those he had once gone out of his way to help. Foujita's widow has not forgotten her husband's anguish, and to prevent further, posthumous abuse, she has stood in the way of many exhibits and publications since his death in 1968. I once remarked to a Japanese artist that Foujita, who so loved publicity about himself, would have been chagrined by this limited access to his works. In an unexpected outburst, the artist replied that Foujita deserved this "punishment" for his behavior during the Second World War.

Despite these obstacles, Foujita's life story has become increasingly better known, both in Japan and elsewhere, which attests to the tenacity of the legend. Now, almost forty years after his death, there are many signs that Foujita is back in the spotlight—where he always liked to be. Foujita's work has been shown in Japan and abroad more frequently, and as proof of loosening constraints, new catalogues of his paintings have recently been published. In 2001, a museum show in Montparnasse centered on the love triangle of Foujita, his then wife Youki, and the Surrealist poet Robert Desnos, with photographs and paintings tracing the course of this *"amour surréaliste."* Other exhibitions have followed, including a major retrospective in 2006.

While in Tokyo, I spent an evening with some Foujita enthusiasts who were trying, in various ways, to flush out every single detail about him. Scholars, collectors, bibliophiles, artists, writers—we gathered at a basement gallery in Ginza. Our group, from Japan, France, and the United States, gave some idea of the international range of Foujita's following. On a warm fall evening after a particularly hot summer in Tokyo, we all had been summoned to look at a magazine put out by Foujita's class while he was attending an elite middle school in Tokyo. Some copies of this class magazine had just been purchased by the gallery. One issue contained an illustrated essay by Foujita, written in his own hand in 1902, when he was sixteen. Each student in the class had contributed samples of work to the magazine; these had been bound together to show the class's accomplishments that year. One student had contributed an essay in passable English, suggesting the high educational level of Foujita's classmates. Foujita, a budding teenage artist, had contributed a selection about his recent trip to Taiwan. He showed an interest in foreign landscapes even then, for his is the only student essay that came with illustrations of Taiwanese leaves and flowers. Thus he began a practice he continued throughout his life of mixing his prose with his sketches: in his adult years, Foujita's letters were often accompanied by clever illustrations.

It is admittedly stirring to hold in your hand the original piece of paper used by the person whose life you are in the process of re-creating. Each of us there that night hoped to gain some insights from Foujita's youthful writing and drawings. The most desperate among us tried to find similarities between his cramped, careful boyhood calligraphy and the casual handwriting of Foujita's later years. No one had the temerity to say that the primitive outlines on the leaves showed the beginnings of Foujita's characteristic mature line. Indeed, he may have had a pre-cocious gift for drawing tree bark, but there's nothing like being in a small Tokyo art gallery, staring at Taiwanese leaves drawn by a sixteen-year-old, to make you feel that you are far from the truth of things. So meager was the knowledge gained from this school exercise that I wondered about the route this essay collection had taken so that we could be reading it that evening. Had some Japanese clerk gone through thousands of middle school essay collections to find the one and only batch that included Foujita's plants? Or had the school anticipated the needs of future biographers and kept Foujita's class productions separately, knowing that a day would come when they would fetch a decent price?

As it turned out, a better way existed to evoke Foujita's presence, and this was close at hand. Unimpressed by Foujita's youthful artistic efforts, our group agreed to adjourn to another gallery nearby. Soon we all—Japanese, French, American—were shuffling down the street on that sultry Tokyo night to see an exhibition of works drawn entirely in pencil. These drawings, dense and ugly, seemed to express many bad dreams, and the artist, who greeted us there, did little to dispel the impression of a person who knew about difficult midnights. She leapt toward those of us who were not Japanese and, in muddled English and French, described her technique. Her language problems were not much noticed, since we had created our own linguistic hullabaloo, speaking together in French, Japanese, and English. Meanwhile, one of the Frenchmen saw that people were handing out business cards, as is the Japanese custom, and so he decided to make a few for himself. After he had set for himself the difficult task of creating a number of *meishi* (name cards) from pieces of sandpaper, he proudly handed them out to everyone.

When we went off to eat dinner, we were joined by the pencil artist's companion, an ebullient man who claimed to be part of the Japanese Mafia. By my side at dinner sat a Japanese researcher who had strong opinions about some disputed events in Foujita's life. While the sake flowed, the researcher and I discussed an obscure episode that involved Foujita's postwar troubles, a rainy night in Tokyo, a forgotten lunch box, and tuna sashimi. The details of this event are perhaps thrilling only to the initiated, but Sasaki-san and I exchanged views about that stormy evening in 1946 over our drinks and a kind of pumpkin pancake I had never eaten before.

Granted, our evening of banter and inebriation was no match for the gala occasions Foujita attended in his heyday. Still, our gathering showed what he faced in his own very active, very multicultural social life. From his early days in Paris, Foujita placed much importance on his public appearances, and he would have known, first of all, that great patience is required to figure out what exactly is going on among the various nationalities at such events. The evening also called for constant diplomacy ("He looks like a nervous wreck," a Japanese woman commented to me about one of the French guests. "She wants to know how old you are" is how I translated this for the Frenchman). Guests need a capacity for dusk-to-dawn activity and quick wits to catch the details in assorted languages. Apparently, Foujita fulfilled these requirements because histories of 1920s Paris provide many accounts of his prominent role in masquerades, excursions to Deauville, and nighttime revelry. Foujita himself did not touch alcohol, but that did not prevent him from outdoing the most intoxicated guests in his display of high spirits.

In the closing moments of our gathering, it seemed fitting to review the story of Foujita's changing fortunes. His biography makes us consider his nudes, cats, white color, and perfect line, which, in his best years, were odd, singular achievements. His creations also ask us to think about the peculiar situation facing a Japanese artist who worked in the Western medium of oil paint during those days. If the Japanese artist wanted to move away from geishas and Mount Fuji, what else was suitable subject matter? What limitations were placed on his choices? And then there is the issue of Foujita's participation in the social doings of his Western friends. His dogged party-going forces us to think about the psychology of a small, myopic Japanese artist jostling for a place in 1920s Paris. Foujita was resolute about driving himself to fit in, and inevitably, there is a sense that he tried too hard. To what lengths did a Japanese have to go to find acceptance in Paris in the 1920s, supposedly the most freewheeling and tolerant of locales? And what did those efforts have to do with the turnabout in Foujita's behavior during the Second World War?

I feel sure that Foujita would have joined our festivities that evening if he had been in the neighborhood. There are many stories about his kindness to colleagues, and he perhaps would have paused to give the pencil artist a few tips about her drawings. He probably would not have been fazed by the hubbub of half-understood conversations, and in all likelihood, a soirée where he understood every word might have been tedious.

I am convinced that Foujita would have joined us, but just as certainly he would have followed his usual custom of keeping himself fit for the next day's work. A friend who often went to Foujita's studio at nine in the morning wrote that by the time he got there, Foujita would have already finished his first painting of the day.

THREE

RESTLESS FROM THE START

What attracted me was not so much the art as the life of the artist, which I imagined to be full of fantasy and freedom to do as one pleased. Of course I had long been attracted to painting and drawing, but the passion was not irresistible, whereas I wanted at all cost to escape from a life of monotony.

—Pierre Bonnard

The childhood of an outstandingly productive and outstandingly rambunctious Japanese artist merits close scrutiny. It is tantalizing to consider the influences behind Foujita's ability to work very long hours and, in his spare time, to attend social events wearing curtain fabrics, lampshades, and loincloths. Unfortunately, the evidence does not fill in the whole tale and frequently leads to ambiguous conclusions. There is no doubt that Foujita was born in Tokyo in 1886, the last of four children, and spent some of his youth in the family home near a sharp bend in the Edo River. Foujita later speculated about the role of geography in the shaping of his character, wondering whether his years beside that divergence in the river's course accounted for his own divergence from convention. More likely, the river's greatest role in his life was teaching him about the flow of the fish during the rainy season: "After long days of rain, the water transported my small golden fish toward the impure torrent . . ." His family origins were illustrious, with well-placed domain officials enhancing the family tree. Later on, Foujita would refer to this privileged background when friends complained about a strain of passivity in his character—frequently, their exasperation focused on his dealings with women. Foujita claimed that he was not demonstrating weakness in these matters, but instead the "delicate sensibility" that he had inherited from his aristocratic forebears, maintaining that "not vulgarity, but elegance and tolerance in all is my ideal."

Because ancestral armor was plentiful in his household, the young Foujita set up the New Year's display of two heirloom suits of armor, marking an early relationship with Japanese at war. Because his relatives had military connections, the martial spirit continued up to Foujita's time. His father, Tsuguakira, was a high-ranking army doctor who stood out as a sometimes fearsome, sometimes benevolent figure. For a military family, Foujita's was more receptive to fresh ideas than most, and foreign travels by relatives brought in news of the outside world. There were members of the extended family who had pursued artistic careers, and Tsuguakira, well-versed in the Chinese classics and history, "was very knowledgeable about literature," according to his son. Still, the home does not appear to have been the kind of permissive establishment where poetic aspirations were nurtured. According to a grandson, Foujita's father took himself seriously and expected the deference due his military rank. Not a winning figure to some members of the family, the father could make his young relatives feel ignorant, dismissing them with such pronouncements as "A frog in a well knows nothing of the ocean."

Foujita's mother died when he was almost five years old, after which he was placed in the care of his older sister. Some speculate that Foujita never forgot the cold hand of his dead mother, which sent a permanent chill into his soul. Others theorize that he was greatly moved by the gentleness of his sisters and their friends after his mother's death, and that this inclined him to appreciate the company of women forever after. It is true that later on, a woman's presence mattered very much to Foujita. He eventually set up a life abroad independent of his family, but as his five wives and other entanglements prove, he could not abide life for long periods without a female companion. In his letters to his wife Youki (who was fond of extended vacations away from him), the world-famous artist Foujita whimpered like a child about his loneliness.

"I am very competitive, and there's a contrariness much concealed in my nature," he wrote in his Japanese memoir *Swimming upon the Earth*, going on to provide proof of this statement. When he was about four, a soldier asked him whether he was a boy or a girl. In response, Foujita displayed his private parts and explained: "I am not Japanese, but a foreign make." Even in his impudent display of his genitals, he showed that, in those days, imported goods of all kinds were considered the best quality. Endowing his four-year-old self with uncommon prescience, Foujita went on to write, "But since I have spent a good half of my life, twenty-five years, abroad, you can say I was right. I narrowly escaped becoming a genuine foreign product."

It is important to remember that Foujita's family was rather well-off. "You only have to look at his family and his education," his art school classmate, the cartoonist Okamoto Ippei, wrote, "to see that he was upper class." This meant that Foujita could indulge in all manner of reckless behavior, aware of being less vulnerable to certain risks. He was different from those Japanese artists from humbler circumstances who viewed starvation in a garret as a final and dreadful expression of their fate. "He was optimistic and seemed to have a streak of good luck," Okamoto continued. "He even approached adventures with the idea that he was going to come out on the winning side and would proceed without any hesitation . . . This was proof that he was a young man of privilege." In defending his friend on all fronts, Okamoto pointed out that Foujita's position as a son from a good family (*botchan*) did not get in the way of his drive to support himself when he was an adult. "As *botchan* go, he was a pretty restless kind of *botchan*."

The restlessness, hardly a defect in an artist with outsized ambitions, drove Foujita to disguise himself as a high-class prostitute for his schoolboy pranks and, in middle age, turned him into a relentless traveler who mounted exhibitions, with little advance notice, in Spain or Rio de Janeiro or San Francisco. Foujita later took to the road for reasons other than his art, sometimes hastily booking train and boat reservations to escape messy romances and once, after a major mishap, the French tax police.

Foujita, with characteristic self-confidence, claimed for himself a talent for painting from the age of four. But before he could fulfill this promise, he had to get certain practical issues settled. Foujita was thirteen when he decided to tell his father about his desire to become an artist. Communication between them was complicated: "For no real reason, my father was a frightful being to me during my childhood." Wary of a direct approach, the young Foujita wrote his father a letter about his ambitions: "I want to be an artist. Let me do something I like. I'll show you that I will definitely succeed." He put the letter in the post and mailed it to the Tokyo home where they both lived. Fortunately, when his father opened the letter, he took a positive view of his son's wishes and gave him fifty yen, an enormous sum for the time, to buy painting supplies. Foujita remembered that he didn't sleep that night, and that the next morning he went to an art shop in Kanda where he bought a real paintbox, a tripod, an easel, and oil paint containers. His first creation was an oil painting of a chicken and an egg, copied from a biscuit tin his brother-in-law had brought back from Germany.

The battle had not been won yet, because his older brother also had to be persuaded about these plans. The brother predicted that Foujita's extreme nearsightedness would prevent him from succeeding as an artist. Upon hearing this, Foujita promised that he would study massage, a traditional Japanese occupation for the blind, so that he could earn his living as a masseur and never be a financial burden to the family if his eyes got worse. "My brother consented grudgingly," Foujita wrote. "You can see that even at a young age, I was stubborn and didn't like to lose." Foujita started off using watercolors, since buying oil paints in quantity would have been too expensive. To achieve an oilier effect, he tried mixing various substances into his paints—cooking oil and Vaseline among them—which produced disastrous results. These were the precursors of various paint brews he would later create, to more impressive effect. He reported that his grades in mathematics were poor, but he excelled in any class that required drawing. By 1900, at age fourteen, he had made much progress, since his watercolor was selected as one of the paintings that represented Japanese middle school students at the World's Fair in Paris: "Having my painting exhibited in Paris was the beginning of everything."

Foujita's father later declared that he'd never objected in the slightest to his son's choice of career, saying, "It did not seem like a bad plan to me. My grandmother was related to Haruki Nanko and Haruki Nanmei, artists who painted in the Nanga style. I thought that my son might have inherited their talents." Still, there was a persistent hope that Foujita would, like his father, become a doctor. The father, seeing that his son was good with his hands, did not envision them wrapped around a paintbrush; instead, he suggested that the young Foujita use these talents as an eye specialist or a dentist. The absurdity of this notion was already apparent, since Foujita did not attempt to fool anyone about the likelihood of his becoming a stern medical professional.

Early on, he earned a reputation for provocative behavior among his classmates. An irrepressible exhibitionism had managed to take root and flower in that sober home. On sketching trips during art school, Foujita stood out at the parties by dressing up as a courtesan, his particular specialty. He used an inn's red quilt for a kimono, a piece of cloth for his chignon, and for footwear, traditional-style women's pillows, which rested on wooden boxes. During one trip, Foujita appeared before his classmates in red underwear and declared himself a female prisoner from the police station next door. His friends, invigorated after a banquet, got into the spirit of things by tying up his hands and parading him around town.

While in his teens, Foujita knew that he wanted to specialize in Western-style oil painting. He also knew that he wanted to get out of Japan and go to France to study. For most Japanese in those days, Europe was, in many ways, still a murky, mysterious territory, and life in France not a subject exhaustively studied. Although there were Japanese artists who had already been to Paris and back by the time of Foujita's adolescence, their reports could not cover all that he needed to know. He would later say that he was not at all prepared for what awaited him. Japanese art publications also did not provide enough information, and many of the names mentioned in the articles meant nothing to him anyway. (He claimed that he had never heard of

Cézanne, van Gogh, or Gauguin when he arrived in Paris in 1913.) Foujita's brother-in-law, who had traveled to Germany, took him to a Western-style restaurant in Tokyo and showed him how to eat with a knife and fork as the Europeans did. Although he began to study French in his middle school days, Foujita did not make enormous progress, and so he could not easily inform himself about French civilization while in Japan.

In 1905—the year Foujita was nineteen and entered art school—oil painting was still a relatively new concept in Japan. During the long period of seclusion that preceded the 1868 Meiji Restoration, little had been known about Western styles of oil painting beyond a few examples that managed to be circulated in Japan. Artists who got their hands on these foreign creations had tried to master the new methods, but it was only after 1868, when new information from abroad came pouring in, that Japanese artists could finally make extensive studies of Western painting.

The break with native traditions could not have been more extreme. Until then, traditional Japanese artists, trained to paint in ink, had evoked a mood with a few deft brushstrokes on a sheet of paper or silk or, showing off a flair for the decorative, had placed colorful objects on golden backgrounds. In some works, meanings were left vague, often carrying Buddhist undertones about the ephemerality of all things. A clutch of irises radiantly portrayed, long-haired beauties in gorgeous robes—these were the kinds of things that had been the subjects of Japanese scrolls and screen paintings. Subtle messages hovered over, say, an ink painting of a shrike perched on a leafless branch.

In contrast to Japanese traditions, Western-style painting demanded expertise with oil paint and depictions of life as it really was lived. This Western emphasis on reality could mean accurate reproductions of ordinary landscapes or a true-to-life portrait of the washerwoman. It is not surprising that some Japanese took one look at the subject matter, as well as the use of perspective and modeling in those works of art, and anguished over whether they could make the transition. The art historian Takashina Shūji has written of the challenge:

The importation of "Western-style" painting to Japan was not merely a matter of appropriating the realistic form of expression based on laws of perspective and chiaroscuro. It encompasses the entire concept of oil painting—materials and techniques which had hitherto been virtually unknown in Japan . . . It was practically equivalent to importing an entire civilization.

Like so many Japanese art students of his generation, Foujita was not to be deterred in his ambition to become a Western-style artist. To begin his studies, however, he required family assistance. According to a much repeated story, Foujita's father consulted Mori Ōgai, a colleague in the army medical corps and an eminent author, about his son's plans for foreign travel. Ōgai understood such youthful yearnings for Europe, since he himself had been tempted and inspired by a long stay in Germany as a young army officer. (In "Under Reconstruction," one of Ōgai's stories, the hero meets a former German lover in Tokyo, and when she tries to kiss him, he brusquely refuses her: "We are in Japan.") While sympathetic to the desire to get away, Ōgai suggested that before setting off for Paris, the young Foujita should study in Tokyo to learn the basics of oil painting and to get acquainted with leading Japanese figures in his field. Since his father was paying the bills, Foujita could only accept this advice with both resignation and gratitude, enrolling in the Tokyo School of Fine Arts in 1905.

At the Tokyo School of Fine Arts, Foujita did not show outstanding promise. For three years in a row, his submissions were refused at the government-sponsored salon where Kuroda Seiki, his teacher and a renowned artist, wielded much influence. Kuroda did not appreciate Foujita's artistic efforts, particularly the oil painting *Self-Portrait* (1910), one of the works he presented for graduation. "I used to fool around a lot and so I did not spend much time at school," Foujita later remembered:

My teachers always scolded me, and my grades were very bad. There were about thirty students, and at graduation, I ranked about sixteenth. Just before we graduated, Kuroda-sensei held up my graduation project in front of everyone and criticized my works as examples of how not to paint. But there were things that I wanted to do, and I found it difficult to go along with what he advised. I wanted to go to France as quickly as possible.

The 1910 *Self-Portrait* is the first of many such pictures Foujita drew of himself. In contrast to his later work, he used broad brush-strokes; there are only touches of white. His teacher, Kuroda, strongly influenced by the bright colors of the Impressionists, objected to his use of darker hues and in particular the predominance of black. Kuroda may have also objected to the cocky attitude of the student in this portrait, whose expression suggests a total lack of diffidence about his future. This student, Foujita, wears an ultramodern high collar and unapologetic red tie. At twenty-four, he seems to look beyond the room and beyond his teachers, who might not have agreed with his lofty as-sessments of his potential. "One teacher, who thought he was another Velázquez," Foujita wrote scornfully of an unnamed art school instruc-tor said to be Kuroda, "let his hair swirl down to his shoulders and wore a bowtie, and velvet shoes. He took a look at one of my paintings and roared out, 'There's no reflection of light from the sky in your land-scape!' I was dumbfounded."

By the time of his graduation, Foujita understood that his opportu-nities in the Japanese art world were virtually nonexistent, especially since the powerful Kuroda scorned his work. He had no choice but to make a name for himself in Paris or to start taking the massage lessons. Years after, Foujita disdained all that he had learned in Japan, saying, "What I learned at art school amounted to no more than learning how to hold a palette or wash a paintbrush." But Kuroda had studied in Paris for nine years and, after he returned to Tokyo, spoke often of his experiences there. It is said that the most important thing Foujita learned from Kuroda was the idea that Paris, and no place else, had to be his destination.

FOUR

AH, FRANCE!

France! Ah, France! I don't know why, but ever since the time I studied world history in middle school, I have childishly loved France. I must say that as of now I have never had any interest in English. But when I utter even one or two words of French, I feel the supreme pleasure of speaking the French language . . . They say there is a great difference between a traveler's dreams and reality, but the real France that I saw was far more beautiful and far more sweet than the France I had imagined. Ah, my France. I have lived until now only because I wanted to find a way to set foot on French soil.

—Nagai Kafū

There is of course no question that Paris inspires strong reactions in visitors from abroad. For American expatriates, Paris has long been an ancient, wise city offering lessons in refinement and worldliness. When people describe American reactions to Paris, Henry James's novel *The Ambassadors* is invariably mentioned, particularly Chad, the character who is captivated, educated, and, to the chagrin of relatives back home, transformed totally. "Chad had been made over . . . ," James writes. "It was perhaps a specialty of Paris." Ernest Hemingway, the exemplar of Americans in Paris par excellence, roamed around Parisian landmarks and experienced the city's complicated enchantments: "Paris was a very old city and we were young and nothing was simple there, not even poverty, nor sudden money, nor the moon-light . . ."

But while Americans in those days allowed themselves to be be-guiled, they never doubted that, in certain areas, they could more than match the Parisians. The Americans knew, for example, that they could hold their own when it came to verve and spontaneity. After all, Amer-ica was the country that had given Paris the likes of Josephine Baker and Isadora Duncan; this allowed the Americans to assume a kinship with the city. Henry Miller, another conspicuous American expatriate, had the narrator of his *Tropic of Cancer* gaze at the Seine in Paris and declare, "I feel this river flowing through me."

The Japanese found themselves on far less comfortable terms with Paris. Many Japanese of Foujita's generation yearned to leave their homeland as soon as possible. They wanted to escape from the tradi-tional Japanese terrors of earthquakes, thunder, fire, and fathers to achieve liberation in Paris. "For us, France was the country of Liberty, Fraternity, Equality," a Japanese once declared, "the true home of those with individuality and originality." Yet in Japan, they had been instilled with Confucian traditions, which emphasized the virtues of obedience, restraint, self-discipline. These were not the traits most useful in adapting to the rowdy, rebellious atmosphere of Paris in the 1920s. The reports that came back to Japan emphasized the joie de vivre and abandon of life there. To Japanese in the early decades of the twentieth century, who had grown up amidst the restrictions of a far more repressive, formal society, this was a daunting kind of free-dom. Though many Japanese longed to go to Paris, they feared that their inhibited personalities would not allow them to muster the vital-ity required. In *Old Toys*, a 1924 Japanese drama, the character who plays a Japanese artist struggles to settle down in Paris. After he mar-ries a Frenchwoman, he tells her, "I hope that the delicate and sensi-tive passions of you who are French will set my soul on fire."

Perhaps there is no better way to understand what Paris meant to the Japanese in those days than to consider the Académie Julian, a pri-vate art school founded in Paris in 1868. By the time the first Japanese art student was admitted in 1891, the Académie was well-known as more casual in its approach to training artists than the official École des Beaux-Arts. The lack of entrance exams increased the Académie

Julian's appeal among artistically inclined foreigners, as did the school's readiness to admit women. Potential artists from Europe and the United States entered the Académie, later remembering their sojourns there as an ideal bohemian experience for those with a taste for art studies and unsanitary conditions.

In *An American Artist's Story*, George Biddle echoes many other former students when he takes pleasure in remembering his studies at the Académie Julian and his wild comrades. He also fondly remembers the school's principal physical features:

> The school was in an enormous hangar, a cold, filthy, uninviting firetrap. The walls were plastered from floor to ceiling with the prize-winning academies [works depicting a nude or semi-nude model], in oil or charcoal, of the past thirty years. The atmosphere of the place had changed little since the days of Delacroix, Ingres or David. Three nude girls were posing downstairs. The acrid smell of their bodies and the smell of the students mingled with that of turpentine and oil paint in the overheated, tobacco-laden air . . . The girls enjoyed the fun; but the work was rigorous, the studio was never aired, and frequently they fainted.

A pamphlet published in Boston for American art students planning to study in Paris warned about the difficulties of the French language; the pamphlet might also have warned about the presence of those nude models, banned in Boston in those days, but regularly employed at the Académie Julian for drawing classes. A gregarious lot, the students apparently made all sorts of sounds while they worked at their easels. Some imitated caged beasts, and others sang a school ditty about the differences between painting in oils and watercolor:

> *La peinture à l'huile*
> *est très difficile,*
> *mais la peinture à l'eau,*
> *c'est beaucoup plus beau.* *

---

*Painting in oil / is very difficult / but painting in water / is much more beautiful.

The Académie Julian gained a sacred status among young Japanese artists because of *The Art Students of Paris*, an extremely popular book published in Japan in 1903. The author, Iwamura Tōru, was the first Japanese art student to enroll at the school, in 1891, and his account is based on his experiences there. Iwamura glorified the charms of Paris and delighted many youths, but at the same time, he stirred up Japanese insecurities about their ability to live in the French capital. I fear that this book brought torment to the hearts of students who, lacking money or courage, were unable to make the journey.

But *The Art Students of Paris* also had the power to inflame the wanderlust in Japanese art students scheming to get away. Such students would have found Iwamura's enthusiasm for Paris unbearably exciting. I can picture them finishing the book and vowing to get to the Académie Julian no matter what. There does not seem to have been a strong tradition of objectivity in the reports by Japanese returning from abroad, and although *The Art Students of Paris* purports to be a reliable account of life in a Parisian art school, the book creates an idealized picture of an absurdly free and inspiring city. Tokyo could have only seemed a backwater to wretches stuck there for the near future.

There is no proof that Foujita read this well-known book, but he would have had to go to great lengths to avoid it. I like to imagine Foujita reading *The Art Students of Paris* after a family gathering, rushing off to read a few pages upon finishing a dinner with several military men who were his close relatives. There would be Foujita, recovering from a family meal and trying to study Western-style oil painting thousands of miles away from its source. I wonder what Iwamura's descriptions of celebrations on Left Bank avenues would have meant to Foujita, whose less racy society took note just because he rode a bicycle to art school. He did not spend his afternoons studying great works at the Louvre and other first-class museums. Foujita more likely got his news about masterpieces from the reproductions in well-worn journals stained with dry grains of cooked rice or bits of noodle. There are accounts of young Japanese artists rushing through the snows of Tokyo's winter to get their hands on a new publication of Cézanne's works. "I struggled to learn about Rembrandt's light from the dim light of my boarding house," wrote a Japanese art student. Many Japanese from the countryside had never seen a real oil painting before they came to Tokyo.

Undoubtedly making Japanese readers feel as miserable as possible, in *The Art Students of Paris* Iwamura insists that Paris, and nowhere else, is the place to go for an artistic education:

London, Rome, Munich, Antwerp—each has famous art schools and there are also many artists there who set up fine independent lives for themselves, as well as throngs of students, . . . but only in Paris have they created a special artistic society of a totally different stripe with a unique artistic life unlike the rest of society.

Iwamura informs his readers that the behavior of the art students in Paris would be considered childish, annoying, or scandalous by Japanese standards. These students like to get together to drink and eat a lot, are talkative and unapologetic about their behavior. They are not always diligent about their work habits. Yet Iwamura does not intend to comfort his more decorous countrymen with these observations, since he has no doubt that what to the Japanese might seem like frivolousness and bad manners is essential to the development of the creative mind. Japanese art students, according to Iwamura, are no different from students of any other humdrum profession. They study in the constricted, dull atmosphere of art schools that could just as well be training doctors or lawyers.

I just wonder how artists or people who have had a lot of contact with Western artists would look upon those folks we call Japanese artists. Could the kind of interactions that are commonplace among Western artists take place in Japan? How can you expect this style of communication in a country like Japan, where people don't like to become close to anyone outside their own circle, don't much like appearing in front of large groups, don't like talking to others, don't like listening to others, don't like confessing private feelings to others?

Only in Paris do they do things properly. There, with the life of the artist apart from the ordinary workings of this world, they produce a unique spirit, independent, free, and able to stand up to authority.

Unlike the Japanese, Western art students are not at all frail and shy. Furthermore, their indulgences—the constant socializing and pranks— never get in the way of their unwavering commitment to their work. According to Iwamura, "When they play, they play with a puppy's en- thusiasm, and when they study, they study with all their energies. That's how these students live." As for the condition of Parisian art schools, Iwamura dwells tenderly, as other students did, upon their ramshackle state. The walls and floors are not in great condition, and no attempt has been made to hide the exposed ceiling beams; the sundry items stuck here and there do little to improve the general ap- pearance. Again, he had no doubt that this is the preferred training ground for an artistic life. All that concern about decor and tidiness is better suited to the bureaucratic mind of the Japanese.

It was not only his book, but Iwamura himself, along with colleagues also back from Paris, who made an impression on Japanese art students. Once home in Japan, Iwamura gave up painting and instead wrote art criticism and taught at the art school Foujita attended. Ironically, Iwa- mura did not always live up to the devil-may-care attitude he described so winningly in his writings. At home in Tokyo, he was known for his fussy habits and for his large collection of books. Such was his fastidi- ous nature that Iwamura refused to allow visitors to read any of his vol- umes without first having them thoroughly wash their hands with soap. Still, he and other Japanese artists who returned from study in Paris tried to ham it up in public once back in Japan. Their apparent lack of inhibition was another source of joy and grief for artistic youths.

As these older artists sauntered around Tokyo, they seemed to in- carnate all that had been described in Iwamura's writings. The effect of these returning artists on the younger generation was enormous. "With berets on their heads and heavy boots on their feet," wrote Wada Eisaku, one of their younger contemporaries, "they wore corduroy clothes with red woolen sashes, as they paraded around the streets. They introduced behavior considered eccentric and ground-breaking for those times like drinking Western liquors at the Hakodate-ya in Ginza. We looked upon them with envy." And Wada spoke for more than one generation of young Japanese art students when he described the bliss he felt strolling around on a sunny Tokyo afternoon in the company of Iwamura and a friend:

With a bright sun in the sky after the rains had cleared, Iwamura and Okada Saburōsuke and I ate grapes while we walked
from . . . Roppongi to Iwamura's home in Kasumichō . . . As we
walked along the street eating grapes and talking about art, I
felt that this was exactly the same way that Parisian art students lived. Iwamura talked with boundless enthusiasm. This
was the first time that I had met Iwamura, and from that time
on, I felt he had acquired the cleverness, the good cheer, and
the vibrancy of a young French art student. Right before my
eyes I was observing the Paris art student's life that I had long
yearned for. I remember that this made me very happy.

FIVE

LET LOOSE IN PARIS

*Montparnasse! City within the city, where everything takes on an
artistic distinction and moves toward ideal beauty. The sweetness of
your boulevard evokes visions of the steppes, of tragic northern seas,
of miles and miles traveled in dreams of trans-Siberian trains during
the great days of world transformations.*

—Montparnasse, *February 1923*

In 1913, Foujita took the *Mishima-maru* from Japan to France and
posed on the deck two days before disembarking at Marseilles. In
this photograph, Foujita was almost twenty-seven, setting out on the
adventure of his life. He had campaigned for years to get an allowance
from his family so that he could go to Paris and establish himself as a
full-fledged, Western-style artist. At last, after all the delays, he was
about to reach his destination. As this photograph attests, Monsieur
Foujita, eager to meet the citizens of France, had taken much care with
his clothing. On the ship, he wore a mauve frock coat and a white solar
topee, a head covering more often seen on British colonialists in tropical lands. "This was the first edition of a series of outfits which would
provoke the astonishment of Paris and London," a French writer noted.
Foujita's facial expression announced that he was ready for anything,
while behind him flowed the endless waters taking him to a new world.

When Foujita reached Paris, he stayed at the Hotel Odessa, an inex-
pensive hotel in the heart of Montparnasse. The hotel, which has not

lost its seedy allure, is now crammed among shops selling foie gras and rubber reproductions of Donald Duck. But Foujita was satisfied with his fifth-floor accommodations, though French food did not agree with him for the first few days. He went to a café in the neighborhood, where he admired the beautiful women and enjoyed the band supplying background music. He tried to get accustomed to the sight of women sitting on the men's laps, and he was especially taken aback by the public kissing. "I was surprised because they do it all over the city, not just in cafés," he wrote in one of his first letters home. He was amazed, too, by the oil lamps, the buildings with their many flights of stairs that were dark at night, and the tasks he had to perform by the light of a match. "I was surprised by the difference between the Paris I had envisioned in my dreams and the real Paris, which was old and made of cold stone, but this delighted me also and in the end I became a total captive of the city."

Another photograph was taken when Foujita was still striving to hit just the right fashion note in the streets of Montparnasse. For this photo, Foujita wore a black bowler hat with a suit and vest, complete with a dangling watch chain, and on his feet were the formal polished shoes of a true continental. He had acquired a moustache and a world-weary posture. No wonder Foujita captured the attention of women as he promenaded down Parisian avenues. "The very day of my arrival," Foujita confessed, "I was walking down the boulevard Pasteur, when an obviously beautiful woman looked at me and cried, 'Oh, he is *mignon* [cute]!'" He did not understand what the word meant and repeated it to himself several times until he got home. He rushed to his dictionary, and when he discovered the meaning, he was "pleased, satisfied, and proud." Later he was sitting in the Rotonde café, soaking up the atmosphere, when a woman patron gazed upon him with a certain look in her eye. Foujita did not comprehend what she was trying to signal to him, and so he, taking the easy way out, tried to stare back at her in the same fashion. The woman was moved to send the waiter over with a message: "I have a crush on you." Here Foujita's French proved inadequate to the occasion, and so, "without a dictionary close at hand . . . the adventure ended there."

In his hilarious book *The Japanese Guys of the School of Paris*, Tamagawa Shinmei describes the adventures of various Japanese living in Paris before and after the First World War. His account—which likes to take jovial detours away from the hard facts—follows the adventures of an intermittently euphoric, downcast, enterprising, confused bunch of Japanese. There was the Japanese man who was so impoverished that he ate the grass by the banks of the Seine; another lived in a room so small that he suspended the chair reserved for guests from the ceiling and would lower it whenever anyone came to visit. Tamagawa also takes up the case of the Japanese man who passed himself off as the wife of the Japanese delegate to the postwar peace conference and managed to interview world leaders. This same determined Japanese came to the aid of a Japanese judo champion who was idling away his days at the Parisian flea markets. Tamagawa of course has a grand time with Foujita, who conquered the city: "The Parisians love those with superior talents no matter what country they are from. They showered affection on this Asian whom they called 'Foujita! Foujita!'"

Tamagawa outdoes himself in conjuring up Foujita's big moment of social triumph after his arrival in Paris, at a party given by the Dutch artist Kees van Dongen.* Around this time, van Dongen, along with Picasso and other artists, had moved to the Left Bank's Montparnasse, thus creating an important artistic center out of this less developed part of Paris. "When I first set foot in Montparnasse," a Japanese expatriate wrote, "the vendors of goat's milk would be blowing their horns along the main streets while milking their goat to the side. This kind of pastoral atmosphere enveloped the whole area."

Once established in Montparnasse, van Dongen liked to have crowds of friends over. He was an important figure in the social scene, and his parties brought out women in golden tunics and a host in a red devil costume. Foujita would have known that an appearance at a van Dongen party would help him make his mark in Parisian art circles. He also, in general, liked to have a good time. Given the opportunity, he knew, he could call upon his own social intuition—incorporating sexy cuteness, an air of perfect confidence, and good timing—to win over

*Van Dongen was the artist who created a scandal in the 1913 Salon d'Automne by exhibiting a female nude deemed indecent by authorities and seized by the police.

the other guests. "Look, when it comes to making a big splash at parties, I've been confident since my art school days that no one is a match for me," he supposedly boasted.

With the help of the Russian sculptor Oscar Miestchaninoff, Foujita did manage to wangle his way into a van Dongen soirée. Here an unexpected development gave him a fright. "Foujita was taken to van Dongen's studio near Notre Dame des Champs," Tamagawa reports in his version of this episode, "and had certain expectations in mind, but what he found there scared him out of his wits." Just off the boat from Tokyo, Foujita was shocked to discover that van Dongen had paintings of nudes everywhere—on the walls of his studio, dining room, corridors, bedroom.

Foujita soon recovered his composure and entered into the midst of the wild goings-on. "The other guests drank, sang, danced, and let themselves go," Tamagawa writes. "Miestchaninoff got drunk and unbuttoned his shirt, baring his chest. He turned to Foujita and kept yelling, 'Hey you, fancy boy over there, sing a Japanese song for us!'" Foujita was well prepared for what might happen and hid himself from the others to prepare for his debut. When he reappeared, he had only a towel wrapped around much of his head and a blanket over his slender body. The astonished Miestchaninoff, mindful of his manners, quickly introduced Foujita to the others, who gradually became silent. "Foujita suddenly let out with a yell, '*Ara essa-sa!*' and then started waving the blanket around like a matador. He wound the towel around his loins as an impromptu loincloth and stood there, otherwise naked . . . Next he started waving around the dishwashing implement he had in his hand, while shaking his hips left and right. This was his rendition of an old Japanese folk dance called 'Scooping Up Loaches.'"

SIX

A CITY FOR ARTISTS

You are asking me a singular kind of question. Certainly here, just like every place else, you can work, if you have the will to do it. But Paris offers you, in addition, an advantage that you will not be able to find elsewhere, that is, the museums where you will be able to study the work of the masters, from eleven in the morning until four in the afternoon. You can see how you can divide your time. From six until eleven you will go into an atelier to paint from a living model; you will have your lunch, and then from noon until four, you can copy, either at the Louvre or at the Luxembourg, a masterpiece you admire. That means nine hours of work; I think that is enough, and with such a schedule, it won't be long before you see results.

—Paul Cézanne, letter, March 3, 1861

The dance at van Dongen's party does not tell the whole story of Foujita's first months in Paris, although some Japanese remembered him only for such carryings-on. The French may have been won over by his clowning, but his compatriots, astounded by Foujita's ability to participate in Parisian life, were also disgusted by his need to draw attention to himself. Unfortunately for Foujita's future reputation, many such disapproving Japanese wrote lasting accounts of his career. They chose to ignore the other, more disciplined, side of Foujita's days in Paris, berating him instead for shallow and decadent ways. To anyone studying Foujita's life story, such Japanese critics are unavoidable, since they are agitated, articulate, and plentiful. The vitriol not only damages their credibility, but also forces speculation about why Foujita's fellow countrymen lashed out at him so viciously. Foujita, of course, eventually managed to acquire enough fame and fortune to inspire much jealousy, but the nastiness goes beyond mere envy. Foujita's critics also found him guilty of ignoring accepted Japanese norms of behavior, a vague combination of refined, modest qualities that were supposedly known to all Japanese. There was a general feeling that Foujita had violated this essential "Japaneseness" and, worse still, had abandoned Japan to become a citizen of the world.

Finding a measured description of the more serious side of Foujita's experiences during this period requires some searching, and in the end, Foujita himself is the best source. He captures the other part of his life better than anyone, though he succumbs to the bad habits of many autobiographers when he tells his life story; he glosses over certain aspects of his personal history and exaggerates often. Foujita's personal writings therefore do not qualify as absolutely accurate reporting. Still, despite his preening, Foujita does allow us to follow his youthful dreams and struggles.

For example, Foujita claimed that, miraculously, just days after arriving in Paris, the Chilean artist Manuel Ortiz de Zárate took him over to visit an artist named Pablo Picasso on rue Schoelcher. The truth is that Foujita did not go to meet Picasso until about six months later, and even then he got the opportunity only because he tagged along with the Mexican artist Diego Rivera, who had actually been invited. Once inside Picasso's studio, Foujita took a look at everything. By then, Picasso had already gone through his Blue Period and had painted his harlequins, the portrait of Gertrude Stein, and *Les Demoiselles d'Avignon* (1907). Nonetheless, Foujita described himself as composed and clearheaded in the master's presence. "Picasso already lived in a grand atelier overlooking the Montparnasse Cemetery, which was obviously much envied. Lining the walls of the room next to the studio were dozens of sculptures made by black-skinned people from the South Seas. I immediately understood that he was attempting to create a new art form out of this unusual native art."

Other artists have remembered seeing *Les Demoiselles d'Avignon* in Picasso's rue Schoelcher studio around that time, but even if that groundbreaking work was there that day, Foujita passed it by in discovering Henri Rousseau, who would be a great influence on his work. Foujita wrote of being stunned by this first encounter with Rousseau's straightforward style, so firm in its idiosyncrasies. Foujita found much to learn from Rousseau and his seeming simplicity, which reached out toward the unfathomable. At that time, Picasso owned Rousseau's *Portrait of a Woman* (ca. 1895), and Foujita must have stopped to contemplate the matron in the painting, who stands by a brightly patterned curtain in a severe black dress. For the curtain, Rousseau's colors are bright and direct, seemingly applied with childlike pleasure, but the woman's harsh facial expression and the puzzling branch she holds in her hand take us in a scarier, less knowable direction.

Confronting Rousseau for the first time, Foujita experienced joy as well as embarrassment at his own ignorance. There was also the immigrant's anger at his native country, which had been cut off from such artistic developments and only produced teachers of narrow experience:

> I, who did not even know the names Cézanne and van Gogh, now opened my eyes to look out in a radically different direction. I saw that my artistic education up to then had been confined to the artistic styles of one or two people. Suddenly, I understood that paintings were free creations like this and could take a wide variety of forms. I suddenly realized that I should forge ahead, with a completely free spirit, to break new ground with my ideas. That day I threw my box of painting materials down on the floor, realizing that I had to start all over again from the beginning.

Though the discovery of Rousseau startled him, Foujita recovered quickly and charged off for the artistic struggle ahead. In letters home, Foujita wrote repeatedly of his great ambitions, of his wish to match the established artists in Paris and gain an international reputation for himself. Because of his poor showing as an artist in Japan, he longed to prove everyone wrong by returning home a success. To educate himself, Foujita received permission to copy paintings in the Louvre. As in all his activities, Foujita approached this task with unflagging energy. "For the first seven years after I came to Paris, until I started selling my works, I spent more than half my time at the Louvre. I studied so hard that I had pretty much memorized all the works there." He followed the example of the art masters whose biographies he had studied, and made the most of each day. "I practiced getting a deep sleep out of a short number of hours. I worked from ten in the morning until twelve, and in the afternoon from one until eight. At night, after eating supper, my study hours were from ten until five. I slept like a log."

He also devised his own work methods at the museum. If he was interested in eyes, he studied as many eyes as he could find, ancient, modern, Eastern and Western, in terra-cottas of the Etruscan period and eyes from Raphael, Leonardo da Vinci, Rembrandt, and up to Toulouse-Lautrec. He took in eyes looking up, eyes looking down, angry eyes, laughing eyes, crying eyes, eyes with a faraway look in them. He didn't stint on noses either and spent as much as a month on front views of noses. He then went on to noses in profile. Decades later, Foujita was still insisting upon the excellence of this practice to young artists. The Japanese artist Murayama Shizuka, who arrived in Paris in 1954, remembers Foujita repeatedly urging him to study all the arms, noses, and chins in the Louvre.

Foujita next made friends with some of those ebullient art students in Paris. Again, his self-confidence and his social skills among the Westerners were astonishing. Recently, I asked Kajiyama Miyoko, a Japanese friend he met much later, why Foujita had been able to manage so well in France, and she replied without hesitation: "It was his personality. He never went through culture shock and just adjusted. No other Japanese could do that." Proud of his ease in a foreign country, Foujita scorned those Japanese who socialized only among themselves in Paris and knew nothing about the West even though they were living there. He also found his new Western friends kindred spirits in discovering inventive solutions to their wardrobe problems. "If they don't have shoes, they think nothing of going around barefoot," Foujita wrote of his new acquaintances. "If they have no clothes, they put a hole in a blanket and simply stick their heads through that." Not one to grumble about a little dirt, he was enthusiastic about the Parisian cobwebs blessing the windows and the sinks noble with grime:

> I enjoyed socializing with this band, who threw themselves into living without any money just like the greats of old. Two or three of them lived together in one studio, and since they had only one pair of trousers among them, the other two wouldn't be able to go out and would have to wait on the bed for the one wearing the trousers to come home . . . But they are not at all unhappy about their circumstances . . . If you're afraid of life, you can't accomplish anything. I gradually realized that you have to approach things as if your life depended on it.

At first, Foujita's French language ability was meager, but he, unlike his more timid compatriots, was not cowed by mocking, uncomprehending looks from the native speakers. Embarrassment did not deter him, since only perseverance counted. In fact, to the end of his life, grammar and vocabulary were not strong points, and a Frenchwoman has described his French as "fluent but bad." He later said, "In order to understand the temper of France, you absolutely have to speak French . . . I made it a habit to frequent cafés, and the many waiters I encountered there became my French teachers." Then there was the matter of the French people themselves, whose manners could intimidate Japanese. Seeing himself as a model of tolerance, Foujita took a practical approach toward international understanding: "I tried not to be afraid of Westerners or to find Western things odd. Instead I tried to grasp France's good points and weak points." Moreover, he looked for the similarities between the French and Japanese civilizations: "The French, like the Japanese, are a people who have a great love of 'elegance.'"

Throughout his period of adjustment, Foujita kept on working. The act of painting enthralled him, and from the moment of his arrival, Paris inspired him still more. "I wasn't looking to create a masterpiece . . . I was satisfied with creating a painting of a kind never seen before which expressed my own individual talent. I did not think one should worry about fame or money." It seems that at least when he was starting out, Foujita possessed the instincts associated with a true artistic calling. Too much success and too much ballyhoo on the streets of Montparnasse would later blur his achievements and raise questions about his admission to the Temple of Art. Yet in writing about his youth, he described the solitary rewards of his craft with precision. Clearly, in addition to being enthralled by Paris, Foujita also experienced the most austere of satisfactions: "No matter how important the work may have been, I was only interested in it while I was in the process of creating it. Once the work was finished, it was a thing of the past for me." Foujita toiled at his art, in good times or bad, for long hours. He worked so hard that he lost at least one wife who grew bored with his diligence, and some claimed that other failed liaisons were not helped by his long working hours.

Foujita always gave a lot of credit to Paris, which in turn gave him the opportunities he would never have found back home. *Hana no Pari*, "Paris, that flower," is how the Japanese often referred to Paris, and for Foujita, too, the city had that special kind of beauty. In Foujita's descriptions of his first experiences there, Paris, that flower, does seem magnificent. Back home in Japan, he did not lack for friends and relatives to advise him, without pause, about what to do with his hair, his clothing, his health, his breakfast. "It's good to have relatives, but then again, they can meddle in your affairs and even have an effect on your paintings," Foujita once wrote. In Paris, he tried to get to know the locals, including the artists from dozens of different countries who gathered in Montparnasse. And like so many other new arrivals, he delighted in the pleasures of Paris itself: "In the spring, the blooming chestnut trees and the lilacs give off their scents, and in winter, with the freezing moonlight on the paved streets, the sounds of the horse-drawn carriages ring out even clearer."

But Foujita did have problems communicating in French at first, and while he was a well-born Japanese military officer's son, this meant little if no one understood what he said. Because of his bad French, he was cut off from many conversations and newspaper articles. His race brought him other difficulties. Foujita was harassed by children who threw stones and called him a "Chinaman"; at a French market, he was once surrounded by a group of Frenchmen and chased away.

Yet in the end, Foujita was more fortunate than many of his compatriots, since a great gift came to him early in his stay:

> One day when I was in the outskirts of Paris, I drew a landscape. The bright sunlight illumined the loneliness of the Paris fortification wall in autumn. It seemed like an expression of my own situation at that time, without a trace of falsity. I grappled with that landscape as if in a dream, mustering all my strength. Then I was enchanted by the completed scene. Truly, that painting resembled none other in the whole world. It was a painting that was completely mine. I had created my very own work. I had found my way. At last, I thought, I have grasped the key to the secret.

SEVEN

SETTLING DOWN

The School of Paris had its own universities and experimental laboratories: the cafés at the Vavin crossing and the cités scattered around the Fourteenth Arrondissement.

—Jean-Paul Crespelle

Cité Falguière, on a dead-end street in the Fifteenth Arrondissement, is a well-known spot among Foujita's admirers. He moved to no. 14 cité Falguière in 1913 and used his time in the neighborhood to prepare himself for entry into the Parisian art world. A walk down the cobblestones brings back those days of artistic experiments and bug-infested studios. Cité Falguière is now not only revered by lovers of beauty and history, but also coveted by developers, who have managed to demolish most of the old buildings. After the Paris World's Fair of 1900, when art had more clout than the real estate agents, wood from the exhibitions was recycled to build artists' studios there. The extremely famous, as well as lesser lights, have camped in these ateliers over the years, and so the surviving studios are perennially evoked in documentaries or in elegiac newspaper articles.

The structure at no. 14 cité Falguière, where Foujita lived, has been razed ("replaced by apartments for the rich," as one television documentary complains), but at no. 11, just beside it, the old studios are approximately as they were in Foujita's time, sheltering another generation of creative artists. To visit no. 11, a visitor goes down the cobblestones to a dilapidated building with large, battered windows. Inside, there is a narrow corridor and then the surprise of a line of ateliers with vine-splattered city gardens. A rickety staircase leads up to the apartment of Kaminagai Mineko, a Japanese woman in her eighties. She is the widow of the Japanese artist Kaminagai Tadashi and has lived in the same atelier-apartment since her arrival in Paris in 1957. Inside, the generous windows and cramped quarters give the visitor a sense of the space Foujita once inhabited. The windows reach up to the ceiling, ensuring freezing winters and infernal summers for the inhabitants ("More than a thousand times, I awoke to the early winter mornings of the cité Falguière studio," Mrs. Kaminagai's son has remembered. "Heroics were required to light the stove to warm up the place.") Mrs. Kaminagai has many stories about the renowned figures from the art world who have visited the premises. Her husband told her that before she came to Paris, he saw the artist Pierre Bonnard waiting in the rain for an absent friend on the outside staircase; the art dealer Ambroise Vollard also used to sit on the steps and play with the cat.

Foujita's spirit cannot be effaced from the dead-end street, and although Mrs. Kaminagai has done her best to allow him to rest in peace, the stream of reporters and researchers makes this impossible. Often interviewed about the former inhabitants of these quarters, she is especially hounded by students of Foujita's life. "Reporters interrupt my dinner, call me at all hours from Japan," she told me one day after I, too, asked her about her friendship with Foujita. Nowadays, the feisty, warmhearted Mrs. Kaminagai remains situated in her longtime residence and between two cultures, trying to provide insights into the expatriate life. "Do you think it was easy being married to an artist here? But I lived through the war in Japan, and after that, I suppose I could stand anything." She shifts between French and Japanese, frequently unaware of what language she is speaking. She circulates just as easily between the living and the deceased, serving tea to visitors by the stacks of her late husband's paintings and the picture frames, crafted by him to earn extra money, which still hang from the second-floor balcony. Her blunt way of speaking—"All artists are like babies, you know"—can cow the meek, but red cheeks and an optimistic disposition sweeten the impression. In French or Japanese or both, she talks about the detective novels she reads constantly, about the artistic profession, and about Foujita: "Foujita had a samurai's strong spirit about him and also a sense of morality. When he came to eat dinner here, he would be formal at first, but then he became more natural. Foujita and my husband used to talk about the times when they were poor in Paris. They both agreed that the worst part of being poor was walking around smelling the tempting aromas from the bakeries. They felt terrible because they couldn't afford to buy anything."

After talking to Mrs. Kaminagai, it is easier to picture Foujita in cité Falguière. The front steps, where Bonnard waited for his friend and Vollard played with the cat, provide an ideal spot for imagining Foujita at work on watercolors in his second-floor studio. Back then, fledgling artists from around the world also were tenants, and in particular, the place was sought out by Japanese in search of cheap rent. Hope and genius struggled to triumph over extremely chilly interiors. "An enclosed space with only twelve rooms to rent and twenty studios," a Japanese artist wrote about the conditions at cité Falguière, "it was a hangout for poor artists." In those days, the proprietor of the establishment was Madame Durchoux, who also owned the nearby café. She was understanding to a point about unpaid rents from her artist-tenants, but her patience had its limits. She was driven to throw out her impecunious tenant Amedeo Modigliani, but later, after he achieved posthumous renown, she deeply regretted having used the paintings he left behind to repair the box springs of a bed.

Foujita was living at cité Falguière during the First World War, and disruptions at the banks cut off his allowance from Japan. This forced him to use his ingenuity to acquire food and other supplies. "We artists in Paris had already been waging war with poverty," he wrote. "But with the outbreak of this unprecedented war, our problems became even worse. Psychological suffering kept pace with suffering over the lack of material goods and tormented everyone." In one of Foujita's tales about his wartime deprivations, he described his daily pilgrimage to the local butcher to buy leftover meat bones, which he said he was going to use to feed his cat. Actually, he made hot soup for himself from those precious ingredients. When at last the butcher, annoyed by his requests, asked whether he really had a cat, Foujita was forced to confess, "The cat is really me."

With the outbreak of the war, most expatriate artists returned to their native countries or fled elsewhere, but Foujita and a few other

colleagues decided to stay on in Paris. He worked for a Red Cross society, caring for the sick and wounded. In his wartime accounts, he
portrayed himself as brave in the face of the danger, and it did take
much courage to remain so close to the battlefields. "I decided to stay
in Paris as long as the old people and children did. Even after the exploding gunfire drove the Japanese Embassy and the French government to Bordeaux, I still stayed on in Paris." He looked down on those
Japanese who fled home in fright and gloated about his own resolve to
remain. Brave Foujita certainly was, but also realistic. Part of his decision to remain in Paris hinged on the recognition that if he did go back
to Tokyo, he might never get out again. Better to face enemy artillery
than to be clamped back into the vise of Japanese society.

At the same time that Foujita carried the wounded on stretchers
and fought starvation, relics of more affluent days, his frock coat and his
tuxedo for example, were traded for cash. He also sold his bed and slept
on the floor, Japanese-style, just like a poor student in Tokyo. After he
disposed of his forks and knives, he ate his food with the handle of his
brush. "If I wake up a success one morning, I can build myself a castle
in one day and that night will have no problem constructing a palace.
But now, with frankly penniless empty hands, I must fight these difficulties!" (While he certainly endured deprivations during wartime,
Foujita did like to romanticize his sufferings in his autobiographical
writings. He neglects to mention such boons as the loans he managed
to get from the Japanese Embassy, which seem to have been paid back
by his father until 1916.)

Since Foujita could not afford to buy oil painting supplies, he con-
centrated on watercolors. Works from this period show him toying with
Cubism, which was then in vogue around his Montparnasse neighborhood. *The Fortune-Teller* (1914), depicting his subject in a reverie over
her cards, was a shift toward abstraction, which he followed with several hundred other Cubist works. Later on, Foujita said that he might
have become a Cubist had the war not intervened.

In his cité Falguière atelier, Foujita maintained his arduous work
schedule despite the war and freezing temperatures. The drive to keep
warm required a special kind of sacrifice. "I saved only fifteen of my
works and used about five hundred others that I felt would embarrass

me in the future to fire up my stove and cook my rice. I burned my table and my chair in the fire too. One day, when I ran out of things to burn, I threw my shoes in; only my shoes wouldn't catch fire no matter what I did." During bombing raids, Foujita sometimes kept on working in his studio rather than fleeing to the basement, since fear of death was beneath the dignity of this army officer's son. A friend used to shout at him angrily, ordering him to go down to the basement and to be sure to bring his money purse along. "I'd say, What's the point of having a money purse by your corpse when you're hit by a bullet?"

Foujita decorated his quarters with his Japanese mementos. He had no easel, since he worked, Japanese-style, seated cross-legged on the floor at a low table. During wartime, visitors to Foujita's studio were surprised to come upon him busily engaged in the day's project, seemingly cut off from the tumult outside. The sun came shining in upon a serene single-mindedness. Still, Foujita recognized that his doorstep might become a battleground at any moment. In preparation, he bought a used baby carriage and packed all his art materials in a bundle inside. For good measure, he stuck on a small Japanese flag. If necessary, he planned to walk all the way to France's west coast, pushing the carriage.

His studio was spotless and orderly, in contrast to the filthy disarray that came naturally to his friends. Not even a crumb lasted long on Foujita's floor, and lack of money, mixed with a Japanese taste for spareness, kept the clutter down. One commentator declares that Foujita had the cleanest atelier in Montparnasse, but with many artists' habitats a grimy horror, he did not face overwhelming competition. He toiled in this tidy environment when not joining the amusements around town. Crucial to his efficiency, Foujita did not drink alcohol, which was unusual in a social circle known for late-night binges. Still, he threw himself into festivities and enjoyed the canteen that the Russian Marie Vassilieff ran for impoverished artists. "Meals were fifty centimes," Foujita remembered. "Three artists cooked: I did the Oriental things, the chop suey. Modigliani came, and Picasso—Picasso played toreador, and people sang and danced."

While at cité Falguière, he proved himself resourceful and intrepid, earning money modeling, painting houses, and cleaning toilets.

Although he would take up any job to survive, Foujita had trouble hold-ing on to his earnings. He could not resist spending whatever he re-ceived, and for this reason, he followed the example of a friend who showed him how to put a little cash aside. As soon as he got some money, Foujita stood in the middle of his studio with a few coins in his hand. He then scattered these into the far reaches of the room. When his financial situation became desperate, he scrounged around in the corners for this small change.

Short on funds and frequently cold, Foujita nonetheless under-stood how much he benefited from his time at cité Falguière. Forever after, he remembered the lessons he had learned from his neighbors. He had been able to study the techniques of some struggling Western colleagues with names like Amedeo Modigliani and Chaim Soutine. These two worked at their art and battled melancholy in no. 14. In some of Foujita's works from this period, the faces and torsos do have a Modigliani-like length and pensiveness; their expressions show the darker sides of his imagination. Foujita's emotional turmoils were of a different order from those expressed in Modigliani's nudes or Soutine's bloody beef carcasses, but nonetheless, he produced his sort of mourn-ful shadows in works like *Woman in Blue* (ca. 1917) and *Life* (1917), both depicting long-faced women in distress. Hayashi Yōko has pon-dered Foujita's stay at cité Falguière. Because of the proximity of Modigliani and Soutine, she argues, Foujita understood that he had to come up with a style as distinctive as theirs if he wished to estab-lish himself in France. The influence of these two Western artists made Foujita look again at his Eastern heritage. "Foujita worked with Modigliani and Soutine," Hayashi writes, "and thanks to them, he tried to discover his own originality and began to examine Japanese art, in order to discover his own style." Hayashi is unwavering in her belief that it was this search for originality that sent Foujita back to Japanese traditions when he was starting out in Paris. In this, she stands apart from Foujita's Japanese detractors, who have seen only commercial motives behind his embrace of Japanese effects. The difference in opinion is crucial—Hayashi sees an artist in pursuit of his own vision; the others scorn a money-grubbing fabricator of Japanese knickknacks.

Recently discovered correspondence from these years does much to corroborate Hayashi's position, since, in lengthy and repetitive letters,

Foujita not only touted his genius, he also swore that he would do what no other Japanese had done before him. In a later memoir, *Profile of Paris*, he repeated the sentiment: "I decided that since I was a Japanese, I would try to create Western-style paintings that contained Japanese ideas . . . I decided at all costs to create something that Westerners could not. Yes, those Western folks were talented, but I wanted to create works they could not imitate."

Aside from the artistic influences, Foujita was proud of his ability to make friends with these dedicated, occasionally mad Western artists at cité Falguière. In his memoirs, he can sound boastful about his connection to Modigliani, who is a significant figure in Foujita's version of his youth. "He recited Dante, but since I was an Oriental, he used to recite [from the Indian poet Rabindranath] Tagore for my benefit." Foujita told of having had a secret affair with Jeanne Hébuterne, who was also Modigliani's lover. He described that "cold and sad" day of Modigliani's funeral, and when Jeanne killed herself, Foujita offered to wash the blood off her corpse. "In those days Modigliani, Utrillo, and Soutine were all very poor," Foujita recalled. "Modigliani, for example, would wear the same shirt all the time. He drank round the clock, and there were times when he would be drunk from the morning on, would fall down on the main streets, and stop the trains."

Foujita also liked to reminisce about his intimacy with the Lithuanian Expressionist Soutine. "There were many bedbugs where Soutine was living, and he sprinkled water around the room to get rid of them. The bedbugs were really a big problem for him. Once a bedbug got into his ear. To get the insect out, he poured water in his ear, and this gave him a middle ear infection. It turned into a big commotion because he had to have an operation." Himself an enthusiast of hygiene, Foujita was always eager to demonstrate his ability to thrive among the dirt and eccentricities of Western artists. He seemed to believe that friendships with Modigliani and Soutine, who were as dirty and eccentric as one could wish, certified him as a deluxe bohemian.

A few more words about the bedbugs: In *Profile of Paris*, which was published in 1929, Foujita's unflinching discussion of things like bedbugs surely impressed and annoyed his fastidious readers back home.

Again, the Japanese would have felt wonder at his cool, open-minded personality, which allowed him to accept such disagreeable living conditions—yet they also would have felt offended by his disregard for Japanese proprieties in so openly discussing such matters. Still, Foujita could not resist shocking his prissy fellow countrymen and continued to *épater les japonais* at every opportunity. He rejoiced in reporting that you could take someone else's wife out to dinner or to a play in France without starting a scandal ("Why? Because the husband does not consider his wife his slave") and writing about his visit to a lesbian bar.

He even had nerve enough to write about France's toilets, a feature of life there that appalled some Japanese (Mrs. Kaminagai, who arrived more than forty years after Foujita, still remembers her horrified reaction to the first cité Falguière toilet she encountered). "There is no city that has as many public toilets as Paris," Foujita happily declared. "They are simple round sheds big enough to hold three people. You find one on practically every other block. The roofs are used for advertising. There are many advertisements for plays and other entertainments. Inside the toilets, there are advertisements for venereal disease cures which are in keeping with the character of the place." The apartment houses had their own arrangements: "Very few living quarters have their own bathrooms. Everyone uses the common toilet. In awkwardly constructed buildings, there are toilets only on the topmost floor and the bottom one. The people who live on the middle floors have to go to the toilet closest to them."

Cité Falguière provided the setting for Foujita's most memorable toilet story, which has not yet found a place in art history. The incident involved his friend Modigliani, who, according to Foujita, was too absorbed in his work to visit the building's facilities. Modigliani took the easy way out and put his waste in a newspaper and then shoved it under the bed. A stench greeted visitors to his studio. "I wondered why his place stank so," Foujita wrote in his genial way, "and that's why I asked him about it one day. A lot of excrement from the past month came out from under the bed."

EIGHT

EAGER TO LEAVE

Many of the Japanese in Paris are afraid to talk to Westerners and avoid them. These Japanese eat Chinese food or go to Japanese clubs, and so they become friendly with bad characters and get caught up in gambling. Or they develop a liking for the racetrack. Their relationships with women become troubled. Then, after three or four years pass, they are ordered to go back home. They don't have enough money for their school fees, and so they have no other choice but to work at other jobs. Soon they get weaker physically, develop lung trouble. Some of them even die. There are many tragic stories. Even the toughest of them don't find it easy to persist to the very end.

Those of my compatriots who studied hard before returning home and those who have still not gone home truly deserve congratulations.

—*Foujita*

To appreciate Foujita's jauntiness in the face of foreign customs, it is useful to turn to those of his countrymen who had a different reaction to life in France. Indeed, while some Japanese were as exhilarated as Foujita by their overseas experience, others spent their days in misery. For such Japanese, life abroad brought the terrible strain of confronting newness in everything—language, food, skirt lengths, walking styles, couples kissing in public. All foreign visitors face these adjustments, but Japanese travelers of Foujita's generation probably felt the strain more keenly. The effects of their country's centuries-long separation from the outside world showed up in their wide-eyed wonder and terror at all they encountered. Their cocoon had been thicker and was constructed with more complexity. Getting out was hard, and once out, Japanese visitors found it harder to feel at ease moving about in alien territory.

Kaneko Mitsuharu, a Japanese poet who spent a year in Paris in 1930, once wrote, "Three months after arriving, anyone who isn't asking himself why he came to such a place is either genuinely crazy or a fool or the grand-daddy of Japanese bums like us." A number of expatriate Japanese proved their soundness of mind by constantly agonizing over their reasons for making the journey. Battling thick French sauces day after day, many uprooted Japanese were clearly more prone to gloom than Foujita. For example, there was the artist Sakamoto Hanjirō, who took a ship to Paris in 1921 and encountered trouble almost immediately.

> During the boat ride over, I really suffered from the food. Since I was a second-class passenger, all they served was Western vegetables. This was difficult for me since I was accustomed to eating *misoshiru* soup and pickled radishes. The only thing I enjoyed eating was the pickled onion I sometimes found at the edge of the plate. As a result, I got very thin. By the time we passed through the Suez Canal, I was suffering from malnutrition, and suddenly blood came out of my rear end. I was surprised when the ship's doctor told me that I would have to be hospitalized.

Shimazaki Tōson was a Japanese author who wrote at length about his lugubrious mood in Paris. Tōson stood out from other creative artists because he did not go there to satisfy any vague artistic ambition. On the contrary, Tōson had very concrete reasons for his departure from Japan. After his wife's death, Tōson impregnated his niece and, in order to escape public censure, fled to France, leaving his niece behind in Japan to face the outcry alone. In a Japanese work with the French title *Étranger* (1922), Tōson wrote of his battles against despair in Paris. At times, he blamed French furniture for his dejection.

I returned from seeing my friend off in a lonely mood and tried sitting down in the chair in my room. The chair I sat in was not one purchased on a whim or to use during rest periods or only in the daytime while I was working. It was a chair suitable for a person like me who no longer had to bend his legs to sit cross-legged on the floor. In my room, there was only a thin rug on the floor by my bed, and the rest of the floor was made of wooden floor boards. Those wooden floor boards were used instead of [Japan's straw] tatami. I was accustomed to sitting on the tatami for long periods, but like it or not had to give up this old custom . . .

At night, I thought that perhaps I would be able to enter into European life more at some point, and I looked forward to this as I climbed into bed. Many bedbugs, emerging from places unknown, crawled into my bed . . .

There were times when Tōson's mental state appeared to improve:

During the past five months, I felt as if I was spending my life standing all day long. There were times when I felt like crying like a baby. That is how unable I was to distance myself from old customs. Yet even I became a little bit accustomed to chairs after some time and could manage to make sitting down on them part of my life. Once I got used to everything, I found that I was no longer bothered by the tall buildings in the towns and cities. The terrifying sounds which emanated from the cobblestone streets and reverberated through the town also no longer bothered my ears.

This positive mood did not last long:

Sometimes I threw off my Western clothes, removed my shoes, and took pleasure in wearing the kimono that I had brought from Japan for home use. I sat perfectly still on my bed all alone. But even this did not make me feel better, and at such times, I could only think about how I wanted to fall to my knees on the floor, press my forehead to the cold wooden boards, and let the tears flow.

Yashiro, a character in Yokomitsu Riichi's novel *The Sadness of Travel* (1946), also finds himself making the journey from Japan to Paris. At Yashiro's first glimpse of France, his overseas adventure seems ill-fated, since he does not seem receptive to the new experience: "From the time Marseilles came into view, he thought constantly only about Japan. Paradoxically, it was as if the closer he got to Europe, the more Japan seemed to come closer in an all-out attack on his mind." Once Yashiro reaches Paris, the situation does not get any better. The reader feels Yashiro's anxiety in this new land of steepled roofs and cobblestone roads.

> He first arrived in Paris at night, and since he could not see much in the dark, he thought that Paris was the countryside, contrary to his expectations. But when the night yielded to the next morning, he realized that he had not come to just a big city, but to a kind of temple, a very ancient place many hundreds of years old which he had never gazed at or heard of before. Yashiro had come from Japan, where there seemed to be only fresh vegetables and water, and for the moment he could not feel any attachment to these streets of dried-up black stones. Yashiro was a Japanese man who had lived in a region of plentiful moisture, and when his skin came in contact with the dry Paris air, he responded just like a frog, which regulates its respiration by expelling internal gases from its wet skin. Yashiro felt as if his pores had closed up, his senses weakened with each passing day, and he kept catching cold. He walked around and looked at the amazing sculptures, paintings, and buildings, but he became depressed when he could not discern any of the beauty people made such a fuss about. Even though he salivated with hunger at the delicious food spread out before him, he ate a few mouthfuls and felt like throwing up. He drank only coffee and water.

NINE

OVER A LONG DISTANCE

Marcelle, with black hair, smiling, good and sweet, taught me how to eat soup without making any noise and not to slurp dessert from the spoon.

Large Gaby always walked her Pekinese while singing. She's the one who pointed out the artists Chevalier, Damia, Polin, Montéhus, on the rue de la Gaîté.

The beautiful washerwoman Marguerite, always with a powder puff at her nose and fresh see-through blouses, took me into the woods and showed me how they kiss in this country . . .

—Foujita, "How I Became Parisian"

n describing his ability to adjust to Paris, Foujita was successful at skipping over the messy parts. He cheerfully told about the mauve suit on the ship and the blooming chestnut trees. There was mention of miraculous meetings with important artists; other reports detailed the French toilet situation and his friendship with Modigliani. But when it came to trickier matters, Foujita showed more reticence: for example, he did not like to emphasize that he was already married when he reached Marseilles in 1913. His wife was Tokita Tomi, a schoolteacher in Japan. While Foujita was in Paris, encountering women whose flirtatious words he could not comprehend, his wife, Tomi, was back in the Japanese countryside, trying to earn money to join him in Europe.

In another state of mind, I would be writing Tokita Tomi's life story. She is the kind of biographical subject often resurrected these days. She is female, she is determined, and she has a taste for adventure. In addition, she has been largely omitted from the writings about her celebrated ex-husband. Looking at things from her female point of view, I could point out how she longed to escape a predictable future for life with Foujita, a very nearsighted and unpromising Tokyo art student when she first met him—the same art student who had failed to get a single work accepted in the Tokyo salon.

Foujita said he met Tomi while he was on a sketching trip along the coast south of Tokyo and claimed that their love affair got under way when a sudden thunderstorm sent Tomi running into his arms. Afterward, Foujita visited her each week at the school where she taught. One of Tomi's students later recalled spying on her teacher's admirer, "a short, dark man seated all by himself beneath the dim light." Foujita and Tomi went so far as to run off together while waiting for their parents to consent to their marriage. "Let me marry her," he wrote to his father. "Without her, I will die. If I can't spend my life with the woman I love, there's no reason to live." Foujita's father, fearing that his son had become besotted with a geisha or a model, was relieved to discover that Tomi came from a decent family. Finally, both families relented, and around 1912, Foujita married Tomi, whom he remembered for her simple old-fashioned hairstyle, so like one in an illustration from an old storybook.

In recent years, I have read of such Japanese romances and am familiar with the details. The man is rich, talented, and ambitious. The woman has artistic dreams of her own, but mostly she is pleased to have escaped convention with a man not so steady but able to stir her to dream in a new way. Once she breaks away from ordinary life and marries this man, she hopes to say farewell to straitlaced society, regular mealtimes, censorious neighbors. I can see Tomi in her new residence (which was provided by Foujita's family) after her marriage, pleased by the daubs of paint on the studio walls and the smell of turpentine. She was even willing to allow her husband to leave her soon after the wedding for his long-dreamed-of journey to Paris. She understood that an atypical union required audacious choices. If I were her biographer, I would admire her willingness to face these difficulties. At the same time, I would be ready to cast a cold eye on her husband's selfish nature.

After Foujita set off by ship to Paris not long after the marriage, Tomi taught again at a school and took on the additional job of dormitory supervisor. Whether their plans were ever realistic or not, they hoped to gather money quickly for a reunion in France. In the interim, he sent her letters and postcards about his doings abroad. He wrote often at first, including detailed news about his daily life, and photographs of himself, his friends, famous sites, as well as pressed flowers direct from France. At the beginning, his tone was loving, full of plans for the life they would live together in Paris. To Foujita's Japanese friends in Paris, his attachment to Tomi was obvious; he showed them her letters and spoke of her with fondness. Evidencing her great attachment to him, Tomi carefully preserved each piece of correspondence. Years before world fame came to Foujita, Tokita Tomi awaited his letters from Paris.

Long after Tomi's death, these letters were discovered by her descendants just as she had left them, wrapped in cloth and stored with some old Parisian fashion magazines that Foujita had also sent her. "Of the people who came to see me off, please go to thank those whose addresses you know," Foujita, the punctilious husband, requested while still on the ship to Paris in 1913. "Next time I will send you detailed maps to the homes of Wada-sensei and Okada-sensei. It would be good if you go to see them . . . I'm doing all right on the ship and don't feel very nervous. You too should come to France quickly. All you have to do is know English. Think of me—I'll be speaking in English until we reach Marseilles." No one can miss the sincerity of his affections and the speedy dispatch of this first letter. Less pleasing is his second one, which he did not get around to writing until he had been in Paris for nine days. "I intended to write you an especially long letter about my doings," he apologized. "Since I wanted to write something long, I've been putting it off, and now it is August 15th." His exhilaration about his being in Paris is clear as he tries to convey the details of his daily life. "I'm staying at the Hotel Odessa . . . where Japanese often stay at first. The husband and wife who run the place speak worse English than I do. They have sixty rooms . . . It's a fine place and costs three or four francs a night . . . I've been going around to the museums and the universities to look at paintings. I also went to the upper Seine."

While his considerable ambitions thrived on the Parisian air, Foujita often remembered Japan in alternating bouts of pride and shame. These passionate feelings about Japan haunted him forever after: To the end of his life, Foujita lurched between patriotism and fury, never able to break free of his native country. At times, Japan seemed far away: "I can't even begin to comprehend how much my thinking about painting has changed in the past two or three days. I now realize that it is necessary to create an utterly polished painting, a final victory, one that has vitality into the future and forever. I am so happy—this change in my thinking has excited me to a really surprising degree. Really, I have already got myself into the French spirit. I have also understood that Japan is not a country for artists." In later letters, Japan was on his mind as he dreamed of future success. "I applied to the Louvre and got permission to copy paintings there," Foujita wrote in 1914. "I am working hard from ten in the morning until four in the afternoon, trying to create excellent, valuable copies of works that will be good enough to become part of a collection in a Japanese museum later on."

At times, he bragged about surpassing other Japanese in his social skills: "I went to visit the most important avant-garde artist, Picasso. [Diego] Rivera . . . came too. They served us tea. There is no other Japanese who mixes so frequently with Westerners . . . [My Japanese friend] Kawashima and I are thinking of buying land together near the upper Seine, about twenty or thirty minutes from Paris. We're both saving our money . . . Kawashima and I have opinions completely different from the other Japanese. The others are passive and withdrawn. We've decided to work together and strive toward making names for ourselves." In fact, disdain for other Japanese is a central theme of these letters. At various times, Foujita railed at the Japanese for not shaking off the small-mindedness of their island nation, for their inability to express their affections openly, for being meddlers and gossips and as sinister as snakes.

Frequently and at length, Foujita also wrote to Tomi about the pleasure he took in his work and his hope that she would soon live with him in Paris. Yet in one of his letters, he also included some ominous news. He had written to his father, much ahead of time, to tell him that he had no desire to return to Japan after the three-year stay in Paris that they had agreed upon. His attitude toward Japan had hardened, and this did not bode well for his marriage. "Even if I could go back there after three years with adequate results, I would find it unbearable to be in Japan, where there is nothing obvious to learn, no stimulation, and also many of my relatives."

Foujita later wrote to Tomi about the start of the First World War and about how all the Japanese had left the city, seeking safety in the countryside. All, that is, except for himself and his new friend Kawashima Riichirō, who decided to stay behind in Paris and tend to the wounded. His descriptions of the dangers and disorder of Paris during wartime could not have calmed a wife far away. "If I die, I would be sorry not to be able to see my father, brother, and sisters and especially you again, but this is fate. Resign yourself to this. Resign yourself to the fact that we were destined to be together only until then." Eventually, the situation became too difficult even for Foujita and Kawashima, and they left Paris to become caretakers at an old chateau. After some time, Kawashima's family summoned him away, and Foujita, left alone in Dordogne during wartime, admitted to some disheartenment: "Now that I am by myself, I feel quite lonely in the mountains."

Foujita could not make money, and so, after briefly toying with the idea of going to the United States, he fled to London. Once there, his emotions notably cooler toward Tomi, he wrote a brisk reply to her request for more information about himself, failing to mention a love affair in a tent that had started a scandal:

It would be fine with me if I stayed here [in Europe] for my whole life. I don't think I would be able to do real work if I didn't stay on. I don't know how many times I have written this to you . . . Originally I planned to have you come here to live once I had been here for about three years. I even bought land in France for that purpose. But the war destroyed everything, and all my plans came to nothing. I've had various other problems. Why have I endured all this suffering and why do I want to remain here? Because I am thinking of nothing but my final success. If I succeed, I will have discharged all my obligations and my excuses will be at an end. I will have fulfilled my filial obligations toward my father and brought honor to my country.

Tomi would have found this letter hard enough to bear, but Foujita managed to add another unkind touch: "I find letters to Father difficult, and I cannot get myself to write to him. When you go from Chiba to Tokyo—and that shouldn't be hard—I'd like you to take this letter and go to see him. Please explain the situation well and comfort him." It was at the end of the letter that he told of his worst nightmare. Back in the provincial Japan of his imaginings, Foujita saw himself clearly: "To put it briefly, in Japan, I'm afraid I'd become a braggart or get disgusted by what I have to do to earn a living. I fear becoming a completely despicable human being there."

Yet perhaps no letter is so cruel as the one he wrote when he was holed up in the mountains during the war with no money and no prospects, but still full of braggadocio about his future. Meanwhile, Tomi, far away in Japan, was having serious problems. She was "married" to Foujita, but then again, not married enough to avoid being ignored by her in-laws. Foujita's father had allowed their marriage ceremony, but he had balked at placing Tomi's name in the all-important family register, which would have made her Foujita's legal wife. The father gave various excuses for not registering her name, but as the couple's separation became prolonged, the father must have seen no reason to formalize a marriage he had never been keen about in the first place. Insulted in various ways by her in-laws, her husband's emotions more distant with each letter, a never-ending war making her trip to Paris impossible, Tomi finally took steps to improve her situation at home. She took (and passed) a government exam to advance her professional status. Foujita, giddy with his freedom in Europe, was disgusted by this practical decision: "I am telling you that your thinking is too passive. I would like you to do one big thing and become more aggressive. Once you come here, you will understand that first of all, Japan's Ministry of Education and then all the other academic organizations are wrong about everything and that everything about Japan is ridiculous."

Gradually, he wrote more postcards, instead of the letters that he had filled with descriptions of his activities and drawings of clothes he had sewn himself. Perhaps the chances of Tomi's reuniting with her husband would have been slim even if Europe had remained at peace. But the First World War destroyed her travel plans and her marriage, since her family was not going to allow her to take a ship to France under such dangerous conditions. By then, her relatives had perhaps also heard rumors about Foujita's escapades with other women. In 1916, Foujita informed his father in Tokyo about his desire for a complete break with Tomi. According to reports, the father worked hard to convince her that such a long-distance relationship was futile. She resisted at first, but finally agreed. Descriptions of that last scene must include her wrapping Foujita's letters in a piece of cloth, Japanese-style, before storing them away forever with the French fashion magazines.

Japanese commentators who stand ready to pummel Foujita for everything have taken him to task over his treatment of Tomi. If I were her biographer, I would mull over their comments. "When Foujita first went to Paris, he was already married," writes Kikuhata Mokuma, one of Foujita's most dedicated foes. "After a while, an abrupt letter of divorce was sent from Paris to the new wife whom he'd abandoned. Foujita was surrounded by the women of Paris, by women from all over the world, and his virtuous wife, who was just a teacher at a girls' school, must have already seemed like something from his distant past. The rootless Foujita, who had turned his back on the reality of Japan, became part of a foreign circle in Paris. Piece by piece, he wrapped himself in only the superficialities of Europe."

In coming to the end of Tomi's story, her biographer would not be able to resist noting the different fates that awaited an artistically inclined Japanese man and his wife around 1916. Foujita went on to success on the Left Bank in Paris. About two years after her divorce, Tomi married a dentist. In 1932, at age forty-five, she died of a cerebral hemorrhage.

But I am not writing the woman's story this time around. This time, I have vowed to scrutinize the situation from the man's point of view. Proving the fickleness of a biographer's loyalties, I have managed to shift my attitude without much difficulty. Moreover, I required only a small amount of evidence to feel comfortable looking at things from Foujita's perspective. In my quest, I turned to Sasaki Shigeo, a former banker and now a bibliophile supreme. At his Tokyo home, which serves as the headquarters for his Document Center for Modern Art, Sasaki has amassed a vast collection of materials—from magazines, newspapers, books, and other sources—about every phase of Foujita's life, covering such crucial and not-so-crucial subjects as his artworks, his biography, his wives, his travel itineraries.

Seated at home among his documents, Sasaki, who is in his seventies, seems relaxed and confident, with Foujita's lifetime activities assembled close by. Given the fervor of his obsession, it is a surprise that Sasaki's appearance is determinedly un-arty and like that of any other retired Japanese banker. His attire is only barely casual, a shirt without a tie or jacket, though these would not have seemed out of place. His clothes, his daily schedule, his organization of materials reflect a profoundly ordered mind. I am not the only one to have asked him about whatever could have impelled him to get so involved in tracking down everything he can find by and about Foujita. In his puzzlement at the puzzlement of others, Sasaki does not consider his zeal unusual. He has said that his project had its origin in his childhood when, on August 15, 1945, the Japanese emperor told the nation that Japan had lost the Second World War. "I am of the generation of Japanese who were completely misinformed about what was happening during the war. We are determined not to be deceived again." He began with the accumulation of voluminous materials about Japanese war paintings, commissioned by the military during the Second World War and since then mostly kept out of public view. Foujita was the most prominent of these government-sponsored artists. In 2000, to much fanfare, Sasaki organized an exhibition in a Ginza gallery on Japanese war art—the first such exhibition since the end of the Second World War. It is not immediately obvious, drinking a cup of tea with Sasaki, that a brave campaign to tell the true history of Japan's wartime activities is under way in his quiet and exceedingly narrow home.

Sasaki's collection of documents is a response to the Foujita family's attempts to control information about their renowned relative. What to do when primary sources are not readily available? Sasaki's answer has been to collect multitudinous pieces of published evidence and build the story from there. His materials on Foujita fill his Tokyo residence, sitting atop staircases, windowsills, and flower-arrangement alcoves, and under valuable Chinese vases. "Recently, I have been struck by writings which clearly show an intentional bias, with factual misinterpretations that bolster a particular point of view and a complete support of those misinterpretations," Sasaki has written. "These have been aired on television and have been circulated by major newspapers." Armed with a sheaf of documents, Sasaki publicly battles against those who contribute to the manufacture of a Foujita legend.

On an autumn day in Tokyo, with a virtuoso's poise, Sasaki tried to reconstruct the breakup of Foujita's marriage for me from various sources. The marriage to Tomi is one of those events, critical to an evaluation of Foujita's character, that Sasaki yearns to view accurately. Foujita's marital problems may seem like a small issue, but for Sasaki they are part of another, greater tale. If you don't get the facts straight about what went on between the young couple, then you are likely to be off the mark later, when it really matters: you are going to make a mistake in evaluating Foujita's controversial role in the Second World War.

"Look at this list of Foujita's letters to Tomi," Sasaki urged as we studied a reference work. "According to this list, some of the envelopes were found empty."

Indeed, the records show that wrapped in Tomi's cloth bundle of mail from Paris were ten empty envelopes addressed to her by Foujita. Since we know that Tomi treasured the letters from her husband in Paris, meticulously saving each item, it is unlikely that she lost any letters or carelessly tossed one out with the day's garbage. Speculations now swirl about these empty envelopes. Sasaki, pained at the thought of documentation turned to ash, suspects that Tomi destroyed those letters that she could not bear to read again. She may have saved the empty envelopes to remind herself of what they had contained.

"Tomi came from a rich, established family, and her father died soon after Foujita left for Paris. She received a sizable legacy," Sasaki told me. "This would have surely been enough to buy her boat fare to Paris."

For more information, Sasaki referred me to *Memories of Half of My Life* by Ashihara Eiryō, Foujita's nephew. In these memoirs, Ashihara often looks with dismay upon his famous uncle's behavior. Moreover, this nephew's descriptions, charged with an insider's knowledge, are very convincing. Yet when Ashihara takes up the issue of what actually went on between the newly married couple, he declares Foujita the wounded party. In particular, Ashihara describes the time when the financially strapped Foujita decided to prolong his stay in Paris. Ashihara claims that Foujita wrote to Tomi in Japan, appealing for money. According to Ashihara, Foujita asked that she send him money she had saved—two thousand yen to be precise—and that Tomi refused her husband outright. The nephew believes that Foujita's first marriage was destroyed by Tomi's refusal to give him the money: "At this time, his distrust of all women became firmly established."

A biographer trying to sympathize with Foujita's plight readily imagines him receiving such a letter of refusal from his wife. ("This story has its believable aspects, since an exact figure like two thousand yen is mentioned," Sasaki, the former banker, notes.) Small rooms in foreign cities are excellent for pacing and for ruptures in relationships; unfamiliar smells and furniture can be a breeding ground for recklessness. Foujita would have been living in one of his bedbug-plagued ateliers when he received the letter from his wife denying him financial assistance. As witnesses have affirmed, Foujita's studios were always clean and neat despite the bugs, with Japanese touches throughout. I can picture him at twilight writing a response to Tomi, one of the letters that have now disappeared.

But then, just as I am about to settle on this version of the story (bedbugs, dusk, Japanese woodblock prints on the walls), Sasaki comes up with another piece of written evidence that provides yet another view of the situation, and a new inventory of explanations suddenly becomes possible. Even Sasaki, master of many documents, realizes that facts preserved on paper are no match for emotional nuances that have eluded the record-keepers. He cites a newspaper article published in 1938, many years after these events. When asked about why this marriage failed, Foujita made no excuses for his attitude: "While I was struggling in Paris, my passion cooled for my wife in Japan, who was much taken up with appearances."

TEN

DACK TO THE GREEKS

Thus all the luxury of Paris, all the great scintillation of Paris is worthless! Come with me to the ancient Greek kingdom of Epirus! We don't have cars there, nor even roads! There may be problems within the country, but even so you will see only extraordinary dances! Not a single unharmonious movement!

—*Raymond Duncan*

While much is uncertain about this period in Foujita's career, the evidence suggests that he had worked himself up into a belligerent mood. More or less at the same time that he broke with Tomi, he decided to relinquish all financial assistance from home. In a 1942 memoir, Foujita included the dramatic letter he wrote renouncing his allowance. Since he was breaking his promise to return after three years, he asked his father to stop supporting him. "I am now thirty. At thirty, I am a full-fledged man . . . No matter how much suffering I may endure, I want to remain here . . . There's no need to send money to an unfilial son. I refuse it." His father did not write for six years.

Foujita surely included this letter in his memoir to present himself as plucky and steadfast during his years of struggle. A stoical samurai, facing all comers on the Left Bank, would have seen his life force being depleted by dependence on others. In Foujita's telling of his personal history, that same indomitable, self-denying personage turns up time and again. He portrays himself as surging on ahead alone, a model of autonomy and grit. Getting his paintings shown at a gallery for the first time? He claims to have arranged that by himself after trudging around Paris in the snow. Making contacts with important names in the Parisian art world? He charmed everyone instantly and, boosted by his amazing good luck, kept up his single-handed, public relations campaign during his years in Paris.

Actually, Foujita was quite beholden to others in making his way forward, receiving help he never acknowledged. To arrange that first show in Paris, he got at least some essential assistance from a resourceful Frenchwoman. In addition, he was able to meet the leading lights in the Parisian art world, not only because of his own perseverance, but through the intervention of others. There is another occasion soon after his arrival when acquaintances provided him with crucial guidance that he never adequately recognized—when Foujita decided to leave the modern world behind him and immerse himself in Greek culture. Soon after his arrival in France, Foujita decided that the Paris of his day was too far removed from the origins of Western civilization. So, seeking authenticity and purity, classical art and dance, Foujita turned to the Greeks.

Foujita came under the influence of the American Raymond Duncan, the very odd brother of Isadora. In Paris, Raymond had founded a school, called the Akademia, which advocated "a return to the Greeks." The Akademia offered courses in such subjects as Hellenism, dancing, literature, weaving, philosophy, carpentry, and oratory. Duncan had many guiding principles, among them vegetarianism and careful readings of Greek plays in the original. In his letters to Tomi, Foujita explained that he had been attracted to this movement out of a desire to leave the "vulgar" world behind and live in accordance with nature. His new pursuits would bring him close to the "simple" but "highly spiritual" art of the ancients, helping him express nature's truths in his own work. Foujita, a black belt in judo, later said that Duncan's belief in the connection between physical exercise and the development of the human spirit had also appealed to him. ("The words *gymnastic exercise* do not refer to muscular exercise," Duncan wrote, "but to human exercise, exercise which involves simultaneously the body and the soul, muscles and the intellect.")

Foujita also could feel an affinity for Duncan that went beyond a mutual admiration for Greek culture. Duncan's life moved between extreme flamboyance and serious purpose, matching Foujita's own natural tendencies. The Duncan family had long been devotees of the Greeks, Isadora perpetuating the classical style in her dancing, while brother Raymond supplied a kind of intellectual backup. An American newspaper described Raymond's role in Isadora's performances: "a diaphanous younger brother distributing strophes from Ovid in the background . . . Miss Duncan's melancholy brother kindly read extracts from Theocritus and Ovid as an accompaniment." Raymond once headed the family effort to build a dancing school near the Acropolis in Greece. This edifice, under Raymond's supervision, was to be a stone-by-stone re-creation of Agamemnon's palace. He remained untiring in his efforts to complete construction, even after a water supply could not be found in the vicinity. "Raymond was in his element," his biographer declared. "He carefully retraced the path ancient goatherds and their animals had made as they climbed the Acropolis of Athens centuries before the Parthenon." In the end, he ran out of money and set off for new arenas.

The next stop was Paris, where Raymond arrived with his Greek wife as well as with the handmade Greek shawls and blankets he sold to the public. He had learned to make a sturdy, comfortable Greek sandal, which he also peddled in Paris; satisfied customers included Gertrude Stein and her brother Leo. Raymond strode around Paris in a Greek tunic and those sandals, sticking to this style even in bad weather. "His long hair done in coils about his head and his draperies were all exhibitionism done in self-defense," the American expatriate Robert McAlmon speculated in his memoir, *Being Geniuses Together*. "He didn't want to be just Isadora's brother."

Foujita's other mentor in Greek culture was an expatriate Japanese artist who seems a mild sort compared with Duncan. Kawashima Riichirō, mentioned in letters to Tomi, had studied art in the United States and was the first Japanese to have a work accepted by the Salon d'Automne in Paris. Kawashima seemed to be Duncan's favorite disciple at the time he met Foujita, who was in 1913 just off the ship from Japan. "In those days, I went around like a real eccentric," Kawashima once said. "Just one look at my clothes, and you could see that I stood way apart from the world inhabited by other budding artists. I wore Greek clothes, a tunic with a sash tied around it. There was a stone necklace around my neck and a brimless leopard-skin cap on my head. I used to walk around the side streets like that, feeling very proud of myself." Although Kawashima later said that Foujita came over to his studio to meet him for the first time, there are those who believe that Kawashima was dressed in Greek attire and preaching about the Greeks on a Paris sidewalk when Foujita first spotted him. Seeing an obvious kindred spirit before him, Foujita went over to strike up an acquaintance.

It is certain that Foujita visited Kawashima at his live-in studio, an appropriately spartan establishment. The bed consisted of a large box filled with straw on the concrete floor, and drinking water was pumped from the common tap in the courtyard. In these plain quarters, Foujita was won over by Kawashima's ardor for the Greeks. "I'll definitely join you!" he shouted. The rapport between the two expatriates was instantaneous and intense. Not at all shy about imposing himself, Foujita next offered to move in with Kawashima so that they might create an "Akademia" of their own.

Because of Kawashima, Foujita was soon seen around town in his own Greek tunic and sandals. He took up Greek dance and, under Kawashima's influence, modeled himself after figures from Greek paintings and sculptures. The dancing in turn helped him clarify his own approach to art: "Dance is composed of only the most beautiful lines, and without knowing this, creating a true work of art is impossible." Clearly, Kawashima was the perfect guide for Foujita's introduction to Paris. This was not only because Kawashima was knowledgeable about Hellenism and wandered the boulevards in Greek clothes; Kawashima had also lived outside Japan for many years and so, unlike most Japanese, felt extremely comfortable among Westerners. This suited Foujita, who was dying to distance himself from his compatriots and throw himself into a new society. Kawashima knew many people in the

Parisian art world, and such contacts explain Foujita's encounters with well-known artists early in his stay.

Foujita eventually acquired his own loom and wove fabric for his Greek wardrobe himself. Proud of his Greek fashions and his sewing skills, he was delighted to cause a stir in public. An Englishwoman stopped him at the Louvre and said that in forty years in Paris, she had never seen anyone dressed so strangely. He admired his own appearance in the mirror, where he saw what he considered a true work of art. "Throughout the world, those who become famous have thrown themselves deeply, deeply into strange things," he wrote at the time. "Those who do what everyone else does will accomplish nothing."

Often Foujita and Kawashima went out on the streets of Paris together, both wearing their Greek outfits and sandals. "They were a great success at parties," wrote the British artist Nina Hamnett. Diego Rivera was enough taken by Foujita and Kawashima's Greek phase to paint their portrait, and a photograph of these two Japanese men—holding hands like shy, well-dressed lads from Athens and wearing Greek tunics, beads, caps, and sandals—demonstrated, at a glance, why their parents probably never wanted them to leave Japan in the first place. Foujita enjoyed telling about the time they were walking down boulevard Saint-Michel in their Greek clothing when two drunk Frenchmen threatened Kawashima: "What are you doing in a get-up like that?" When Kawashima got scared, anticipating real trouble, Foujita threw himself into the fray. In no time, he had triumphed over these ruffians with a few quick judo moves. "Ah," Foujita reminisced with pride, "it happened in front of a café near the Pantheon. Everyone saw us."

Foujita continued to go to the Louvre, but he expanded his investigations to include the ancient art of Greece, Egypt, Assyria, Rome, and Pompeii. He carefully copied a section of an Egyptian mural and drew a lively watercolor of a woman performing a Greek dance in the open. Some of his figures, with their stretched, flat faces and barely detailed features, look as if they belong back in the time of the pharaohs. In another work, a rather Japanese-looking man in a toga poses before a tree drawn in the archaic manner. Perhaps most quirky is Foujita's *The Kiss* (1914), a response to Constantin Brancusi's sculpture of the same name, which had been in the Montparnasse Cemetery since 1910. Brancusi's work, an abstract stone rendering of a couple kissing, tells part of the story, and then Foujita takes the tale further in his oil painting by fitting out his Brancusi-like figures with the hair and robes of long-ago Athens.

As Foujita had written to Tomi, he and Kawashima put their funds together to purchase a small plot of land in Montfermeil, where Duncan had a colony of devotees. The Montfermeil purchase was about a half hour from Paris and just up the road from where the French artist Jean-Baptiste-Camille Corot had once lived. The two friends constructed a hut for themselves with a red roof and planned to paint their replicas of Greek art on the walls. They made their own clothes and cultivated vegetables in the backyard, seeking to match the old Greek spirit. Since Raymond Duncan held Akademia's recitals nearby, Foujita and Kawashima joined the pyrrhic dancing in the woods. Foujita did his own laundry, sometimes dressed in a revealing Japanese-style loincloth. When he wore the same loincloth to a Greek dance session, the Western devotees expressed their surprise and admiration. It goes without saying that Foujita's comings and goings, in his very international costumes, did not pass unnoticed in that Parisian suburb. As he tried out his homemade bow and arrow or took an afternoon nap in the open fields, Foujita could not get over his good fortune at being able to do as he pleased. Delighted by the fruit trees around his hut, he savored a freedom impossible in Japan.

In June 1915, with wartime conditions worsening, Foujita and Kawashima moved farther off, to Count Alphonse de Fleurieu's chateau in France's Dordogne region. The call-up of able-bodied men during wartime had caused a labor shortage, and so the count asked the two Japanese artists for help in taking care of his property. In exchange for a place to live, they were responsible for drying out the excessive humidity in the count's chateau by lighting the stove each day. Foujita wrote that the offer sounded good when he and Kawashima heard about it in Paris, but once they arrived, they had their reservations. The chateau that they were supposed to inhabit part-time was rotting away from the moisture and had been built into the side of a cliff that Foujita feared would collapse onto their heads when it rained. Foujita believed that the count had invited the two of them—ignorant

Japanese—because none of the locals would spend time in such an unhealthy environment. Moreover, the count, a cheapskate who even hoarded all the available eggs, hoped to recruit Foujita and Kawashima as farm workers, but in the end, they managed to avoid such chores.

Still, Foujita and Kawashima found much to please them in an area where they could fish for their meals and eat vegetables fresh from the fields. Sometimes they broke into song atop a precipice, while one of their drawings shows them in front of the count's clammy chateau performing a Greek dance. Through it all, the two men kept working at their painting, sure they would start an artistic revolution. "Cadmus was a prince of the Phoenicians," Kawashima wrote in his diary. "He was a man of wisdom and courage who was determined to bring the sixteen-character alphabet to ancient Greece . . . Foujita and I are modern-day Cadmuses teaching the world a new alphabet of art." Foujita was much impressed by the prehistoric ruins in the vicinity, particularly the wall paintings in the caves. Guided through those caves by the renowned French archaeologist and cave expert Abbé Henri Breuil—an experience he remembered to the end of his life—Foujita wrote home enthusiastically about the well-preserved depictions of mammoths, foxes, and other animals. Since Foujita had already been bowled over by Henri Rousseau and by classical art, the forms in these prehistoric works, which were rich with the emotions of centuries past, gave him proof, once again, of the power in the primitive.

While most of the art he created in Dordogne has been lost, for Foujita, there was one lasting accomplishment: his trademark hairstyle was created one night during their stay. This haircut, much like an upsidedown rice bowl, would be endlessly photographed, imitated, and caricatured in the future. An entry in Kawashima's diary for June 23, 1915, describes how Foujita came to spend the rest of his life in bangs: "Tonight there was a great revolution in hairstyles. By the lamplight, Foujita cut his long hair without any regrets. After he did this, the spirit of ancient Greece emerged. We joined hands and celebrated this event."

"When I look back on those days," Foujita said years afterward, "I feel that my clothing was very crazy. But at the time, I thought it was extremely artistic. I thought that I myself had to become a work of art in every way." Although he had reservations later, the passion of Foujita's "return to the Greeks" was real at the time, but more important was his daring in a new environment. Certainly, much daring was required for a Japanese to walk down Parisian streets in a Greek tunic, and daring, in those foreign parts, was half the battle. In addition, the times called for liveliness, despite wartime privations, and Foujita displayed the requisite high spirits day after day. "We also went to the galleries and the museums together," Kawashima said later. "Foujita was always more flashy in his behavior than I was and bolder, too. He behaved like my older brother. I was actually half a year older than he was and had lived in Paris and abroad longer than he had, but compared with him, I was just a sweet little boy."

Kawashima's diary has numerous references to his own coughs, colds, and lung troubles, as well as to the maladies of other Japanese artists: "I heard that Yasui [Sōtarō]'s illness (lungs) was not good and that he went home first class by ship. The company's apparently fully booked up to the eleventh. The weaklings are fleeing in great numbers." Foujita seems to have remained robust throughout, ready to join Kawashima whenever he was able, for nights on the town or, on special occasions, for demonstrations of the Japanese arts. One evening, wearing Greek clothes, they attended a costume ball hosted by Russian artists. After changing into a kimono, Kawashima performed a sword dance, while Foujita recited a Chinese poem to great applause.

When he could no longer manage amidst the dangers of wartime France, the hardy Foujita departed in January 1916 for a year in London, where he thrived in his new surroundings. There are stories of him working as a designer and tailor at Selfridges department store and as a restorer for an antique shop owned by a Japanese merchant. Isadora Duncan introduced him to her social circle; he joined a touring Japanese dance troupe and, despite a total lack of experience, claimed to have been a great success. There are conflicting reports about Foujita's liaison with a "very well-known" woman and the tent they shared in the countryside. Perhaps encouraged by his triumphs in Greek sandals, Foujita became more reliant on a distinctive wardrobe to announce that he had arrived in town. Even on a tight budget, Foujita made his mark. But London was ready: On one of his visits, *The*

Times reported sighting "a Japanese phenomenon, wearing a violet costume and with bangs on his forehead, walking down Piccadilly."

Once the wartime hazards lessened, Foujita returned to Paris to build his reputation as an artist. The sickly Kawashima went off to the Spanish coast, where he recuperated from his lung ailment and took a castle tour. Eventually, after a stay in the United States, he returned to Japan in 1919.

Kawashima had helped Foujita get established in Paris, and he later complained about being completely ignored in his friend's discussions of his youth. But Kawashima, who knew Foujita better than most, had no doubt about his roommate's superior fortitude: "Foujita is thinking about both of our futures all the time," Kawashima wrote as a young man in 1915. "He is a person of great strength, and I rely on him for everything. Having agreed to take responsibility for me, he intends to work hard at this task."

ELEVEN

CARP AND
CHERRY BLOSSOMS

*In cité Falguière, wondrous slum of the arts, where Montparnasse's
great past still seems to hang upon the bushes and dangling leaves
that clog the stones and the staircase, Toda reigns.*
  —Paris-Montparnasse, *September 15, 1929*

Foujita and Kawashima were not the only Japanese in Paris to
choose outlandish clothing. Toda Kaiteki, a Japanese artist who
went to Paris in 1923, could match them, seam for seam, in
every unforgettable detail. Toda caused a stir when he walked down
Parisian boulevards, since, as a rule, he wore only Japanese robes whenever he went out. A photograph in *Paris-Montparnasse* shows how much
Toda stood out in his adopted country; Toda posed in his cité Falguière
studio, dressed in his customary Japanese formal wear with the requisite white *tabi* socks and sandals on his feet. Beside him is a collection
of Japanese swords and, on the wall, a single Noh mask. He wore his
hair gathered in the back, in an old-fashioned style also found on retired samurai.

Before leaving Japan for France, Toda must have sensed trouble
waiting, since, according to one account, he made careful preparations
for his journey. He cut off his little finger, placed it in a jar of alcohol,
and presented the bottle to the head priest of a Buddhist temple. Toda
requested that this memento of his earthly body be buried in the
temple grounds if he died outside of Japan. Aside from pickling his

finger, Toda created a Buddhist name for himself, to be used after his death. He then attended a party to celebrate his departure. In a joyous mood, Toda danced and drank the night away before leaving for France.

Once in Paris, he chose to present himself as a pure specimen of Japaneseness in his art as well as in his personal appearance. Toda had started out as a sculptor, but in Paris he became a specialist in very Japanese-looking paintings on silk, principally of fish. More precisely, Toda was a master of painting carp. He could also do squirrels, cats, birds, and tigers, but Toda made much of his money from carp on silk ("I don't even bother to count the number of scales I speedily draw on a carp like this," he told a potential customer. "But it always comes out thirty-one"). Although he was like Foujita in occupying a studio at cité Falguière, Toda differed from his Japanese colleague in keeping a glass tank filled with water in the middle of his quarters—no doubt stocked with his principal subjects. He was known for his hard work and kept up his strength by constantly nibbling on raw garlic, which filled his studio with a distinctive aroma.

Toda's inability to speak French was well-known, and among the few phrases he had mastered were *méthode orientale* (Oriental method) and *poisson Toda* (fish Toda), which he went around yelling all the time. Toda's carp paintings found customers, but much of his income went to pay for his frequent drinking bouts (Toda could also pronounce "gin" and the names of his bars). The combination of alcohol and Japanese martial arts traditions could have dangerous consequences in Paris: according to Montparnasse legend, Toda—presumably costumed in one of his Japanese outfits—once started a big ruckus when he drew his sword in a Montparnasse café.

Foujita considered Toda "a free spirit . . . He always draws pictures of carp, and though he draws the same thing a hundred times, he has the strange ability to do it well a hundred times." Eventually, Toda's health failed, and as he had feared, he died in France in 1931, far from home. His friend Foujita had him transported to a first-class hospital for his final days, and when Toda died, the proprietors of his drinking spots contributed one thousand francs each to pay for the funeral. By that time, Toda had made an impression on Robert McAlmon, who wrote that Toda "had a wild, primitive quality. His magnificently shaped head and indeed his entire appearance made one think of the legends of the Samurai knights in the days before upstarts from the Western world invaded Japan."

In every aspect of his life abroad, Toda sought to emphasize his connection to *le pays du soleil levant* (the land of the rising sun)—the quaint phrase often used by the French to refer to Japan. His behavior, however, was not a mere desire for spectacle, but an astute marketing strategy. One might say that Toda Kaiteki strolling down the Champs-Élysées in Japanese garments illustrated an extreme solution to the problem faced by Japanese artists in Paris.

Every Japanese artist in France at that time had to contend with the phenomenon known as *japonisme*, the French love affair with Japanese art. *Japonisme* began to be a force in France in the mid-nineteenth century when Japan, after the long years of isolation, opened itself up to trade with the outside world. Suddenly, many examples of Japanese arts and crafts appeared in France, often sold alongside objects from China. Over the years, various French individuals have claimed to be the first to understand the importance of Japanese art and thus to be deserving of recognition as the "originator" of *japonisme*. The most winning story centers around Félix Bracquemond, a French artist and printmaker, who, around 1856, discovered that wondrous pictures from a Japanese album had been used to pack imported porcelain. He next acquired his own copy of this album, which happened to be a collection of woodblock prints by the Japanese artist Hokusai. Armed with his Japanese treasure, Bracquemond showed Hokusai's works to every artist he encountered and so introduced the Japanese woodblock print to France.

Among French artists, a passion for Hokusai and other Japanese printmakers followed, as did a quest for more information about Japanese art. At approximately the same time that Japanese artists in Japan were trying to master the principles of Western oil paintings, their French counterparts were attempting to fathom Japanese artistic techniques. The French, enthusiastic about Japanese woodblock prints (particularly *ukiyo-e*, which often featured courtesans, actors, and other denizens of the "floating world"), screens, ink paintings, and other artistic creations, pored over works by the Japanese masters. By 1868, when Édouard Manet completed his *Portrait of Émile Zola*, the profound Japanese influence on French art was indisputable. Manet depicted Zola seated at a desk by a Japanese woodblock print of a sumo wrestler and a Japanese screen, as if to announce the writer's ease among such recent imports.

The French admired the ukiyo-e for their colors, so flat and bright and bold. They learned much from the decorative motifs, and in the lively, uninhibited subject matter found their liberation. Awakened to new possibilities, French artists also strove to match the lines that could capture a whole person, animal, or scene in a few strokes. They went on to imitate other Japanese practices, such as the fondness for cutting things off midway. Soon there were French paintings featuring truncated boats and human figures.

Any mention of *japonisme* must include Toulouse-Lautrec, who was ardent about applying what he had learned from the Japanese. He revolutionized the French poster by using thick, audacious lines to portray his cabaret performers, and his brash color schemes owed much to the Japanese masters whom he considered his brothers. Toulouse-Lautrec's art often relied upon the Japanese technique of showing only parts of people, and posters have never been the same since he depicted La Goulue dancing at the Moulin Rouge with only a partial view of her partner, Valentin "the Boneless." In van Gogh's championship of Japanese art, there was predictable urgency. "I envy the Japanese artists for the incredible neat clarity which all their works have," he wrote. "It is never boring and you never get the impression that they work in a hurry. It is as simple as breathing; they draw a figure with a couple of strokes with such an unfailing ease as if it were as easy as buttoning one's waist-coat." In 1887, van Gogh was moved to create the oil paintings *Bridge in the Rain* (1887) and *Plum Tree in Bloom* (1887), his versions of woodblock prints by Hiroshige.

While the French craze for Japanese art had died down by the time Toda and Foujita arrived in Paris in the early part of the twentieth century, the spirit of *japonisme* lingered, and the French could still eagerly seek out a Japanese artist's depiction of plum trees in the snow. Temple roofs emerging from the fog, pleasure boats on the Sumida River— the French could not get enough of such Japanese images. This special position occupied by Japanese art greatly inhibited those Japanese artists who had traveled to France to master Western painting. Expatriate Japanese may have been eager to learn about how Renoir, Cézanne, and others achieved their effects, but the more Japanese artists employed these techniques, the more the French berated them for ignoring their Japanese heritage and merely copying the West. No one asked Picasso to paint bullfights to keep in touch with his Spanish background, or Modigliani to include motifs from the Italian Renaissance in his portraits, but French critics and customers insisted that Japanese artists evoke their native land in paintings, perhaps with moonlit autumn grasses or some other touch of the Japanese exotic.

Was it any wonder that Toda, facing starvation in his Left Bank studio, painted carp by the dozen and always dressed as if he had just returned from an all-Japanese funeral? He cannot be blamed for trying to catch the eye of buyers enamored by *japonisme* in order to earn his living. Viewed in this light, the carp were a sensible solution. As late as 1929, a French art critic praised one contemporary Japanese artist exhibiting works in Paris for "not forgetting all the artistic resources of Japan" and another for "showing himself as a person completely of his race" even when painting landscapes of Paris. Later on in that same essay, the critic struck a more admonitory note:

> There are other [Japanese] artists, whom we will not name, who have submitted to indisputable European influences, but let them beware. An artist never wins by trading away his originality, if he has one, for someone else's. Very fortunately, most Japanese artists understand that by walking upon the path of their Japanese ancestors, while at the same time adapting to their own epoch but remaining faithful to the spirit and the sensibility of their race, they will develop their personalities more surely than by making themselves into servile imitators of celebrities in modern cosmopolitan painting who have often themselves achieved nothing but dubious glories.

Ishii Hakutei, a Japanese artist who had lived in Paris from 1911 to 1912, felt moved to come to the defense of Western-style painters from Japan. In a plaintive 1923 essay, he begged the French to understand that centuries had passed since the days when artists depicted subjects like hawks and pine trees, which the French so adored: "In Japan," Ishii wrote,

> there is no longer a single artist who blindly continues to practice his art according to the principles of the Tosa, Kanō, Nanga, Shijō schools or of the ukiyo-e print ... Since we [Japanese artists] all receive a mostly European education and because we take European works as our models, we would be going against the nature of things if we did not conform to that influence ... Certain Europeans believe that imitation is the driving force among us Japanese artists who paint in oils ... I must say that this is an erroneous opinion. Contemporary Japanese artists receive their impressions of nature almost like Europeans. And like Europeans, they find a way to express themselves directly through oil painting. Of course, [the Japanese] lack experience in that tradition of European art, which inevitably leads to defects in the drawing, in the coloring, and even in the material practice of their art. I cannot deny this.

TWELVE

A WOMAN'S ROLE

*In winter, through the cold, short, and often hungry days, we hung
about in the Rotonde from morning to night. What else could we
do, where else could we go? . . . Most of us were chronically short of
coal and gas and had long since fed the stove all that could be
burned; the water in our studios was frozen.*

—Marevna

With *japonisme* still a force to contend with in France, Foujita
was back in Paris from London by the beginning of 1917. He
attempted to eke out a living, but the ongoing war continued
to limit opportunities in the art world and otherwise. Though short
on funds, Foujita had, as usual, enough energy to spruce himself up
for the entertainment of his friends and innocent bystanders. He kept
to the same hairstyle he had devised during his Greek period—the
bowl cut called *kappa* in Japanese after a similar look on a legendary
water sprite. "I had bangs, a necklace, and earrings; it is amazing, what
I did," he later said. Since Foujita had worked as a tailor in London, his
sewing skills had much improved; years later, a friend remembered arriving for visits and often finding him at work at his sewing machine.
He made an outfit for himself out of the floral-patterned curtains that
he found in his living quarters, a creation that made such an instantaneous impression that an elderly woman stopped him on the street to
inquire if he was a man or a woman. "Unfortunately, I am a man," Foujita replied.

Dressed in the former curtain, Foujita headed toward a Montparnasse café and a romance crucial to his future. Garbed as he was, his arrival did not pass unnoticed: "As he came through the swinging doors, 'various movements' rippled across the tables of the Rotonde."* Foujita soon saw the Frenchwoman Fernande Barrey seated at a table with her friends. Jean-Paul Crespelle describes her appealing freshness, with her bright eyes and turned-up nose. Her high spirits could not be missed, nor could anyone ignore her rough voice and the vocabulary that went with it. Theirs was not love at first sight, and one can understand that Fernande would have qualms about the peculiarly attired Japanese man who came over to speak to her. "Nice dress," he said as an opening. She brushed him off, but her tone must have offered encouragement, because Foujita, unfazed by the cold, snowy weather that night in March 1917, followed Fernande home. "He intended to follow her, no matter how far she went," writes Tanaka Jō. Foujita's resolve was not much tested, since she disappeared into her apartment on rue Delambre, only a few moments' walk away. Having ascertained Fernande's place of residence, Foujita next returned to his own lodgings and set to work. His sewing expertise again came in handy when he made Fernande a blouse out of a deep-blue fabric he had bought in London. The next day, he traipsed off in the snow to deliver his present.

Fernande apparently appreciated the gesture, for as the story goes, she invited Foujita into her apartment. That wartime winter of 1917 was particularly frigid, and heating coal very difficult to obtain. (It is said that a government minister had to intervene in order to send a supply to the dying Rodin.) This mighty Frenchwoman could respond to necessity, for despite her straitened circumstances, she had

---

*Montparnasse vivant (p. 152) says that Foujita met Fernande at the Rotonde in March 1917, but the Buissons believe that Foujita and Fernande met across the street at the Dôme, because the Rotonde had been temporarily closed down by police who considered it a refuge for "deserters, defeatists, germanophiles, and drug users." Klüver and Martin write that the Rotonde was not closed by the police until the end of 1917, which means that it was still open in March, when the couple's initial meeting took place. They also say that the Rotonde faced additional "trumped-up charges of selling American cigarettes." See Sylvie and Dominique Buisson, Léonard-Tsuguharu Foujita (Paris: ACR Édition, 1987), p. 46; Billy Klüver and Julie Martin, "Carrefour Vavin," in The Circle of Montparnasse: Jewish Artists in Paris, 1905–1945, ed. Kenneth E. Silver (New York: Universe Books, 1985), p. 71.

inherited a Louis XV–style chair from her father. To prove her muscle and determination, she took up a hatchet to demolish the chair, using the pieces to feed the fire and warm her freezing apartment. The hand-made blouse, together with the chopped-up chair, were sufficient proofs of their mutual affection, and Foujita began to live in Fernande's apartment. Thirteen days later, the couple was officially married, on March 27, 1917. The groom did not have money to pay for his wedding expenses, but a waiter at the Rotonde loaned him the funds, to be deducted from the cost of Foujita's painting his girlfriend's portrait. Foujita made a studio for himself out of what had once been a stable in the courtyard of Fernande's building and worked, as was his custom then, seated at a low table without an easel. He remembered Japan in the large paper lanterns he used as decorations and the supposedly "magical" green tea he brewed himself.

The French took this marriage and Foujita's subsequent alliances in their stride, but the Japanese could not hide their envy, indignation, shock. Unquestionably, Foujita's marriage to Fernande stirred up the Japanese expatriate community. "In that period [marrying a Western woman] was unusual for a Japanese," writes Hayashi Yōko. "Japanese usually lived in a circle of Japanese and left Paris at the end of several years. Japanese believed that Foujita had started living a life like that depicted in La Bohème. Foujita found himself more and more isolated from other Japanese who lived in Paris, and forgotten or scorned in Japan."

Even his Japanese friends could not bring themselves to utter a kind word about his new wife. The judo expert Ishiguro Keishichi (who eventually distinguished himself by establishing a judo school in Paris) considered Fernande too plain, and like other disapproving Japanese, he disliked her constant nagging. For such Japanese observers, Fernande's lack of refinement marked her as Foujita's obvious social inferior. This is a familiar nightmare, experienced then and now by the horrified who must stand by as their friends or relatives abroad seem to forget their station in life and latch onto supposedly unsuitable mates. Satsuma Jirohachi, a wealthy patron of the arts, also had little tolerance for Foujita's women, especially those encountered in Montparnasse cafés. Satsuma disdained these cheap women who "smelled of urine." Another Japanese friend, sure that Foujita had a masochistic streak, saw Fernande as another example of his appalling taste in female companions.

Taken together, these attitudes reflected a belief among Japanese men that foreign women were a blight upon a male's existence, to be taken on with much caution. "If Asians cannot spend one or two hours a day in contemplation," wrote one of Foujita's former classmates, "they tend to feel that their whole sense of life has been lost. However, if an Asian follows this practice and has a foreign wife, she gets worried and starts to pester him about whether he's sick or doesn't love her anymore."

Japanese male prejudices aside, there must have been some truth to the descriptions of Fernande, since Nina Hamnett also found "Madame Foujita" hard to abide for long periods: "She was French and had the most beautiful legs, but her body was shapeless and enormous. She had the most terrifying face I have ever seen and I was frightened of her. She screamed at Foujita most of the time . . . Foujita was angelic and never answered back or said a word." Later on, after Foujita had become successful, Fernande continued to resist the lure of decorum. To a reporter's questions about her early career as a model, she replied, "Model? I was a street-walker!" Actually, her accomplishments were notable in spheres she probably considered too respectable for the crude impression she preferred to create. At the time she met Foujita, she was an art student and eventually had works displayed in the Salon d'Automne.

In his book *The Japanese Guys of the School of Paris*, Tamagawa Shinmei proves himself that rarity among Japanese men. He goes so far as to suggest that a non-Japanese female might serve a beneficial purpose. Tamagawa makes his position clearer when he titles a chapter "In a Foreign Country, Guys Who Aren't Popular with Women Probably Can't Succeed." Tamagawa concedes that while Fernande may have rattled certain people, she, unlike Foujita (who still spent his days in a haze of linguistic confusion), could communicate fluently with influential figures in her native French. She could help Foujita with language problems, instruct him about French customs, and in general get him to feel more at home in France. In addition, Fernande was herself a budding artist with contacts in the Parisian art world.

Whether or not Fernande was as difficult, foul-mouthed, and promiscuous as reported—"I liked to have a good time," she admitted; "I had about ten flirtations a day"—she seems to have dedicated herself to promoting Foujita's career. According to her version of events— widely circulated despite the obvious embellishments—she urged Foujita to concentrate on his painting while she took care of earning money and selling his pictures. She claims that she showed his work to gallery owners, lugging examples of his creations around town herself. She did not have much success until she was caught one day in a rainstorm and looked for shelter in the Galerie Chéron on rue La Boétie. As Fernande told it, the owner, Georges Chéron, showed no interest in Foujita's work, but she borrowed an umbrella and left her husband's paintings behind as a guarantee. In true legend style, a wealthy customer arrived at the gallery later and happened upon Foujita's works. After buying up everything available, he asked for more, but Chéron, who had no idea where to find Foujita, had to wait a month before Fernande came by again. A contract with Chéron and Foujita's first solo exhibitions followed.

Foujita, annoyed about hearing time and again about the heroic role Fernande played in his career, later challenged her account of those days. In his version, it was snowing, not raining, the day of that first meeting with Chéron and, more important, Foujita himself pounded the pavement to sell his work and negotiated with the dealer:

This rumor [about Fernande's role] is totally untrue though my wife Fernande always talked about it. Also, she was not a woman artist, but only someone who went around acting like an inexperienced woman art student. She did errands like delivering my works to the galleries, but she did not help me become a success. On the contrary, she often did things that got in my way . . . She was a woman who talked a lot and spread nonsense in the Montparnasse cafés. She was a good person, but that's all.

The debate continues over whether Foujita's account is more proof of his inability to admit receiving help from anyone or a necessary correction of history. In any case, Foujita's version came out rather late, long after Fernande's tale had captivated readers of early accounts of his life. For this reason, Foujita's testimony has, so far, made a very faint impression on the biographical record.

Although the circumstances surrounding the meeting with Chéron remain clouded, the dealer, definitely impressed, signed Foujita to a seven-year contract at 450 francs per month. Chéron's business practices have been criticized—there is, for instance, a story about how he kept Modigliani working down in his basement with some wine bottles and the maid for a model—and years later Foujita did not recall his first dealer with affection: "Chéron would get the artists drunk and present them with contracts to sign." Fernande, on the other hand, appreciated the good food that Chéron served to his hungry clients, in particular the *moules marinière* and *haricots rouges*.

While the contract may not have been entirely to Foujita's liking, the steady income was welcome, and to celebrate their good fortune, the couple purchased a cage with two canaries. Foujita's first exhibition was held in the Galerie Chéron in 1917.

THIRTEEN

RISING STAR AT CHÉRON'S

*All these paintings [by Foujita] have something of the spontaneity
and freshness of vision so striking in the Douanier Rousseau. At the
same time, Rousseau's innocence is a consequence of his untutored
technique—supposing one can use that word of a painter whose genius so largely took the place of technique—whereas Foujita is far
from being naive.*

—Jean Selz

In discussing Foujita's life, French writers sometimes refer to him as
Héritier de la Paix, Champ de Glycines (Heir of Peace, Field of Wisteria), the literal translation of the four Japanese characters used to
write his name. Such French translations make it easy to imagine
the numerous social occasions when French people asked Foujita
detailed questions about his Japanese background. How did he write
his name in Japanese? What did the characters mean? Which is the
family name, and which the given name? Why is the order different
from what we write in the West? The curious may have gone on to
wonder, Did Japanese men still carry samurai swords on the way to
work? Is it true about the geishas and the raw fish? Such questions
pose a problem for all expatriates who have, after all, purposely put
themselves at a distance from their places of origin. Certain expatriates
bristle and refuse to answer these queries, but others revel in their for-
eignness. These go out of their way to supply information about their

hometowns, childhood toys, New Year's festivals, and the meanings of family names.

Clearly, Foujita was the sort who was willing to talk at length about his Japanese background. He, like his friend Toda Kaiteki, no doubt understood that emphasizing his Japanese glamour was good for business. I can see him flourishing a Japanese calligraphy brush for his audience in France as he drew the characters used to write his name. The first character means "wisteria," and the second one "field," he must have said, summoning the Mysterious East in every gesture. He could have disarmed the French further by going on to discuss his ancestors and the genuine samurai in his background. These discourses achieved their purpose, since at least one French writer asks whether readers have heard of Foujita, "from a samurai family of Chiba Prefecture and a man currently in fashion."

Kondō Fumito, who has written a biography of Foujita, is sure that despite the calligraphy demonstrations, Foujita had no desire to become a Toda-like cartoon of a Japanese. Kondō sees Foujita always aiming for a wider fame than was available to an artist specializing in carp on silk. At the same time, Foujita's turning his back on Japanese traditions would have displeased French critics and customers. This was Foujita's quandary, and he took some time to find his way.

For his first exhibit at the Galerie Chéron in 1917, Foujita presented 110 watercolors. He fiddled with his original Japanese name, Fujita Tsuguharu, changing it to what he must have thought was the more French-looking "Tsugouharu Foujita." This mouthful was gradually abbreviated to "Foujita." Having given himself a French-looking name, he showed some confusion by calling attention to his Japanese origins. In the catalogue for the Chéron show, he introduced himself as "Son of General Foujita." Certain critics questioned the necessity of bringing in his father's military position when he introduced himself as an artist. Even so, for his next show, Foujita continued to advertise his background by including a reproduction of his family crest in the catalogue. He already had friends in important places, since the noted poet and critic André Salmon wrote the introductory essay for the catalogue. Salmon praised Foujita, writing, "The unfettered art of Foujita will offer all the joys one expects in ancient spectacles made anew in the light of a foreign mirror." At the same time, Salmon began the tradition of Japan-besotted prose that would often greet Foujita's work in France. In his brief essay, Salmon managed to mention samurai, the Japanese imperial family, and the woodblock print artists Hokusai ("the old man mad about drawing") and Kunimasa, before moving on to other parts of Asia with references to Chinese art and the Korean emperor.

Foujita took pride in telling how Picasso attended his first exhibition and stayed for several hours. "Picasso did not only look at what was depicted in my works," Foujita immodestly claimed years later. "He also looked at the works and thought about how I would develop from there, what kinds of works I would create after ten or twenty years." (Other artists were not as happy when Picasso spent much time studying their creations, since he frequently appropriated their ideas. "Picasso, when he's in your studio," complained the sculptor Alberto Giacometti, "looks at your work not with two eyes but with two cameras, and the next day does the same thing ten times over.") Sales at Foujita's show were excellent, leading to another show at the same gallery in November 1917. As a rising star in the art world, Foujita could afford to include more oils in his show at the Galerie Devambez late in 1918.

Few of Foujita's works from this period have survived, but among those extant, there are beautiful exercises by an artist still seeking to discover his strengths. In his watercolors, Foujita drew long-bodied, slender women in moments of repose and stillness. Holding a watering can or a simple sprig of flowers, these graceful women seem to be contemplating a memory more haunting than any other. He brought much self-assurance to the delicate lines defining their thin fingers and wispy, diaphanous wraps. In such works, Foujita could take credit for moments memorably expressed. During this period, Foujita favored elongated faces reminiscent of those painted by his friend and former neighbor Modigliani. While the critics went out of their way to find assorted Japanese influences everywhere, to a more casual observer these are not so apparent.

During these years, Foujita tried out bright and contrasting colors that pushed against each other unrepentantly—a woman in an orange blouse, for example, set against a green background with her brown hair and shawl. He could also present his thoughtful, long-faced women with Cubist touches, their exaggerated arms and fingers adding more riddles to the works. Foujita also turned repeatedly to children, and in these early works, he shows them seated obediently but resisting innocence; unsettling insights seem to spill out from their large, brooding eyes. The earthy tones in some of his watercolors would not have been out of place in the cave paintings Foujita had seen by candlelight in Dordogne. He produced more evidence of studies of the ancients in bathers and flute players, as well as in a portrait of his wife as Nefertiti's contemporary. His religious works reflect a lasting interest in Catholicism.

Gradually, Foujita moved away from the distinct patches of color to his rigorously restricted palette. In a landscape such as *Suburban Landscape in the Snow* (1918), he had the courage to limit himself to mostly black, brown, and white. He shunned the fine points on the storm clouds, but showed off his brushwork in depicting all the slats of an intricate fence. In this landscape and many others, Foujita drew upon Henri Rousseau's technique and subject matter. This was shown not only in the stark scenery, but also in the sense of ominousness sweeping over Paris's snowy fields and suburban streets. Foujita drew hundreds of Paris scenes, particularly of the sparsely populated outskirts, which show his fascination with his new home, as well as a foreigner's anxiety and loneliness. The highly praised landscapes did much to improve his reputation, for Foujita looked upon Paris as an outsider would, and his fresh view of the city—which one critic praised as a "revelation"—charmed the French.

In considering these early works, art historian Shimizu Toshio insists on Foujita's adroit use of the new knowledge he had acquired in France. "This was not just *japonisme*," Shimizu declares in a 1988 essay, "but a synthesis of all Foujita had learned since his arrival in Paris." Shimizu goes on to cite those influences, including Cubism, prehistoric art, the classical age, the Renaissance, Christianity, and Henri Rousseau. Despite the evidence of such wide-ranging studies, many French critics overlooked them, preferring to marvel at Foujita's more familiar Japanese effects. "There are some Japanese who have come to Europe to be educated as painters in our ateliers," a French critic wrote of Foujita's 1918 show:

They have taken much interest in their praiseworthy efforts, but we have seen among these artists only those who have completely lost their own personal flavor in the compositions they have forced themselves to paint in the European style. We are inclined to regret that they do not remain rigorously faithful to their traditions and their ancient models. What is true for them is not true for their compatriot Fugita [sic].

Later on, Foujita wrote angrily about those reviews, "Most of the art reviewers did not even try to write conscientious critiques. They were completely gripped by foolish racial prejudices and saw Japanese as a yellow race or cunning monkeys. Even when it came to art, they ranked Asians and Europeans differently. They did not have the generosity to look upon us equally. They wouldn't have dreamed of viewing a Japanese on par with a great French master."

FOURTEEN

TO THE SOUTH
WITH FRIENDS

The School of Paris exists.
—André Warnod, 1925

More in demand, Foujita responded in his usual manner: by painting constantly. His output accorded with the long hours he spent in the studio. Between June 1917 and November 1918, he exhibited close to four hundred works.

Despite this, Foujita still had enough energy left over to enjoy his free moments and did not lack for cronies to join him on his jaunts around town. Though he had enough friends to take up such duties, it is striking that Foujita, despite his French wife, associated mostly with foreigners. The Japanese Kawashima Riichirō had been his indispensable companion; the Mexican Diego Rivera had taken him to see the Spaniard Pablo Picasso; the Italian Amedeo Modigliani was a cherished friend. Were there no French artists in Foujita's circle?

The truth was that in those days, a horde of artists from all over the world had flocked to Paris and chosen to stay on indefinitely. Picasso settled there for good in 1904; Rivera arrived in 1909; Piet Mondrian, a Dutchman, in 1911; and Foujita, the Japanese, in 1913. Many Jewish artists from Eastern Europe came to escape from persecution and oppressive traditions. "The sun of art shone only in Paris," Marc Chagall, a Russian who arrived in Paris in 1910, once said of those days. This international community, as the art historian Romy Golan has pointed out, grew even larger in the period after the First World War. At that time, France was eager for immigrants because so many citizens had been killed during the war. Foreign artists, who swept in along with the workers filling conventional jobs, became so numerous that some French told of walking down certain Left Bank avenues without hearing their own language spoken properly. Golan quotes a French critic's disgruntled description of a Paris landmark: "The Rotonde . . . where all the dialects on earth are spoken, sometimes even French . . ."

Still, the French had good reason to take pride in their ability to welcome and absorb so many nationalities. The foreign artists were in turn grateful for the sense of emancipation, the cheap studios, and the independent academies with their liberal admissions policies. The café owners tolerated customers who ate little and stayed long hours, while galleries were willing to sponsor exhibits of these innovators from outside the country. The times encouraged Fauves, Cubists, Expressionists, Futurists, Dadaists, and Surrealists along with anyone else trying something new and controversial. It was generally believed that these expatriate artists lived out a dream of creative mayhem in Montparnasse.

The presence of so many international artists fortified France's position as the world's art capital, but after a while, the French envisaged the ruination of native traditions by these unruly outsiders. In 1925, the Salon des Indépendants decided that works by artists from all over the world would no longer be exhibited together but instead would be grouped by nationality. This would keep the baleful non-French works safely apart. Golan sees long-simmering French xenophobia and anti-Semitism taking its toll on the School of Paris, which had once encompassed the entire jumble of postwar art in France. Gradually, the idea of the School of Paris was narrowed to refer only to the foreign artists and thus distinguished from the French School (École Française), which was composed of only French artists. Golan shows that since many of the prominent foreign artists were Jews (Moïse Kisling, Jules Pascin, Jacques Lipchitz, and Marc Chagall, to name a few), the School of Paris came to be thought of as a group of recently arrived Jewish artists in Montparnasse.

Picasso, Rivera, Foujita, and many other non-French, non-Jewish artists would also be included among the members of the School of

Paris, but that did not mollify the French purists who continued to be disgusted by the undignified behavior of the foreign society in Montparnasse. Some French artists, as Golan writes, "abandoned the metropolis in favor of the French countryside, often going back to their home provinces . . . This kind of return to the soil was hailed as invigorating, virile, and moral, a pointed contrast to the goings-on of the metropolis." The Jews were not the only ones to make the French artistic establishment uncomfortable. A 1925 edition of a literary review delved into the dangers posed by the "Orient." This Asian onslaught possessed such a poisonous potential that one article was called "Let's Not Lose Our Confidence in Western Thought!"

Perhaps nothing better illustrates what the French most applauded and feared about the School of Paris artists than the trip to the countryside undertaken by poet-turned-art-dealer Leopold Zborowski (Poland) with Modigliani (Italy), Soutine (Lithuania), and Foujita. Here in one expedition to the south of France was the School of Paris's artistic brio, spontaneity, and determined break with the past, as well as its disruptive habits and filth. This 1918 journey is a tale of international friendship tested along the Mediterranean and catches unknown artists in a raw state, before fame shaped their reputations.

In a portrait by his client Modigliani, art dealer Zborowski looks gaunt and weary. This exhaustion was perhaps a result of the effort "Zbo" expended to keep his precious Modigliani alive and working. Zborowski would have had difficulties with the depressed, alcoholic Modigliani even in peacetime, but the world war increased the challenges. Many art dealers had departed from Paris for the duration, and while this left Zborowski free to cultivate his competitors' customers, they in turn were, understandably, preoccupied with more pressing matters of survival. In April 1918, Zborowski decided to go on the offensive and take Modigliani to the south of France, where his works would surely find a better market. Zbo felt that Modigliani required companionship on this journey, and so he invited Soutine and Foujita to join the junket to Cagnes.

Foujita was the most solvent of the trio, since he received a regular stipend from his art dealer, Chéron. Zborowski planned to have the three artists live and work in their rented quarters while he went around selling their masterpieces. In fact, the area was packed with rich people, but they did not show much interest in buying anything. The damp climate was also not salubrious to the tubercular Modigliani, who quickly discovered the bars where he could drown his sorrows. Furthermore, he was infuriated because his lover, Jeanne, did not arrive alone but was accompanied by her mother. Soutine was much more pleased about the change of scenery, since he had never seen the sea before, and spent much time staring at the Mediterranean, which made him sleepy. Some say that Foujita gave him swimming lessons.

Soutine may have taken pleasure in the scenery, but he was a man whose happy moments did not last long. Five years later, when he was back in Cagnes for another stay, Soutine wrote to Zborowski, "I want to get away from Cagnes, a landscape that I cannot abide." The paintings Soutine created during his visits to the region testify to the turbulence within him that continued even when the sun was shining from morning until night. The bucolic setting doubtless further stirred up his anguish, since he knew himself incapable of matching that sort of tranquillity. His disquiet erupts upon his Cagnes canvases in fierce brushstrokes, deforming the stone houses of the town and leaving a staircase blood-red. For Soutine, the trees of Cagnes are malevolent, out to move across the land to vanquish everything. His outbursts drown even the grass.

Soutine's depictions of Cagnes seem particularly vehement when compared with the work of his traveling companions Foujita and Modigliani. Modigliani, drawing some rare landscapes, came up with subdued appreciations of the local scenery, despite the ongoing uproar in his personal life. In one work, the red roofs of the Cagnes homes decorate a bright hillside thick with trees. The different greens of the trees and the fields blend together restfully.

As for Foujita, his was a far cooler response to the French countryside. Actually, Foujita later claimed that Modigliani tried to learn a few secrets from him while they passed the days together: "Once at Cagnes, I was drawing, doing a landscape. Modigliani crept up behind me and watched for an hour. Then he tapped my shoulder and said, 'Now I understand.' He loved Oriental things—he had a stylized art." In his paintings, Foujita stayed away from the rich greens and reds of Modigliani's Cagnes, preferring the gray, black, and white he had been emphasizing in his views of Paris. Foujita's Cagnes is a cloudy and deserted place, with a feeling of emotional barrenness drifting around those same trees and red-roofed houses.

In addition to the stimulation of new vistas, the trip created conflicts that would never have surfaced if these artists had stayed in Paris. Out in the open air, Modigliani resented that Foujita won all their fist-fights even though he was the smaller of the two. Foujita reports that Modigliani brought in as a stand-in "a boy of seventeen to eighteen, a husky bad actor who had been in prison." Foujita once again put his judo skills to good use and vanquished this opponent. "Modigliani said to me, 'Let's see what you can really do with him,' so I threw him a couple of times on the terrace, and Modigliani never took me on afterward."

In this saga of ragtag artists and their long-suffering dealer by the sea, there is romance, romance thwarted, liquor, poultry theft, and once again appalling sanitary habits. Foujita is conspicuous as the only clean, sober, and financially secure member of this group. Soutine had never before owned a toothbrush and received his first one, along with tooth powder, as a gift from Foujita, who also instructed him on the use of this equipment. (This increased Soutine's popularity at the local whorehouse.) "[I] cut a collar out of the tail of a shirt, so he was dressed," said his accomplished tailor Foujita, who also helped Soutine wash away the bedbugs brought along from Paris.

Zborowski spent much of his cash on tips to hotel bellboys, to ease his way to potential buyers, but these sales techniques did not yield enough to feed his hungry entourage. Foujita reports that "[Zborowski's] method was to sit reading a paper on the esplanade, or to go into hotels, presumably for a rendezvous with a duke, or some important person, but nothing came of all this." Meantime, the owner of their accommodations, Papa Curel, grew restless when his rents went unpaid. He longed to be free of his difficult tenants, and they likewise longed to get back to Paris. Papa Curel's woman friend scolded him for getting involved with this bunch in the first place: "What were we thinking when we rented our rooms to these circus clowns?" When Modigliani volunteered to paint her portrait in lieu of further payment, she took his offer as an insult. At last, before allowing them to depart for Paris, Curel confiscated their baggage and painting supplies but not their paintings, which he considered worthless. "Papa Curel did not take our paintings," Foujita declared later. "Five years later he would have become a millionaire with the works of Modigliani, Soutine, and Foujita. Papa Curel died strangled by regrets."

Foujita had other memories of that time in the sun, particularly a visit to the ailing and aged Renoir, who lived close by. "I can see Renoir now, sitting thus, arms on the chair arms, bandaged." Renoir spoke about Japanese art and its influence on him and other Impressionists. Although some doubt his version of this encounter, Foujita declared this meeting a great moment in his life.

Modigliani was not so won over by the master, since Renoir steered their conversation in an awkward direction. "Paint with joy, with the same joy with which you make love," Renoir advised the melancholy, impoverished Modigliani. "Do you caress your canvases a long time? . . . I stroke the buttocks for days and days before finishing a painting."

"I don't like buttocks, Monsieur!" Modigliani shot back as he walked out.

FIFTEEN

SALON'S MAN
OF THE HOUR

During that autumn 1918, hope was reborn in Paris despite the flu epidemic (to which Guillaume Apollinaire would succumb) and the disasters resulting from the German bombs.
—Sylvie and Dominique Buisson

Back in Paris, less drenched in sun, Foujita found success. Once the war came to an end, he was spotted presiding over celebrations "clad in a Samurai robe, his thin lips flowering in the most Japanese of smiles, like the blade of a sword." The year 1919 saw the reopening of the Salon d'Automne, which had been closed during the war. Foujita submitted six works—four watercolors and two oils*—and he was incredulous when all were accepted. Describing this event in his memoirs, he tried to strike a self-effacing note: "On the opening day, I walked into the exhibition hall and was surprised. The works of an upstart like me were exhibited in the most prestigious room, along with Matisse, Bonnard, [André Dunoyer de] Segonzac, Maurice Denis, [Albert] Marquet, and others." Acclaim followed upon acclaim in the next few years with more paintings shown in the Salon d'Automne and other places. In 1921, a spectacular year, Foujita exhibited three oil paintings—a still life, a self-portrait, and a nude—in the distinctive style that would be associated with his name forever after.

---

*The four watercolors were *Christ and the Two Thieves, Adoration of the Infant Jesus, Blind Man's Bluff*, and *Motherhood*; the oils, *Eternal Life* and *Church at Concarneau*.

Although the dates remain uncertain, it is believed that the following year he framed his nude of Kiki—Montparnasse's ubiquitous social icon—with a thread-by-thread re-creation of a densely decorated French fabric. "You couldn't get through the crowds in front of my paintings," he wrote in happy recollection of those days, "and all at once I became the Salon's man of the hour." The general public again rallied to Foujita's side when French colleagues balked at naming him an official member of the Salon d'Automne. "Some of my colleagues in the French art world were not happy about letting a yellow-skinned foreigner become a member." The newspapers took up Foujita's cause, which led to an outpouring of support from the public. Foujita became a member of the Salon in 1920 and joined the Salon jury the following year.

Foujita's artistic achievement can be best appreciated if you view his works in a room filled with the colorful oil paintings of his contemporaries. For maximum effect, hang a Foujita among Picasso's loudly dressed harlequins, the deep red and blue of a Modigliani portrait, and a bloody beef carcass by Soutine. Beside these blasts of color, Foujita's stark paintings stand out as acts of courage. For his nudes, still lifes, self-portraits, he depended upon large swaths of white, created with his special paint, and upon this surface, he often added color in thin washes and his very fine, supple lines in the black that looked like Japanese sumi ink. When Foujita really wanted to prove his point, he stuck to only black and white, attaining a result somewhere between a Japanese ink drawing, an ukiyo-e print, a prehistoric cave painting, a Titian, and a Manet (among other East-West influences). Conspicuously strange, his paintings delighted the European critics by mixing Western oils, Western settings, and Western art history with Japanese traditions. Also hovering around Foujita's best paintings is a sense of anxiety that crosses national borders.

To achieve his singular effect, Foujita started off with the milky white ground he had perfected after much experimentation.* The

*In Japan, Foujita's white is often referred to, in French, as *le grand fond blanc*—"the great white ground." However, in France, Hayashi Yōko made a search of French documents dating from the 1920s and did not find any mention of *le grand fond blanc*. I, too, have never seen a reference to *le grand fond blanc* in French materials from that period.

development of this white required artistry and cunning, as well as the patience to nurture a complex brew. In the annals of art history, few buckets of white paint have caused such a fuss. Foujita's white, spread first across the canvas, can often be seen gleaming through the colors added later, but is more emphatically in the nudes, sheets, and walls, among various other white expanses in his paintings. Foujita refused to disclose the white mixture's ingredients, in order to keep the imitators at bay, and this spawned countless investigations. Recent analyses have again tried to solve the mystery by isolating such components as animal glue, lead white, calcium carbonate, and talc. Foujita always said that he used sumi ink when drawing his line, proud of having achieved the seemingly impossible task of incorporating this tradi- tional Japanese material into an oil painting. His claims have been ex- amined closely, since sumi contains water and ordinarily will not stick to oil paint. One theory is that Foujita's white was an emulsion only partially composed of oil, and that this enabled the sumi to sit on it without difficulty. Another theory suggests that Foujita employed other materials to produce his so-called sumi.

In short, maybe those lines were all sumi, and then again, maybe they weren't.

For his lines, Foujita used a fine Japanese brush, and he acknowl- edged the importance of this tool by often including his brush col- lection in his studio self-portraits. Brush in hand, he mustered the confidence and power to create his sweeping lines. Foujita's lines earned every bit of the amazed reactions they received, since those lines can sweep around a naked woman's body with much courage, fol- lowing the curves of hips and calves, seemingly without a break. The lines do not shy away from toes and fingers either, since these, too, are accurately defined along the way. The lines also perform humbler tasks when Foujita draws, with boundless persistence, every inch of fur on a preening cat, at times moving from a thick black hair on the back to the more sparsely furred side and on to the underside of the paws, which he could reproduce especially well. His lines capture the grains on his studio table and creases in the sheets. No wonder he liked to pose his subjects before intricately patterned fabric, since he could then set about reproducing every flower petal and every ripple in the water. Foujita's thin and steady lines—whether outlining a woman's body or describing the contours of a pipe—are at the heart of his legend. For that reason, Foujita liked to stress their mystique: "Before I draw a line, I want to become one with the object and draw from my instincts . . . I want my mind empty of all thoughts as I give myself over to the flow of the line. Beginning with the very first stroke, I draw without any expectations about what will happen. A line drawn without expectations in mind produces the most interesting result . . ."

"No one could equal that line," the conservator Koyano Masako once told me. "It was completely natural, the result of much practice, and came from days when Japanese sat on the floor and wrote with a brush. No one can do that now. Japanese people don't use brush and ink anymore." The line was undoubtedly dazzling, but came with its own perils. An accomplishment possible only for those in the prime of life, drawing the line required great strength and steadiness in the hands as well as an ability to concentrate over a prolonged period.

In his letters to his Japanese wife, Tomi, when he first arrived in France, Foujita had written repeatedly, in long enthusiastic sentences, about how he was not going to be like other Japanese artists in Paris who were too scared to socialize with the locals and stayed holed up in their rooms. Monotonously, with an ego as big as a chateau, he insisted over and over that he was going to explore everything, that he was going to succeed, going to create something original. "I'll create works that the Westerners can't, something containing the art of the East's Japan. Of course the materials will be oils, but the results will be impressive and valuable as works of art."

Foujita at last achieved his goal sometime around 1921, in an oil painting such as *My Room, Still Life with Alarm Clock*, a look at his studio that was shown at the 1921 Salon d'Automne. *My Room* was one of Foujita's personal favorites, and he lugged the painting around with him over changes of residence and mood. In 1941, when Foujita was living in Japan, an editor reported that *My Room*—along with a similar still life—consoled Foujita in dark moments: "He kept those two paintings carefully wrapped in paper. 'You have to take a picture of these,' he told me and brought them out. 'When I find that I can't paint,' he said while untying the strings, 'or feel myself slackening off, I take these two paintings out and look at them in a prayerful state of mind.'"

My Room finds Foujita in that reverential mood, as he shapes hallowed objects out of bits of everyday life. On the table are a red-checked cloth, oil lamp, pipe, doll, drinking glass, each drawn with the meticulous accuracy that brought Foujita his fame. His exact black lines define every strand in the woven basket, every skein of yarn, every turn of metal on the oil lamp. The artist makes each of his ordinary objects worthy of hushed regard. Three mostly white ceramic plates, decorated with country scenes, hang on the white wall; Foujita's distinctive eyeglasses await him, as do an umbrella and sabots. He is restrained about color here, setting off his white—on the walls and in other objects—against the big brown table. Previously, Foujita had earned praise for his landscapes of Paris, which, critics said, looked at familiar places in an illuminating new way. Here, Foujita impressed the critics once again by paying tribute to such items as a commonplace alarm clock and wooden shoes from Brittany.

Foujita also introduced a human presence into this painting without including a single figure. The Japanese artist Foujita, who has left those distinctive eyeglasses on the table and the sabots on the floor, might be off to the side, telling his personal tale. His story praises the quotidian pleasures of French life, like the enjoyment of pottery painted with fruits and lamps of transparent blue glass. The rough table also suits a life of quiet routine. Yet the absent artist does not stop there with a peaceful story; he might be adding a cheeky proclamation. He has included only French objects in this still life, but he has placed them in a spare and pale picture that recalls his faraway place of birth. In his careful rendering of things like a French fabric, Foujita shows his immense confidence. He will not be sequestered, like his quavering Japanese colleagues, in a room bursting with Japanese curios. Master of enough talent and vitality to live amidst red-checked cloths, Foujita claims the French way of life for himself.

It is also easy to see why the crowds flocked to see Foujita's female nudes when they were first exhibited in the Paris salons. With their naked flesh exalted by his white color, his nudes can be found reclining on sheets with multiple wrinkles of a subtly different white. The women stare directly ahead, challenging the world to object to their pose and everything else it implies, while Foujita's ever-so-thin and supple black line outlines their bodies, bringing the flavor of the old Japanese ukiyo-e to twentieth-century France. But before one can give *japonisme* all the credit, attention shifts to the very sincere oddness of the paintings, which shows the influence of Rousseau.

In *Reclining Nude with a Cat* (1921), one of Foujita's perceptive, precisely drawn cats sits beside his naked woman, while in *Nude with a Jouy Fabric* (1922), Kiki is framed by the well-known, complexly patterned French fabric. Again, this cloth definitely stands out here, with its details reproduced by Foujita, in a zealous drive for accuracy, down to the navel on a cherub. In this painting, Kiki is certainly meant to recall the naked women from ages past who have similarly reclined on sofas for artists. None of those older nudes, however, could boast of Foujita's particular shade of white. The white is stunning in the painting of Kiki, for the color, while not quite human, has the moist softness of human flesh. She looks directly at us with her flat, resolute face. And while the artistic influences that went into its creation may be obvious, the flat face is adamant about a contemporary woman's inscrutability.

Foujita's 1921 *Self-Portrait,* which was also included in that year's Salon, makes another memorable comment on his state of mind in those heady days. This portrait is the second installment in his pictorial history of himself, with updates issued throughout his life. Sometimes witty and impertinent, sometimes brash and boastful, Foujita's self-portraits are not confessionals. In the Japanese style, they impart information by indirection, and so the smallest hints matter a great deal. When we last confronted Foujita in his 1910 self-portrait, he was still a student in Tokyo. He did not care to look at the viewer directly, presenting himself as a dandy in Western fashions about to take leave of provincial Japan. By 1921, Foujita did not have to make a point of his sophistication, since he had achieved his escape from home. Austerity has replaced swagger, and Foujita poses against a bare white wall of his studio with only a rough wooden table, a clock, a decorated plate, and his smoking equipment. His black clothing further emphasizes severity while his face works very hard to tell us nothing at all.

By then, Foujita was on his way to becoming a genuine Parisian personality, recognizable to all on the city streets. No longer an attractive young student, he has acquired bangs, a little moustache, and round glasses that do not try to hide his extreme nearsightedness. He has no illusions about his own looks, but this is no longer the point. Instead, he knows that efforts must be made elsewhere, and his monkish vision of himself announces a willingness to do whatever his new environment requires. At the same time, he keeps himself concealed behind bangs and glasses, always at a distance from those who would approach him. There are suggestions of more playful impulses only in the plate on the wall behind him, which shows a boy being chastised by his elders.

The 1921 *Self-Portrait*—Foujita's first work to be acquired by a museum—still belongs to the Musées Royaux des Beaux-Arts of Belgium. Foujita liked to tell the story—whose accuracy is, of course, again questioned—of how the sale was concluded at the last moment, inside the train he was taking from Brussels back to Paris in 1922. "In my whole long life, I had never before nor ever after sold a painting inside a train."

SIXTEEN

SAEKI YŪZŌ'S PARIS

When I went to Paris, I was not very surprised by the beauty of the city. One reason for this, I think, is that I had seen many of Saeki Yūzō's works. Saeki Yūzō's paintings do not show a foreigner appreciating Paris, but express the surprise a Japanese feels about Paris. Of all the Japanese who have looked at Paris, perhaps no one has observed it as well as Saeki.

—Yokomitsu Riichi

Here, just after Foujita's first Paris successes, seems to be an appropriate point to review again Foujita's predicament in France. Clearly, he had great ambitions and sought nothing less than acceptance as a first-rate, international artist. In addition, Foujita was eager to fit into as many spheres of French life as possible; he tried to improve his French, married a Frenchwoman, and studied the techniques of Western masters. Still, he could go only so far. The French, who did not look to him for sun-drenched landscapes of Provence, expected the Japanese Foujita to create in a manner befitting a person from *le pays du soleil levant*. Yet Foujita hit upon a style that satisfied his artistic conscience and the tastes of the French public.

It is instructive to look at the life of Saeki Yūzō for another example of what Foujita did *not* do to make his way in France—for Saeki's story is a cautionary tale for Japanese artists who would not, or could not, appeal to the French. Predictably, Saeki and Foujita traveled in completely different social circles in Paris. Saeki's grim saga had a deadly quest for purity at its core, and his struggle for recognition continues to this day. He is venerated in Japan, but in France, where he created his best works, Saeki Yūzō remains mostly unknown. Saeki, who chose a dangerous model when he identified himself with van Gogh, reportedly decided to go to Paris after he saw one of van Gogh's paintings—of sunflowers—for the first time in Tokyo. The two artists were driven by an unhealthy dedication that set their works apart from those of others, and their mental instability frightened their families and caused their own early deaths.

In 1924, Saeki arrived in Paris with his wife, Yoneko, and daughter, Yachiko. He went directly to cité Falguière, where his friend, the artist Satomi Katsuzō, had a studio. Displaying grooming habits that were no competition for Foujita's, Saeki wore a faded blue workman's outfit and had let his hair grow long during his voyage. The dishevelment was startling, and to Satomi, who had heard reports of the 1923 earthquake in Tokyo, Saeki looked as if he could have just emerged from the rubble, a lucky survivor. Saeki soon set out exploring the stone streets of Paris and took a sightseeing ride in a horse-drawn buggy. He was to earn his reputation with oil paintings of Parisian neighborhoods, and his focus on the sights began immediately upon his arrival.

Saeki's encounter with the French artist Maurice de Vlaminck was a disastrous episode in a tormented life. On a drizzling day in 1924, Saeki and Satomi went to Vlaminck's home in Auvers-sur-Oise. Wet from the rain, Saeki unrolled his painting of a nude for Vlaminck's appraisal. One can almost hear the sound of Saeki's nerves cracking when Vlaminck dismissed the painting as a mere academic exercise. To further Saeki's humiliation, the work then slipped from his hands, out the open window, and down onto the shelter of Vlaminck's three dogs, who started howling. Saeki, in tears by the time he got outside, spent that night at the Café de la Mairie, where van Gogh had killed himself in 1890. Since Saeki liked ghost stories, he hoped to see van Gogh's shade that night. Instead, the bedbugs pestered him, and he did not sleep at all. Before leaving, he visited the graves of Vincent van Gogh and his brother Theo.

After the encounter with Vlaminck, Saeki vowed to make a fresh start. His confidence in painting human figures shattered, Saeki sought other ways to express his feelings about the foreign country before him. His impressions were a mixture of excitement, gratitude, heartache, and fear, which he began to pour into his scenes of Paris and beyond. With the implacability that marked his every action, he forced himself forward, and in 1925, two of Saeki's works were accepted by the Salon d'Automne. Despite this progress, his family in Japan insisted that he return home, since they feared for his health. He had developed tuberculosis, which had already claimed the lives of his close relatives. Saeki bowed to his family's entreaties, but he grieved at the prospect of returning to Japan. "My teachers are van Gogh and Vlaminck," he said at the time. "I don't want to go back to Japan just when I feel myself able to paint my works." Eventually, he set himself up in his studio in Tokyo, but the ill, restless Saeki found his surroundings uninspiring and, in fact, his landscapes of suburban Tokyo are feeble efforts, no match for the disorder he could inject into a painting of a nondescript government building in France.

Though aware of his worsening condition, Saeki returned with his family to Paris in 1927. Suicidal dedication again drove Saeki out with his canvas and supplies. These outdoor painting sessions would have taxed the constitution of a stronger artist, but Saeki refused to wear proper clothing in the bad weather. His insistence upon working outdoors proved fatal, and as he pushed himself to complete many canvases, he drained his physical resources. The feverish brushstrokes in Saeki's Parisian street scenes came out of an artist with little time left. Saeki, who was drawn to tattered Parisian byways in his paintings, could mark any wall with madness. He saved much of his ferment for the lettering in posters and wall graffiti, the distinguishing feature of his work. Saeki had no wish to reproduce these writings literally, and so, with a jumble of calligraphic strokes, his brush announced a forthcoming opera performance as well as his own euphoria and suffering.

It is the saddest of stories. By March 1928, when the bedridden Saeki was obviously failing, his wife tried to cheer him up by bringing home a postman with a resemblance to the postman in van Gogh's portraits. Saeki painted this postman in his uniform but then, exhausted, had to return to his bed. Saeki was thirty years old when he died a few months later in a mental hospital; some say his death was from natural causes, while others consider him a suicide. His six-year-old daughter, Yachiko, who had also contracted tuberculosis, died two weeks later.

In Japan, where they honor him, the selfless, unyielding, and doomed Saeki is often cited as an example of an artist who represented everything that Foujita was not. Saeki lived out the myth of creative artist and then some, willing to sacrifice his life for his art.

While Saeki had his admirers among the French critics, they were considerably more awestruck by Foujita's talents: "Only Foujita has the fine touch which can depict an object's minute points." The French found profound meanings floating across Foujita's milky white surfaces and important perceptions driving his meticulousness: "No fragment escapes him, neither physical nor psychic fragment." They appreciated Foujita's references to Japan, but his starkness also provided the Europeans with insights into their unsettled world:

> [The grounds in his works] were plain, flat, made of a rare material as if everything under the artist's fingers strives to achieve the precious quality of a lacquer chest. Across the length of this screen, he often spreads, for example, a Jouy fabric. The red or mauve which provides shade to his motifs is repeated with the same tireless and smiling application, achieving an unparalleled accuracy of tone, a disconcerting exactitude. Because of this, our eyes come to see the character of an epoch, the naiveté, in a word the psychological peculiarity which emanates from the object and which we would not have understood by looking at the object itself.

In Japan as well as in France, the situation could not have been more different for Saeki and Foujita. Upon his return to Japan in 1926, Saeki was respectfully received in artistic circles. But when Foujita sent his painting of his studio, *My Room, Still Life with Alarm Clock,* back home to Japan, the work did not inspire any such regard. It must be added that the Japanese registered their opinions about Foujita's work only after they realized that he was still alive and making a reputation for himself in Paris. Foujita had left Japan in 1913, and during the First World War, the public back home heard nothing about him. Only in 1921 did a Japanese art journal report on what Foujita had been doing in the meantime: "In Japan, people think that Foujita has died in Paris, but he is much appreciated here in Paris as an artist with a great future."

Proving that he was indeed still breathing, Foujita sent *My Room, Still Life with Alarm Clock* back to Tokyo for exhibition at the 1922 Imperial Salon. His quest for approval in his native country would continue—with the slurs that wounded and enraged him—to the end of his life. The trouble started when the Japanese salon committee asked him to go through the normal selection procedure, like any other artist who was not a salon member. Believing his son distinguished enough as a member of Paris's Salon d'Automne, Foujita's father informed the committee that he would withdraw the work if they required the ordinary screening process. In the end, the committee acceded to these demands, but the family's highhandedness caused much resentment. (Foujita learned about this uproar when a Japanese newspaper arrived in Paris: "More than having my picture accepted, I felt happy knowing for the first time that my father, who hardly ever wrote, truly loved me.")

Since Foujita had been rejected several times as a student, *My Room, Still Life with Alarm Clock* was the first work that he exhibited at an official Japanese salon. One complimentary review acknowledged that Foujita was well ahead of other Japanese artists, who were mere novices by comparison; elsewhere, Foujita received praise for having the courage to create such an *"intime"* view of himself, which would have been an impossible task for other Japanese artists: "Looking at this painting, one feels that one is peering into the artist's soul."

From a far larger contingent of observers came the more caustic appraisals of Foujita's achievements. It must be emphasized that while the Japanese were rather new to oil painting, they had their own ideas about what to expect at exhibitions and would have felt satisfied with, at least, a multihued Impressionist mix of effects. Renoir, Monet, and even the Japanese Kuroda Seiki had trained the Japanese to appreciate colorful landscapes and shifting blazes of light. They were not looking to oil painting for black lines and white spaces, which were abundantly available in their own ancient works on paper and silk. In the eyes of

many Japanese, Foujita's pale *My Room, Still Life with Alarm Clock*—
along with the similar still life he sent to Japan for the 1924 salon—
was a step backward, little more than a hackneyed specimen of
japonaiserie in oil paint. An artist summed up the Japanese art world's
reaction: "There was first of all a complete mismatch in approach.
'What on earth is this thing?' they said. 'Even I can paint something
like this!'"

Foujita's still lifes of his studio convinced many Japanese that his
success abroad had been a result of all his shenanigans in Paris. They
believed that he had gone far because of his hairstyle, clothing, and behavior rather than because of his artistic ability.

SEVENTEEN

AN AMERICAN HEIRESS

Success came quickly. Foujita in total: a type marked by a Montparnassian cosmopolitanism, 100 percent Café Rotonde, café-crème through and through, and a completely Parisian figure.

—*André Salmon*

Even though Foujita was disturbed by such unpleasantness, it would be a mistake to think that he was greatly harmed. After all, he was far away in Paris while his father was fighting to get his painting into the Tokyo salon. The distance to Japan was large, communications imperfect. Furious in the morning, Foujita could overlook much by evening as he strolled along Paris boulevards. With ample evidence of Foujita's reluctance to share his private worries with his friends, he surely did not spend time unburdening himself in the cafés. Foujita, more than most, could lose himself in the blissful forgetfulness of the expatriate.

To get an idea of Foujita's state of mind in these years, I prefer to look to Emily Crane Chadbourne. In 1922, Foujita painted *Portrait of Mrs. Emily Crane Chadbourne*, which now hangs in the Art Institute of Chicago. Chadbourne's fortune came from the Crane Company, the family's Chicago business, whose products included pumps, valves, plumbing, and bathroom equipment. She grew up wealthy, attending performances at the Chicago Civic Opera Company with her father, and was exempt from the household chores performed by ordinary women. At least one family member believes that this made her unprepared for marriage and probably unskilled at the duties expected of her as a wife. Although she did marry, her husband became enamored of a dentist's wife. (A family record dismisses this woman as a "flashing camellia.") After obtaining a divorce in 1905, Emily Crane Chadbourne fled to Europe.

Chadbourne was the kind of wandering and wounded American heiress regularly deceived by fortune hunters in Henry James's fiction. She did, in fact, become part of James's social circle when she lived in London and can easily be imagined at a dinner party, complaining to him about the philistines in the American Midwest. On the whole, though, Chadbourne had more of a taste for mobility than a run-of-the-mill James heroine. She liked to be on the move, preferring to be in the vicinity of world wars and social upheavals.

Because of her Crane Company money, she could remain far from the bathtubs that were the source of her wealth and close to the European specialists guiding her art purchases. Her friends included the artist Augustus John and members of the British aristocracy; she told of having "sat on a staircase with Gertrude Stein during the German bombardment of Paris." Chadbourne attended the coronation of Haile Selassie in Ethiopia, and *The Autobiography of Alice B. Toklas* reports that she went to China, where she joined the campaign against the spread of opium. She was a regular at League of Nations meetings in Geneva as part of her wholehearted support of anti-opium forces. Evelyn Waugh was not charmed when he ran into Chadbourne and her female companion at the Ethiopian coronation in 1930. He writes of

> two formidable ladies in knitted suits and topis . . . square-jawed, tight-lipped, with hard discontented eyes. For them the whole coronation was a profound disappointment. What did it matter that they were witnesses of a unique stage of the inter-penetration of two cultures? They were out for Vice . . . Prostitution and drug traffic comprised their modest interests, and they were too dense to find evidence of either.

In 1922, when she commissioned Foujita to paint her portrait, Chadbourne was fifty-one, with Ethiopia and opium still to come. Foujita, at thirty-six, was just starting to enjoy his fame and would soon become the obvious choice for rich women who wanted their portraits painted. Foujita clearly relished the challenges of this commission and would have appreciated the usefulness of her social contacts. As his portrait shows, he also divined that Mrs. Chadbourne had her share of woe. We will never know whether he traced her solemn expression back to her growing opposition to opium or to a miserable past in her American hometown.

No written accounts of their conversations exist, but the portrait gives us much information about their encounter. I first saw *Portrait of Mrs. Emily Crane Chadbourne* in the studio of the Art Institute of Chicago, where Timothy Lennon, conservator of paintings at the Institute, and Hayashi Yōko, fresh from Tokyo, analyzed the materials that had gone into its composition. Chadbourne would have been pleased about the interest shown in her by this Japanese researcher who was definitely knowledgeable about cities far removed from Chicago. With the Chicago skyline out the window behind us, we turned to the canvas and Mrs. Chadbourne stretched out on a striped couch. For Foujita's portrait, she wore a vest of golden flowers, the Chinese design a prediction of activism to come; green stockings and green shoes completed her buoyant attire. Silver leaf once formed the wall behind her in the painting, but that has now oxidized to black. Despite this, the work remains a rousing bombardment of color, which Foujita obviously painted with zest. By posing Mrs. Chadbourne in green shoes, blue dress, and golden flowers, he tried to bring his scrawny subject out of her gloom. He also took pains with the black cat keeping her company on the sofa.

Everywhere on the canvas were the signs of the care and expense that Foujita lavished on the portrait, proving that Mrs. Chadbourne was a generous customer. That day at the Art Institute, both Hayashi and Lennon murmured in admiration as they scanned the painting's details under a microscope. "Foujita used to differentiate between those works he did for commission and those he considered his own art," Hayashi said. "But he was not yet very famous when he painted this portrait, and so he took great care with it, even though it was commissioned. This portrait ranks with his best works." Aside from the once-silver background, golden flecks are scattered everywhere across the surface—on an earring, a sofa tassel, a flower. Hayashi explained that Foujita was a very "artisanal artist," who liked to do everything himself. He mixed his own paint and stretched his own canvases, and she believes that he applied the silver foil with his own hand. This might explain why not even a silver speck has survived to the present day. "That's very hard work," Lennon said, shaking his head over Foujita's unwarranted confidence. "Not for amateurs. You have to have a perfect touch." Textures and patterns fascinated Foujita, and he strove to distinguish the velour fabric from woven wool in the furnishings. For this reason, even the sofa pillows are thrilling.

There is little sign of Foujita's white ground here, since the whole point is brightness and strong contrasts. His supple line has been put to much use, however, outlining every indentation on the backrest and every strand of hair on Mrs. Chadbourne's head. Wishing to depict his subject in the most glittering of settings, Foujita drew upon decorative Japanese styles for this painting. He harked back to the brilliantly colored Japanese screens in which wild beasts and bamboo were set against a golden background or an imperial entourage lingered on a field of red poppies.

In this portrait, Mrs. Emily Crane Chadbourne, an American plumbing heiress who is a little depressed and a little underweight, struggles to match the vibrancy of her Japanese portraitist and his Japanese influences.

EIGHTEEN

SUCCESS AND
DOMESTIC WOE

Believe me, the bohemians of those days were very much more bour-
geois than any class of people I had known so far. But they were fun.
—Jacqueline Goddard

Around the time that he drew Mrs. Chadbourne, Foujita was enjoying his new celebrity status. Collectors in France and other parts of Europe sought him out, and the Belgians purchased his work for their museum. Among Americans, he also had his admirers. Foujita had traveled from Tokyo to artistic acclaim and financial security on the Left Bank. In a demonstration of his newfound wealth and his old sense of hygiene, he had a bathroom installed in his quarters on rue Delambre. Foujita "passed for a nabob" with this home improvement, since private bathrooms were a rarity in Montparnasse at that time. Thoughtful in his good fortune, Foujita allowed the models to bathe free of charge.

Foujita did not stick with the multicolored style of his Chadbourne portrait. He began to create (very white) portraits of society figures, some dressed in flimsy gowns or lounging on flowered sofas. Commercial opportunities beckoned, and increasingly, Foujita offered his wares to customers. Sleep was not a crucial matter to him, and so he could also keep up his production of his noncommissioned works. "With his brush," wrote French critic F. R. Vanderpyl in 1921, "(which is often equivalent to a quill pen or rather a chisel), he draws our suburbs, the nooks and crannies, our landscapes, our children, our pets, our interiors, and one seems to be looking at them through a strange crystal which revitalizes our vision, increases our capacity for making distinctions, and reveals to us snippets of life neglected since the observant days of our childhood."

Foujita started painting cats with those sitting beside his reclining nudes, but this was only the beginning of a side industry in cat portraits that became a huge and dependable source of income. There was a need for cats (Chardin's and Bonnard's cats proved insufficient), and Foujita stepped in to present his cats in many moods—cuddling their young, blissful in sleep, judgmental. He said that his career in cats began when he brought one stray home, and then acquired some more. After that, he relied on cats when no human model was available. "Since they were always in my studio, I sometimes put a cat at my side in my self-portraits or placed them by my nudes as a kind of signature."

The cats—presented in full, down to the last whisker—perfectly suit Foujita's painstaking techniques. Their value has not diminished, since even now a Foujita with a cat costs much more than a catless production. While his cats enhanced his reputation, he enhanced their significance by letting them speak up for him. Their personalities changing with his own shifting circumstances, the cats are lovable and carefree in the early years but, in dismal times, more desperate and combative. When asked about how he had settled upon his two best-known painting subjects, Foujita offered his well-worn response: "It's because women and cats are absolutely the same. If you treat them nicely, they are submissive, but if you don't, they will turn on you. Just think about it—isn't a woman just like a cat if you put on some whiskers and a tail?"

While Foujita made his name with his paintings of cats and other subjects, he depended on his social life to spread his reputation beyond the art galleries. Once the First World War ended, the partying began among the artists in Paris and continued until the stock market crash in 1929. To commemorate *les années folles* (the crazy years), there were constant dances, costume balls, private parties, and other festivities.

According to one participant, "The war was over. Everyone was happy." In the heart of Montparnasse, they did the tango at the dance hall Bal Bullier, while the windmill marked the spot on the other side of the Seine where the crowds gathered at Moulin de la Galette. "In particular," reminisced the art dealer Daniel-Henry Kahnweiler, "I remember a certain Swedish ball which was magnificent. The alcohol flowed in torrents. There were also mattresses which had been prepared by the organizers for those who could not go on and went there to sleep . . . That night we drank a lot of champagne, but the Swedes mixed it with gin and that produced stupefying effects. As a result our friend [artist André] Masson got dead drunk."

During the years of his marriage to Fernande, Foujita was only gearing up for his full-scale participation in the merrymaking, but even at half-steam, he definitely made an impression. His outfits, his haircut, and the earrings made him popular among the cartoonists, who often drew him socializing in public places. "Fou-Fou," as he was nicknamed by his French friends, had always had a lot of energy, and he approached his social life with the vigor he brought to his painting. Let us pause to think about the time Foujita went to the Paris Opéra with a lampshade on his head. Imagine his aplomb and his glee when he explained to all that this headgear was part of his national costume. Or contemplate the night—frequently cited as extraordinary even for those outrageous years—when he arrived at the AAAA (Aide Amicale Aux Artistes) Ball costumed as a coolie. He was wearing only a loincloth and covered in tattoos. Foujita carried a cage on his back with Fernande naked inside. In a very cheerful mood, she held up a sign that said WOMAN FOR SALE. NO STATE GUARANTEE OFFERED. ("The sign was more than accurate," notes one wry commentator, "since if Fernande wasn't sold, she offered herself voluntarily.")

Fernande and Foujita also faced tragedy when their friend Modigliani died on January 24, 1920. Weakened by illness and his fabled dissoluteness, Modigliani died at the Hôpital de la Charité, near the banks of the Seine. "Cover him with flowers," his brother telegraphed from Italy, and a large crowd turned out to follow the coffin to Père-Lachaise Cemetery. Early in the morning of the twenty-sixth, Modigliani's pregnant lover, Jeanne Hébuterne, committed suicide by jumping from the window of her parents' apartment. Fernande, who had been her close friend, wept over that wretched end: "I'm the one who prepared her for her burial with Jeanne, the wife of Léger. What a beauty she was with her blond braids! You would have said that in death she was the 'smiling angel' of Reims." Foujita once described Jeanne as *"vicieuse et sensuelle . . . maladive, pâle, maigre, mystérieuse."*

Foujita's success came with much activity, the din outside overshadowing events in his own home. In the end, *japonisme*, so important to Foujita's artistic career, touched his life in other crucial ways. It can be said that Fernande had a bad case of *japonisme* (fondness for things Japanese), since she eventually left him for another Japanese artist. The trouble between the couple had been obvious for some time, and over the years, Foujita's Japanese friends, ever willing to *cherchez la femme* in times of turmoil, complained about the way he silently endured tongue lashings from his women. Long-suffering and passive in the face of difficult women is how many men and women remember Foujita. ("He had bad luck with women," his friend Kajiyama Miyoko told me, shaking her head, as we took a walk through a Paris park.) While Foujita did not answer back, Fernande had her own ideas about his personality. "Don't ever think that Foujita is angry because he has a severe look on his face . . . It's when he laughs that you should watch out. The Japanese are like that."

As Foujita's popularity spread, he spent even longer hours on his work. This left Fernande with little to do. He enjoyed the parties, but returned home early enough to be able to begin work the next morning. Fernande disdained such fussy discipline. "I started getting bored with Foujita," she said. "After I finished preparing his tea and had bought him his croissant, I had nothing left to do and, more to the point, nothing to say to him." His friend Satsuma Jirohachi remembered how Fernande had thrown herself into organizing Foujita's life. Though Foujita sometimes disputed this, she apparently had taken charge of hanging his paintings at exhibitions, where she was abrupt with gallery owners and critics. She negotiated with art dealers and supervised his relationships with fellow artists. She managed everything, "even Foujita's mischief." Satsuma had definite views about the reasons for the breakup:

Foujita wouldn't go out with her and ignored her. No matter what a bragging bossy type she was, a woman is after all a woman. If from dawn to dusk, all you do is paint, if you don't drink and have fun with a woman, well then, how is a woman going to stay with you without getting bored? . . . Foujita worked on his paintings from 10 a.m. until noon. Then again, from 1 to 8 p.m. if he wasn't going out somewhere. When he finished his evening meal, he worked again from 10 p.m. until 5 a.m. He basically was working without a break all the time, sleeping from 5 a.m. until 10 a.m. He slept like the dead. He wouldn't wake up even if you tried to shake him out of his sleep.

While the trouble continued in the Foujitas' marriage, the 1923 silent film *La Bataille* (*The Danger Line*) stirred the crowds upon its release in France. The film's Japanese lead, Sessue Hayakawa, had already become an Asian celebrity in the United States as a silent-film star. "In the swooning circles of movie-loving women," a silent-film buff writes, "he was the fantasy, matinee idol. Cruel, exotic and handsome—all the forbidden attributes for which ladies clamor." Hayakawa's appeal extended to those in high positions, since a fan arranged for twenty-three vessels from the French naval fleet to appear in *La Bataille*. In the West, Hayakawa is remembered most for his portrayal of the Japanese colonel in David Lean's 1957 film *The Bridge on the River Kwai*.

Koyanagi Sei, a Japanese artist who reached Paris in 1922, benefited from this adulation, since he bore a strong resemblance to Hayakawa. Some have pointed out that Koyanagi's face did not possess the power of Hayakawa's, but definite similarities guaranteed him a following in Paris. "Sessue! Sessue!" came the cry when Koyanagi went down the street. He claimed for himself a samurai pedigree—an all-too-frequent boast among Japanese in Paris—and, according to *Paris-Montparnasse*, Koyanagi "arrived with the baggage of the well-read man, carrying visions borrowed from our literature. Balzac and Maupassant and Daudet were familiar to him."

Fernande, badly in need of a new focus, soon had Koyanagi living with her in her second-floor apartment on rue Delambre, while Foujita was banished to his ground-floor atelier. "Foujita used to gaze up at the second-floor window," a fed-up Satsuma noted. "Only Foujita could pull off an extraordinary performance like that."

Foujita's oil painting *My Family*, completed around the time of his breakup with Fernande, shows them both seated at a table in front of a mottled white wall. In this portrait of himself, Foujita does not hide his need for the firm and humorless woman beside him; her skin is the white he does not use for his more tinted Japanese self. The household's religiosity is confirmed by the crucifix on their wall, and the key below honors the home they share together. It is a surprise to discover that Foujita had the mundane view of domestic happiness expressed in this painting. This reminds us, once again, that Foujita revealed little of himself, no matter how much of a racket he made. The artist in the painting keeps his paintbrushes and (genuine sumi) ink at the ready while the wife, finishing her tea beside her dog, looks ready to rise up should anyone disrupt his routine. With the staples of monogamous harmony arrayed around Foujita and Fernande, this is the work either of a man mourning a vanished union or of a cuckolded husband living in a dream world.

NINETEEN

YOUKI, GODDESS
OF THE SNOW

Have you never been haunted by an impalpable presence that has
insinuated itself inside you without the slightest external sign?
—*Dominique Desanti*

"I just love Foujita's cats," the French writer Dominique Desanti exclaimed over afternoon coffee. "All cats are mysterious. But Foujita's cats are more than that. There is something metaphysical about them. You can imagine that they have an afterlife."

The day of my visit to Dominique Desanti's apartment, I had only been in Paris for a short while. Having arrived there after a long stay in Tokyo, I was accustomed to the empty spaces of Japanese interiors, and so her crowded sitting room jarred me somewhat. Every surface was packed with artworks, chinaware, tea sets, and treasures from secondhand shops. The many stuffed pillows in the shape of cats told me that I was in the presence of a real aficionado. I did not see any live specimens scurrying around, but the stuffed versions on the furniture presented cats in their most winning moments. Desanti's attachment to these cats seemed appropriate because, in her eighties, she can match any one of them in alertness and impeccable grooming. A gracious woman with strong opinions, she wore a fuchsia jacket over a frilly blouse with an antique pin. Her elegance accorded with a newly arrived American's idea of a French woman writer, and her talk had a slyness that also seemed just right. Desanti, who takes pride in her lack of official academic connections, has written many books—novels, biographies, memoirs among them—and in her fashionable jacket, she did not hesitate to lambaste political leaders of the day. Since an American like me also considers engagé behavior de rigueur in a Frenchwoman of Desanti's accomplishments, I was pleased to hear that she was going to a rally for a Socialist candidate after our coffee.

When we started to talk about Foujita, however, Desanti did not respond as I had anticipated. Again, I realized that I had been in Japan for too long. In Japan, Foujita is not mentioned often, and when his name comes up, it is in connection with the controversial paintings he created for the Japanese military during the Second World War. Mention his name over a beer in Tokyo, and Foujita's defenders and detractors rush forward, speaking not only of Foujita, but of twentieth-century Japanese history. That is why, after coming to France, a researcher on Foujita finds more surprises than just the change of scenery. In Paris, Foujita remains to this day an illustrious, charming presence who lives on as the sparkling artist and bon vivant of his heyday in the 1920s. The French remember him as le peintre des chats, des petites filles, des jolies femmes—the painter of cats, little girls, pretty women—with the glamorous wives and social life. He is part of the French nostalgia for the 1920s, when Paris was the center of the art world and welcomed talented immigrants from all over.

Throughout the city, there are friendly reminders of Foujita as he was in those days. His photograph and those of his wives during those years adorn the walls of restaurants around Montparnasse. A plaque at no. 5 rue Delambre, at the heart of the quarter, commemorates Foujita's sojourn there (when he was married to Fernande), and a street has been named for him near the new national library. In a department store near the Montparnasse train station, the exit named "Foujita" will lead you out of cosmetics. In Paris, I attended a lecture about cannibalism by a woman from Guadeloupe. At the reception afterward, I met her Guadeloupean friend who recalled, with great happiness, an outdoor art fair she had attended decades ago. There, on a sunny day in the Tuileries, Foujita drew a picture of her mouth.

Desanti, who never met Foujita, also took this positive, French view of his life. In Japan, a well-known, politically active intellectual like her would not only have had fewer furnishings, she would also have discussed Foujita with many qualifications. But this was Paris, and

Desanti, to my puzzlement, knew nothing about Foujita's work for the Japanese military during the Second World War. She had learned about Foujita from her friend, the martyred poet Robert Desnos, and also from Desnos's last love, Youki, who was Foujita's third wife. "Desnos won over Foujita's heart, and they became friends. They had a cruel humor in common," Desanti told me. In Paris, as Desanti spoke of times past, Foujita was allowed his stardom and his engaging personality.

The frailty of accomplished men before beautiful women is a matter Desanti has considered carefully over her long life. She knows about Foujita and Youki's marriage only indirectly, but she had the opportunity to observe her friend Desnos's adoration of this same woman. As I listened to her talk, it was my turn to become the American character in a Henry James novel—the inexperienced visitor who requires tutelage about human passion from a sage European.

"Desnos was devoted to Youki. Desnos told me, 'She was given to me by Foujita. It was as if he had given me the crown jewels.'" Desanti continued, "Youki could do anything, and Desnos would not dare to say anything."

Around the time of the German occupation of France, when Youki was living with Desnos, Desanti met her for the first time. "She was elegant, but plumper than when she had been married to Foujita. And she did have that very white skin which Foujita painted so often. One rainy day in 1940 or 1941, Robert said to me, 'Let's go home.' He meant to his apartment on rue Mazarine. In the apartment were wonderful paintings, many by Foujita. Suddenly *une dame* came out of another room. She was wearing a hat and was incredibly elegant, in high heels. 'Oh,' she said to Desnos, 'you didn't tell me. I have an appointment.' He didn't dare to ask her where she was going. She said that she would bring back wine and pastries. Then she went out. This was my first meeting. I knew she had been Foujita's wife.

"I met her again in 1946 after Desnos had died. She was drinking heavily. Where she got her money to live was a mystery. She was writing her memoirs, borrowing money perhaps. She had sold nearly everything, moved out of the rue Mazarine apartment and lived in the suburbs."

Again, I pressed on to see if Desanti had any further thoughts about Youki.

"Youki was like an apparition. She was very surrealistic. It was like a surrealistic novel—'Well, I'm going away,' she said to him that day. She was elegant and polite. That was the time of the [German] occupation, and so it was unusual that they had wine and cookies. They must have got that stuff from the black market. Foujita and Desnos had been friends. You know that Foujita liked to tattoo people? He drew a tattoo on Desnos's arm. I think it was a bear. People in the concentration camp remember having seen that tattoo on Desnos's arm. Foujita tattooed Youki, too. He drew a mermaid on her thigh. Once, when I was visiting Youki, I asked her about her tattoo. She was in a good mood that day and said to me, 'Want to see it?' She lifted her skirt to show me. There was nothing indecent about the way she did that.

"The second time I went to see Youki after Desnos's death, she was unbearable, drunk. I didn't visit her again."

Foujita met Youki in 1923, when he was separated from Fernande. Youki, whose real name was Lucie Badoud, was almost twenty years old; Foujita, with two marriages behind him, was nearing thirty-seven. He still lived in the atelier below Fernande's apartment, but as his romantic history shows, he could not tolerate solitude. He may have worked long hours day and night, but together with supplies of white paint, he needed a living, breathing female close by on a regular basis. A man of orderly habits, Foujita could not abide the erratic rhythms of bachelorhood.

Youki also did not flourish alone and took active steps to find companionship. In her rollicking memoirs, *Youki's Confessions*, she tells of her upbringing in Paris and her vacations at her aunt's farm in Belgium with "male cousins, female cousins, servants, countless animals: horses, cows, pigs, sheep, chickens, hens, ducks, geese, rabbits and even small guinea-pigs which I raised in a barrel filled with straw." During Youki's adolescence, her grandmother died in a fall, and her father later perished in somewhat similar circumstances, cracking his skull during a hasty flight down a staircase while trying to escape from his mistress's husband. Her mother died following a cancer operation soon after, and so by the time she was eighteen, Youki was alone in Paris, with sufficient family assets to pursue her interests in high culture and in living life to the fullest. Youki adored literature and literary notables, and so her chance encounter with a young poet on the subway was crucial, beginning her involvement with Paris's artists and writers.

Very much on her own, Youki was sitting in the Rotonde that night in 1923 when she spotted an Asian man who fascinated her. Foujita had come a long way from his encounter with Fernande in the same Montparnasse café six years previously, but sartorially speaking, success had not affected his general principles. "He was alone, with bangs brown and thick on his forehead, tortoiseshell eyeglasses," Youki wrote in her memoirs, "a red-checked cotton shirt, a mustache in the shape of an M, a costume made out of very beautiful English fabric with the jacket closing on the right, in the manner of a kimono, and cinched at the waist by a cloth belt." For Youki, it was a *coup de foudre* (love at first sight) in a life not lacking in such jolts. Since he left without paying her any attention, Youki consulted another artist, who drew a portrait of Foujita to help her track him down. She was momentarily daunted when she heard that Foujita was already married ("I had not considered that"), but news of his marital problems swept away the qualms. Youki was also taken aback when she showed the portrait of Foujita to one of her friends, who declared that Foujita had a "flat nose." Youki became livid: "A flat nose? You are an imbecile, an ignoramus. You should be saying that it is the nose of Buddha. Isn't he the Buddha himself? He is God, this man."

Foujita was not one to resist such adulation, and soon after Youki located him in his studio, they spent three days together in a hotel. Fernande, still legally Foujita's wife, became frantic when she could not locate him. She searched the morgues for his body, fearing that he had killed himself over the collapse of their marriage. On the contrary, Foujita felt extraordinarily well all of a sudden. "I have fallen in love with a lovely, lovely beauty of almost twenty, and she also loves me," he wrote to a friend. "The two of us have become much, much closer. I have heard that when Goya was forty and already a father, he became involved with another woman and hid out with her in the countryside for something like two years. I also am about thirty-seven or thirty-eight, and my heart is beating as if this were my first love." In addition, he predicted that this turn of events would be beneficial to his work. "I don't get tired of looking at her face. She has a good body too. I now know that in the future my nudes will have to be completely different, with young bodies, curves, and soft contours." She did not like her given name and so Foujita called her Youki, Japanese for "snow." This was in honor of her white skin, whose special beauty began to illuminate his nudes.

Foujita's years with Youki brought him more fame and glamour, and many nights out on the town. The bright lights appealed to them both, and they sought constant exposure. From his studio in Fernande's building, he soon moved with Youki to a more fashionable address on the Right Bank. She soon proved herself capable of spending whatever money was available and of enjoying herself, even without Foujita's companionship. She was his goddess, his charm, his key to bankruptcy. Foujita felt particularly proud that Youki came from a more respectable class of society than his other women. "I am so happy to have a beautiful woman," he wrote to his friend. "She is not a woman from Montparnasse. She lives around the Étoile, is an orphan, and a fine woman."

Foujita's Japanese friends, as usual, were unwilling to bless his new alliance, but he surged ahead anyway with the well-dressed and effervescent Youki by his side. Undaunted by his friends' animosity, he produced some of his best works during his years with her. Foujita had exhibitions in Europe, New York, and Chicago; he created murals for a banker in Antwerp and for the Maison du Japon, which provided living quarters for Japanese students at the Cité universitaire. Because of these activities, a French critic was moved to proclaim that "in the honorable Mr. Foujita Tsugouharu, the East and West are combined." Years before, Foujita had enjoyed a special audience with Pope Benedict XV—who had confessed to him that the Emperor of Japan was the only other Japanese he had ever received. Foujita had drawn the pope's portrait, and this satisfied customer requested that he next try his hand at Saint Francis Xavier. Unable to work up enthusiasm for the saint, Foujita did not grant the papal wish, but he summoned enough commitment when he painted his nude *Youki, Goddess of the Snow*, which was exhibited at the Salon d'Automne in 1924. This nude displayed for all the world to see the new sexual excitement she had awakened in him. He was frank about his admiration of her body, which floats, in a contented sleep, upon an undulating bank of snowy whiteness. Her long hair is beneath her as a watchful dog sits at her side. Foujita's homage to his love, steadfastly remaining in the vicinity of black and white, burns with all the hues of erotic feeling.

In *Before the Ball* (1925), another work created during the Youki years, Foujita presents seven women in varying states of dress and undress. These women could have been gathered together to dispel any notion that Foujita was just another version of an old-time Japanese artist like Hokusai. These seven should be preparing for the evening's costume ball, but a shift of mood has stopped them from completing their chores. In Hokusai's prints, the women have a sense of purpose about them—you know exactly where his courtesan is headed in her layered kimono and his half-naked divers are definitely after abalone. Standing amidst masks and costume fabrics, Foujita's women do not hide their uncertainty. One stares forward, absolutely white and naked at the center of this fairy tale; another, vigilant, is fully costumed in a child's ruffles; yet another is hurrying to cover her exposed bosom because of a frightening sight beyond the canvas. The mood is expansive, mysterious, perilous, but the drawing gets very specific in the strands of hair on the women's heads and the scratches on the wood floor. In this grand painting, Foujita ponders the askew universe of his Venus.

In other works created during this period, Foujita often portrayed two nude women together, their white skin set against various white backgrounds. These paintings went well with contemporary controversies about women's lives, notably Victor Margueritte's 1922 novel *La Garçonne* (an English translation is called *The Bachelor Girl*). This book alarmed segments of the French public with its presentation of a new-style, postwar Frenchwoman. Unlike her milder predecessors, the heroine of *La Garçonne* goes in for short hair, masculine dress, and lovers of both sexes. Sales of the wildly popular *La Garçonne* were given a further boost when the archbishop of Paris condemned the book for obscenity, eventually forcing Margueritte to return his Légion d'honneur medal.

In *The Two Friends* (1926), Foujita's vision of two New Women is gentle, though the archbishop might object to their lack of embarrassment. With short-cropped hair, they sit naked on a mostly white sheet against a mostly white wall—giving Foujita a chance to display his skill with his favorite color. Their sensuous, perfect white skin, fleshier than Kiki's, is dramatically outlined with his expert brushstroke. Again, Foujita's black and white conjures up recognizable traditions of Japanese art. And again, he goes further when his precise brushstrokes tackle something as diffuse as imperfect human relations. One woman places an affectionate arm around the other, who seems less inclined to respond. In this nude couple, Foujita found a way to add both volume to his women's bodies and some disquieting insights.

Foujita also made his mark during these years with more self-portraits, which toyed with the public image he worked so hard to create. *Self-Portrait in the Studio* (1926) has Foujita, the most famous Japanese in Paris, seated cross-legged on the floor in the manner of his native land. He further emphasizes his Japanese connections with the ink stone and the fine brushes on his low work table. With one such brush at the ready, he prepares to draw more of his fine lines on the paper before him. In case there is anyone who does not remember what his trademark subjects were, Foujita has a woman's portrait pinned on the studio wall and a cat nuzzling at his shoulder. It does not come as a surprise that the artist of this portrait within the portrait also keeps his colors to a minimum. With self-mockery, Foujita gathers together the reasons why he has gained so much attention. He includes his line, his white, his drawing skills, and his promise that he will not tell anything much about himself.

As a result of his success in France and elsewhere in Europe, Foujita became an even more popular portraitist of society women. He appreciated the income but not the difficulties he faced in trying to please these customers. "In those days, I drew portraits of the Countess of Montebello, the Countesses of Clermont-Tonnerre, and of Ganay . . . It disgusted me. The concierges made me take the service elevator because I was not well dressed enough for them. The countesses apologized, but the same thing happened again." One of his clients demanded that he paint her naked as Diana the Huntress. Her mother-in-law, who objected to such a portrait, insisted that Foujita place a mask on his subject. Foujita refused to go along when the mother-in-law next requested that he disguise the woman's body as well.

Foujita had more problems with his portrait of the aristocratic poet Anna de Noailles, who was unable to stay still long enough for him to draw her likeness. As Youki describes the scene in *Youki's Confessions*, the countess talked incessantly while she posed, disturbing Foujita's concentration:

"What does it mean, Foujita?"

"It means 'Field of Wisteria.'"

Enchanted she started clapping her hands. "Oh, that's great, just great. That's just perfect. My verses flow like wisteria."

As she spoke the last sentence, she made a great movement with her left arm and leaned toward the floor. Foujita tried to catch her as she went down. It was rather funny.

"And what is your first name?"

"Tsuguharu," Foujita said, unnerved. "And that means 'Heir of Peace.'"

"Ah! Peace!" (Great movement of her right arm) "I have often extolled it, peace. But I am the poet of peace, the peace of gardens, the peace of the heart, nature, of beauty."

Thus, she kept moving.

Foujita spent a long time trying to complete this *Portrait of Anna de Noailles* (1926), but his subject was still dissatisfied with the result. "No, Foujita, you have made my eyes too small. They are huge, my eyes (in ecstasy). My eyes are like lakes. And my forehead! Take a look— what do I think with? My forehead is like a tower." To other observers, Foujita has perfectly captured this passionate poet. Noailles poses in a dress of gold and flowers, reproduced by Foujita in all its filminess and reminiscent of the richly patterned robes in Japanese artworks. While remembering Japan, he brings us a fragile, gifted European woman who looks capable of writing lines like "Already the blazing life leans toward the night / Breathe in on your youth" and of winning the friendship of Marcel Proust.

From the whitest of backgrounds, Anna de Noailles comes forward to tell of her distress.

TWENTY

MOST FAMOUS
JAPANESE IN PARIS

For several years, Japanese artists have rushed to Paris en masse.
The success of Foujita is the bane of his compatriots' lives . . . Today
every Japanese ship that anchors at Marseilles brings several Japa-
nese painters in eyeglasses.

           —Alejo Carpentier

As usual, Foujita's social life during this period also kept him busy. There is the photograph of Foujita on the beach in Deauville, posing with the singer Suzy Solidor. He is pleased to ham it up for the camera, dressed in loud trousers he sewed himself and taking notes with a giant pencil. There is Foujita again front and center at a Montparnasse costume ball, wearing a funny hat, white-face, and a white boa. He is surrounded by other guests in leopard skins and pirate vests, but surely, more than the others, he deserves his prominent position. At the Moulin de la Galette, he is in drag, having borrowed a flattering dress from the star of the film *Nana*.

Featured in more caricatures as his renown grew, Foujita is pictured in one publication wearing a Japanese-style jacket as he enjoys the essentials of his life—a palette, a painting of a nude, and a bag of money; in another, he is drawn in his earrings and a gaudy cravat, holding court at La Coupole. (He had joined the crowds at the 1927 opening of this Montparnasse landmark when ten thousand canapés, three thousand hard-boiled eggs, a thousand pairs of hot sausages, eight hundred cakes, and more than fifteen hundred bottles of Mumm champagne were consumed.) Foujita had always been quick to understand the professional benefits of this kind of publicity and defended himself against those who said that he went too far: "Those who think I became famous because of my kappa hairstyle and my earrings should compare me to the automobile company Citroën, which spent a fortune to advertise on the Eiffel Tower with the biggest electrical device in the world. Can't you say that my way gives me clever publicity for free? Really, publicity is important. There's nothing that beats the combination of ability and publicity."

His name spread even further across France when Foujita figured in a protest involving a naked woman and artistic freedom. He drew the rejoicing, unclad woman for a poster advertising a ball to benefit artists, and this was displayed all over town. The next day, subway officials, fearing the effect on public morals, ordered the poster removed, and soon five hundred famous artists signed a petition to protest this censorship. While the subway commission recognized the artistic value of his poster, Foujita recalled, there were concerns about "the rascals among those waiting for the trains who would draw graffiti on the posters of the nude." Because of the publicity from this dispute (which was eventually resolved), poster sales were excellent, and the ball completely packed.

In a comical collaboration with a compatriot, Foujita participated in a judo demonstration at the Paris Opéra with the judo master Ishiguro Keishichi. Such luminaries as the president and prime minister of France were in the audience. Ishiguro was eager to appear in the show to get publicity for his new judo school, while Foujita, who had been a student of martial arts in Tokyo, seized upon the chance to show off his physical fitness. Foujita agreed to pose for a newspaper photograph before the match, but only if the picture showed him winning the judo throw. Ishiguro, who had a reputation to uphold and a martial arts school to promote, found a way to get around this. He had Foujita execute the kani-basami (crab-scissors) throw, which Foujita performed correctly, but the victory was apparent only to an aficionado who understood the technique. To the uninformed readers of the newspaper, Foujita seemed to be falling to the ground with his two legs around the upright Ishiguro. The next day, Foujita met friends in Montparnasse, expecting congratulations for his triumph. Instead, they greeted him with, "Foujita, I saw a picture of you getting thrown" or "There's a photo of you losing."

At the actual judo demonstration, the two men performed on a silver bridge on the Opéra stage, and Foujita played to the audience when he flashed a genuine Japanese sword at the VIP box. But he got carried away during a throw and was next discovered hanging dangerously off the edge of the bridge. Rescued, he had sustained slight injuries and needed a cane the next day. Still, Foujita was pleased to have had the chance to advertise his far-ranging talents. Artist, rich sophisticate, lover, he-man—Foujita could not get enough of such moments.

The list of social events goes on and on, a testimony to Foujita's vitality by itself, but more staggering when taken together with his huge artistic output during that same period. For his society portraits, he received payment worthy of his fame and his customers' wealth. He was also sought after as an illustrator of books, particularly those with Japanese themes. His other works were regularly exhibited around Europe. Sales were brisk, even though prices were "astronomique."

Youki writes about the present she received from Foujita for her twenty-first birthday in 1924: a custom-made car with a bronze miniature of the Rodin sculpture *Man with the Broken Nose* as the radiator cap. Along with the car came the Basque chauffeur José Raso, the jai-alai champion with "eyesight like a lynx and impeccable reflexes." At first, Youki feared that their artist friends would tease them for such extravagances, but no one had any complaints about this luxurious mode of transport. Soon Foujita and Youki were going on drives to the countryside with their friends. Foujita was "as content as a child." In an unpublished memoir, model Jacqueline Goddard remembers what it was like to be around Foujita then:

I became his favorite model. No end of drawings of my face were all over Paris. I grew very tired of meeting my face so frequently and muttered to myself, "That B[itch,] me again." Going out with [Foujita and Youki] was quite an experience. He was like a jewelry shop window. Big earrings, an enormous watch to hide a tattoo, rings galore; his love of gold was manifest. He believed in being noticed at all costs. It was difficult for me at times, to arrive at the Dôme with them. It was a ceremony. The uniformed chauffeur would open the door to let Foujita emerge first, then the overdressed Youki, and ultimately, but not importantly, me. A table was kept and the chairs dusted before we were seated. Waves of the hand to salute our friends that I sensed found the whole show a bit much and comical. Their car was enormous too and was the most noticeable of Paris. It was yellow, really yellow with a little bit of black . . .

Foufou was very protective and fatherly to me. He taught me jujitsu to protect me from all sorts of attacks including rape. He would try to take me by surprise in false alarms. It must have been hilarious to see me calmly posing for a drawing, [and then] suddenly jumping on guard [in response] to an attack that was a mock one at that.

Foujita's endless public appearances would have been considered merely entertaining if he had been a French artist who painted nudes. If he had been French, he would have been dismissed as another of those artists who vaulted up bridges or dressed in funny clothes to gain notoriety. And as a matter of fact, the French were, in general, amused by Foujita's energetic role in the festivities. "He quickly stirred the curiosity of Paris," reads a 1928 French profile, "as much by his natural abilities, which he used so marvelously in certain landscapes of our land, as by his way of life, which he immediately assimilated into our least traditional customs."

Unfortunately for Foujita, the Japanese continued to be intensely critical of his boisterous public image, and more unfortunately for Foujita, their opinions would matter to him in years to come. As his fame grew, the Japanese heard more about his marriages, his loincloth costumes, and his tattoos, and associated him with unacceptable wantonness. "Traditionally, artists in Japan are expected to have noble characters," writes Hayashi Yōko, "because this is seen as necessary in members of the cultural elite."

More than seventy years later, the Japanese actress Nagaoka Teruko, one of the few people still alive who visited Foujita during these Paris years, conveys a sense of that disapproval. Nagaoka, who exudes concern for all humankind even when seated on her living room sofa, played a good-natured housewife in Ozu Yasujirō's *Tokyo Story* and *Good Morning*. She was ninety-two when we met at her Tokyo home, and her animated, great-grandmotherly face attested to her miraculous robustness.

To prepare for her long career in film, theater, and television, Nagaoka went to Paris in 1928, at age twenty. "I met Foujita during his brightest, flashiest period. In the store windows, there were mannequins made to look like Foujita wearing the latest clothes. That's how famous he was. Whenever people in Paris found out that I was Japanese, they would ask me if I knew Foujita." Nagaoka met Foujita for the first time in his studio, at a party in honor of someone who had caught many fish. Foujita received his guests in face powder and rouge, wearing a gaudy Japanese fisherman's coat. "The cotton cloak," Nagaoka recalled, "had pretty flowers on the back. It was really very gaudy. Foujita asked me, 'So what do you think of it? Too young for me?'" Not at all shy with this new acquaintance, Nagaoka asked him about the tattoos on his fingers and wrist. "He had a tattoo of a watch on his wrist. It always said twelve o'clock. Japanese don't consider tattoos very refined, you know. In England, I think tattoos are more acceptable. I heard that their crown prince had a tattoo. But Japanese people associate tattoos with gangsters. So Foujita must have tattooed himself on purpose, to shock people."

Some of Foujita's home decorations also left a lasting impression. "Foujita had a wooden box with a carving of a woman with her legs open, and there was a slot between her legs where people put coins in." She continued with a giggle. "He told me that this was the charge for 'Paying respects to Foujita.' 'What a bad man you are!' I told him, and he was so pleased. 'I really am naughty, aren't I?' he said to me. 'I am so happy to hear you say that! You make me feel like a young student.'" Other activities were more offensive to Nagaoka's conservative nature and remain so to this day. "There were many poets, writers, and women journalists there. And how they behaved! Flirting and carrying on. I remember being disgusted by what they were doing. I was a cool sort of person then. I didn't want to become an adult like that. I wanted them to behave in a more dignified fashion, have more pride."

Foujita's Japanese friends in Paris also brooded about the turn his life had taken. His male friends are the ones who have left memoirs, and it is no surprise to learn that some pointed to Foujita's women as the cause of his excesses. Satsuma Jirohachi claims that Foujita was "without artifice," "childlike," "unmaterialistic," "content with only a paintbrush in his hand," and blessed with "an unlimited abundance of inner strength." According to Satsuma, it was Fernande who first dragged Foujita away from his pure devotion to his profession. His marriage to "bossy" Fernande transformed Foujita into a commercial property. Similarly unimpressed by the next Frenchwoman in Foujita's life, Satsuma blames Youki for Foujita's further deterioration. After all, he was "a saintly person who wouldn't touch alcohol," but the allure of Youki's flesh turned Foujita into a dissolute creature who frequented the city's hot spots dressed like a "gigolo."

While gadding about in costumes seemed to suit Foujita's temperament and the uproarious times, there is reason to wonder about the feelings of a Japanese artist who had once been stoned by Parisian children and kept from membership in the Salon because of his race. As Japanese commentators have noted, Foujita, like many Japanese of his generation, must have experienced great discomfort and feelings of inferiority when living among Europeans. A Japanese artist of those days might have been driven to extremes in order to be accepted in French circles, believing he was not going to be welcomed on account of his talents alone. Perhaps pedaling down the boardwalk on a child's bicycle in Deauville was necessary to make his mark? Foujita threw himself into these evenings so relentlessly that some contemporaries could not decide whether he was really having a good time. A Japanese journalist remembers seeing Foujita for the first time, dancing the night away at Le Jockey: "To the standard bourgeois or to common people, he looked very comic. I couldn't tell whether he had decided that this 'comic' style was a necessity in his kind of life or whether this comic style came naturally to him."

And finally, in his old age, when he was bitter about so many things, Foujita dismissed all the stories about his wild past as "scandal-mongering, absolute fabrications."

At least one event celebrated chez Foujita seems so wonderful that no one could have possibly raised any objections. This was the performance of the miniature circus created by the American artist Alexander Calder. After Foujita and Youki moved into a four-story house on square de Montsouris, they invited guests over to see *Calder's Circus* in their fancy new home. Youki described Calder as "a huge charming devil with the body of a giant and the face of a child." The very little circus "performers" were all handmade by Calder from wood, wire, tin, leather, rubber tubing, cork, cloth, and any other scraps he came upon. They included an elephant and a mule, and as Calder wrote later, these animals "could be made to stand on their hind quarters, front quarters, or heads." He fitted his clowns with strings so that they could be manipulated to sit on the elephant's back. James Johnson Sweeney describes a circus equipped down to the smallest detail:

> A bit of green carpet was unrolled; a ring was laid out; poles were erected to support the trapeze for the aerial act and wing indicators of the "big top"; a spotlight was thrown on the ring; an appropriate record placed on a small portable phonograph; "Mesdames et Messieurs, je vous présente—," and the performance began. There were acrobats, tumblers, trained dogs, slack-wire acts *à la japonaise*; a lion-tamer; a sword-swallower; Rigoulot, the strong-man; the Sultan of Senegambia who hurled knives and axes; Don Rodriguez Kolynos who risked a death-defying slide down a tight wire; "living statues"; a trapeze act; a chariot race.

For his show at the Foujitas', Calder did his best to create a genuine circus atmosphere in the fourth-floor studio, using soap crates as seats and arranging them around his small circus ring. In addition, he brought along two large bags of peanuts in the shell and, to avoid disturbances, requested that no drinks be served during the performance. Foujita, who had set up the lighting, sat on the floor beside Calder. A photo taken that evening shows Foujita playing the small drum that accompanied the trapeze act. Beside the drum is a record player, which repeatedly played "Ramona," the circus's French theme song ("*Belle brune de Barcelonne, tes baisers me donnent des frissons d'amour*").

A very international audience sat on the soap crates as Calder manipulated his circus players. "Sometimes the horseback rider didn't want to perform jumps on his horse, and the trapeze artist did not want to use the trapeze," Youki wrote. "The audience, breathless, waited in total silence." At the end, there was much applause and also a great rush to the bar, since everyone was thirsty from the peanuts. All were elated except the maid, who had to clean up the shells scattered throughout the house. The next day, Youki tried to placate her by explaining that eating peanuts was an American custom. "That shows you—it's a country of savages!" the maid exclaimed.

Youki told Baron Robert Rothschild a somewhat off-color story while she was preparing his drink. Forever after, whenever she met Rothschild at a social gathering, he would yell out, "Here comes Youki Foujita. She's going to tell us some dirty stories!"

TWENTY-ONE

GREEN SHEET OF
THE TAX COLLECTOR

Foujita is about to leave us. People talk a lot about Foujita. In a good way and bad. They often remember the exaggerated details, the reports, the photos, etc. . . . The imbeciles and those who are jealous burst their blood vessels trying to find ways to make fun of him, but Foujita tries to create a masterpiece from seven in the morning until late at night. This man with his excellent heart, who has always welcomed friends less fortunate or less happy, returns to his homeland after seventeen years away.

—Paris-Montparnasse, *August 15, 1929*

Kondō Fumito does not look like a man at the center of a very messy situation. He appears tidy and calm when I meet him at the offices of NHK (Japan Broadcasting Corporation), where he is a producer. In his attire, mode of speech, and gestures, Kondō does not stand out from the many other employees at NHK. Accustomed to the shifting responsibilities at his job, he displays neither weariness nor a sense of triumph. There was no sign of the talent for nerve-wracking diplomacy that must be his strength.

Since 1999, Kondō has emerged as the person most active in reintroducing Foujita to the Japanese public. This comes after the decades of meager information that followed Foujita's death in 1968. Kondō has not had much competition, since more fainthearted researchers, scared off by the vigilance of Foujita's widow, Kimiyo, have not dared to venture onto this terrain. "After I die, there will be many exhibits in my honor," Foujita predicted late in life. He would have been flabbergasted about the near extinction of his reputation since then. Foujita Kimiyo, exercising her rights as his copyright holder, has often impeded exhibitions and research.

Kimiyo has complained about the careless approach to copyright in Japan, and some say she has done all artists a service in fighting against unauthorized publication and exhibition of Foujita's works. "The attitude toward copyright is definitely vague in Japan," she wrote in a 1975 magazine article, during a visit to Japan from her home in France. "In France, copyright is strictly protected, and since I am used to living in a place where that kind of idea is generally accepted by society, I find the situation in Japan—where it's as if there's no such thing as copyright— extremely strange." She has also complained about the proliferation of fake Foujitas. "I'm not saying that I can authenticate all of Foujita's works," she told a newspaper on another visit back to Japan in 1986, "but then again, it's odd to believe in the total correctness of assessments of people who never visited Foujita's atelier during his lifetime . . . When he was still alive, Foujita said that Japan is a scary place. You can sell fakes or make them, and it's not considered a crime and no one gets punished."

Kimiyo has certainly not been able to shake off her anger at the criticism aimed at Foujita after the war; particularly in Japan, her invocation of her copyright powers can seem like her way of avenging her dead husband's suffering:

> There must be printed collections and exhibitions of his works, but with the situation the way it is, would there be any point in doing such things in Japan? When I start to think about that, I get very irritated. There was talk of holding an exhibition in France and Japan several years ago. I told them that if they focused on Foujita's role as a member of the École de Paris, I would be willing to hand over all the works I have. But then the talks came to nothing. People said that I had made trouble and wrecked those plans. There are a lot of bad things said about me. Really, sometimes I wish that everyone would do me a favor and just forget about Foujita.

Like it or not, Foujita Kimiyo is the star of Foujita's afterlife, with scenes devoted to lawsuits and bitterness about the Japanese who mistreated him.

Kondō has succeeded in winning over Kimiyo, now in her late nineties, and this has been no small feat. That achieved, he next set about reshaping Foujita's image for the Japanese, many of whom know or remember little about him. Perhaps because age has weakened her opposition to research on her late husband, Kimiyo granted Kondō access to Foujita's private papers. In addition, she told him her side of the story, apparently at some length. Among other Foujita-related activities, Kondō has produced television documentaries, written a biography, and edited a collection of Foujita's memoirs. In his work on Foujita, Kondō lets Mrs. Foujita vent her fury and then tries to make a fair judgment. The results—like so many works "authorized" by a subject's close relatives—have been both praised and disparaged. However, no one can dispute that Kondō has brought forth new information about Foujita, a Japanese artist no longer a prime subject in the newspapers.

"At first I thought that Foujita was a complicated person full of the torments we associate with artists," Kondō told me when we met over coffee at NHK. "I imagined him as someone like the Dostoyevsky character Stavrogin in *The Possessed*. But now I realize that Foujita was really not such a complicated person at all. In fact, I consider him rather simple in his ways of thinking."

Kondō hoped to find emotional outpourings in Foujita's diaries, which he has been allowed to read. But Foujita apparently avoided wrenching disclosures about personal upheavals, preferring to stick to the details of his daily life. He was very careful about recording his routine activities, particularly his household finances. Although he seemed to spend money freely when he was prosperous, he actually kept close track of his expenses, down to the smallest hotel tips.

"Foujita had very strong feelings of himself as a Japanese," Kondō went on to say, describing another surprise. "He always thought of himself as a Japanese who was working for the good of Japan. None of the other non-French artists who went to Paris and became part of the École de Paris believed that they were painting for the sake of their countries. Soutine and Modigliani, for example, did not feel that way. Hemingway was not a visual artist, but he never thought he was writing to improve the image of America. On the contrary, these artists were bohemian in their behavior and felt that they had left their homelands to find something new for themselves. But not Foujita. He created paintings to improve the reputation of the Japanese. He said many times that he wanted to put all his energies into painting for the good of Japan. This is really a strange thing about him."

Kondō's observations go to the heart of the controversy, and if his views are accepted, Foujita will be well on his way to rehabilitation in Japan. As so many accounts demonstrate, Foujita has been criticized by the Japanese for being frivolous, promiscuous, opportunistic, an embarrassment to Japan, and, more inexcusably, a man who rejected his Japanese background. This has fed the anger directed against him for his cooperation with the Japanese military during the Second World War. Kondō takes a more sympathetic, Japan-centered position, seeing Foujita as misunderstood and always longing for home.

"Present-day Japanese cannot imagine such a person. Japanese nowadays don't think that they are working for the sake of Japan. Remember that Foujita was born in the Meiji period [1868–1912]. Up until then, Japan had been isolated from the rest of the world for a long time. The Japanese had not yet really become accustomed to going to Europe. Their feelings about Japan were very strong, and for Foujita this was true, too. Throughout, Foujita's meals all consisted of Japanese food. He liked reciting *naniwabushi* [old-style narrative] ballads. He would bang the table while reciting these, bellowing them out. He only listened to things like that. A French person may have thought this a touch of the exotic, but Foujita could not live without such things . . .

"As a Japanese of the Meiji period, he had absorbed the ethical teachings of Confucius, who taught such things as respect for superiors. Foujita believed in those Confucian principles. In that way, he was quite simple. Many stories have been told about Foujita, but in his essence, he was a Confucian kind of person. The Japanese think he fooled around with women, drank, and took drugs. That's not true. He didn't drink at all and didn't use drugs, either. But when he went to a bar, he was the one who made the biggest commotion. This was just his desire to please (*sābisu seishin*) at work. He looked as if he were the one who was drinking the most, but when the entertainment was over, he went back home and worked on his paintings."

Kondō is emphatic about this idea that Foujita did not show off at parties because of his own wish to dance on the tables, but rather to satisfy the French, who liked such carryings-on. Foujita's eagerness to please, that *sābisu seishin*—literally, "service spirit"—was essential to his acceptance in French society. "Once a Russian artists' association held a masquerade ball at the 'Bullier' dance hall," Kondō writes in his biography of Foujita.

> Foujita went with Kiki. In front of at least 150 artists, Foujita made his appearance dressed as a woman and arm in arm with Kiki. As Kiki descended the hall's large staircase, she took off her clothes piece by piece. By the time she got to the bottom of the staircase, she was only wearing a small hair ornament of ostrich feathers. He wanted to surprise people with his participation in this kind of clowning, which bursts with his *sābisu seishin*.

At his most ardent, Kondō seems to do the impossible, stripping Foujita of his razzmatazz and giving him the dour aspect of a monogamous, striving, law-abiding citizen. This is just the kind of stolid figure whom his widow wants to offer up to posterity. In fact, Kondō has written, "According to his wife, the rumors about Foujita's relationships with women are absolutely groundless." Kondō strives to be even-handed, but his straitened working conditions cannot be easily concealed: At various times, when one reads Kondō's biography or views his television documentaries on Foujita, Mrs. Foujita seems to rise to her feet, railing against the affronts endured by her husband. As a result, Kondō's approach settles certain disputes, but also brings up questions: Has Foujita been unfairly treated throughout his career, the victim of those jealous Japanese who resented his leaving Japan for a bigger, louder world? Or has Kondō toed the family line too much in trying to sanitize Foujita's legacy? While the answers remain unclear,

Kondō's sincerity is undeniable. Allowed into the inner sanctum of the Foujita home, he has become a believer in the interpretations he espouses. Foujita's widow chose astutely when she selected Kondō to relate her late husband's tribulations.

"Foujita worked very hard to fit into French society and to understand it," Kondō told me. "But the Japanese around him ignored his hard work and felt he was just fooling around and making a lot of noise. This really made Foujita angry, and his dislike of the Japanese grew. He felt very strongly that he was a Japanese and liked Japan very much, but he felt that many Japanese only looked at him on the surface . . .

"It is really sad that a person like that who loved Japan so much died in Europe. He had cancer at the end. There were many people who urged him to get treatment at home in Japan. But he couldn't go home. There were supposedly no good hospitals in Paris. He changed hospitals three or four times. Finally, he went to Switzerland.

"I wonder what he felt about being a Japanese just before he died. He must have had many complicated thoughts."

It is instructive to ponder the items that Kondō takes up in detail and those he chooses to skim over. In his biography, he lingers over certain turns in the story—whether Fernande or Foujita engineered the first exhibition in Paris, a dispute with a patron over the naming of a museum, one postwar sashimi dinner—since these events gave rise to Foujita's major grievances. Then there are the episodes that do not get much of Kondō's attention, and these, too, are noteworthy. Like other male chroniclers before him, Kondō does not go out of his way to give Foujita's former wives and lovers adoring treatment. He takes the view that Fernande and Youki were domineering and/or alcoholic presences patiently tolerated by Foujita. Mrs. Foujita told Kondō about how those two—long after their divorces—would turn up at the home she then shared with Foujita. At such times, the widow saw these reminders of the past in search of emergency funds.

Kondō is definitely on Foujita's side when it comes to his trip home to Japan in 1929. After the performance of *Calder's Circus* but before the stock market crash, Foujita faced his own fiscal unraveling. He decided on a trip home to Japan to rustle up some business. The trouble started when Foujita hired a secretary, mostly because he liked the idea of having a business staff. Then a newspaper erroneously reported that he had lost a million francs playing baccarat at Deauville. Although Foujita did not play baccarat, the mistaken news item spurred the tax office to investigate the records of this free-spending celebrity. Foujita next received a huge bill for taxes, which, as a matter of fact, he had not paid since 1925. Youki says that if she had been present to negotiate with the tax officials, the matter could have been settled. Unfortunately, she was off on one of her many trips away from Foujita. This time, she was in Marseilles because of the gloomy weather in Paris and because her friend was depressed. "In spite of the money he had earned," wrote a French commentator, "Foujita lived from day to day, and one morning in 1928, the green sheet of the tax collector shook the euphoria of rue du Douanier like a thunderbolt."

With Youki out of town, Foujita sent his secretary over to consult with the tax department. "I don't know exactly what happened," Youki wrote, "but it is certain that she did not understand a single thing they said to her." On his secretary's advice, Foujita signed a document accepting responsibility for all the debts claimed by the tax office. When Youki returned from her vacation, she was appalled to find that the agreement could not be invalidated under any circumstances, and so an "astronomical sum" had to be paid in eight days. Foujita's nephew later took him to task for this turn of events, which could have been avoided if a lawyer had been hired, but Foujita preferred to rely on his instincts rather than dry legal advice. ("Don't read books," he once counseled his nephew.) Those instincts told him that there was no cause for alarm, since, after all, Josephine Baker had survived a similar experience.

When Foujita's instincts finally convinced him that ruin was imminent, he decided to leave with Youki for Tokyo. That would be the place to make a quick profit, since the Japanese liked to buy the works of artists back from the West. The chauffeur, José, was charged with selling the car and finding himself a new job. As a sign of his displeasure, Foujita left his Légion d'honneur medal hanging on the mantelpiece.

Kondō, who acknowledges these financial woes in his biography, first invokes Confucian notions of filial piety as the reason for Foujita's hasty trip back to Japan. He begins by explaining that Foujita embarked upon this journey to Japan, after an absence of many years, in order to see his elderly father. Always sentimental about Foujita's connections to his homeland, Kondō imagines the trip home to Japan: "Foujita stood on the deck, and a vision of his father floated into his heart . . . 'I want to do my filial duty to my old father.'" Without a doubt, Foujita often thought of going home to pay his respects to his aging parent, but the tax bill surely lit a bigger fire under him.

Hopeful about solving his tax problem during the long trip to Japan, Foujita had reason to anticipate a rapturous reception as a local boy who had made good. A Japanese maxim describes a person who returns home a success as "adorned with brocade," and if this tradition had been followed, Foujita, a bona fide artistic icon in Paris, should have landed in Japan after more than sixteen years away with golden silks and satins tickling his toes and flowing up to envelop him completely. In addition to his professional credits, he had a striking European woman by his side, and despite the criticisms of such women by Foujita's friends, this was considered another kind of major achievement for a Japanese man of those days. But as was frequently the case when his stature in Japan was involved, Foujita encountered less warm feeling than he expected.

Kondō reports that Foujita got word of unfavorable developments before he landed. "Sign of a typhoon in the Japanese art world," read one newspaper. "An anti-Foujita movement arises because of his excessive waywardness in Paris." "He will not be welcomed in Japan." Kumaoka Yoshihiko, an expatriate Japanese artist enraged about Foujita's behavior in Paris, had reached Japan earlier and started a smear campaign. Upset at this news, Foujita had to be persuaded by Youki to continue his homeward journey. Indeed, the venom of the series of articles Kumaoka wrote for an art journal would have made anyone want to turn the ship around and head off in the opposite direction. Kumaoka berated Foujita for almost everything—his work, his social life, his money—and was particularly agitated about his constant self-promotion. A long list of transgressions, including Foujita's appearance

Foujita as a young boy, with his older brother. (Klüver/Martin Archive)

The wedding of Foujita and Tokita Tomi, around 1912. (Klüver/Martin Archive)

Foujita on the *Mishima-maru*, en route to France, 1913. (Klüver/Martin Archive)

Foujita and Kawashima Riichirō in Greek attire in Paris. (Klüver/Martin Archive)

Fernande Barrey, who married Foujita in 1917. (Klüver/Martin Archive)

A cartoon by Lee Conrey of Foujita carrying Fernande on his back at a costume ball, from *The American Weekly*, October 23, 1932. (Klüver/Martin Archive)

Foujita posing with a store-window mannequin of himself in Paris, around 1925.

(Lipnitzki/Roger-Viollet)

Foujita in his square de Montsouris house, around 1928. (Harlingue/Roger-Viollet)

Foujita with Youki at the horse races in the 1920s. The man with them is most likely couturier and art collector Jacques Doucet. (Klüver/Martin Archive)

Foujita and Youki. (Klüver/Martin Archive)

On the beach at Deauville. Foujita is at the center of the can-can line, and Youki is to the left. (Klüver/Martin Archive)

Foujita with his father in Miyajima, Japan, 1929. (Klüver/Martin Archive)

Foujita and Madeleine with the Cuban artist Armando Maribona,
Havana, 1932. (Opus Habana)

Madeleine in a recording studio in Osaka, around 1934. (Klüver/Martin Archive)

Foujita as a war artist in China, 1938. (La Maison-Atelier Foujita)

Foujita and Kimiyo on their return to Japan from besieged France in 1940. (*Asahi shinbun*)

Foujita at home in wartime Tokyo, around 1942. (Domon Ken)

Foujita coming out of his air-raid shelter in Tokyo during the war. (Domon Ken)

Foujita leaving Japan in 1949, never to return. (Domon Ken)

Foujita in front of his home in Villiers-le-Bâcle, France, 1965. (La Maison-Atelier Foujita)

in a suggestive cigarette advertisement ("All the women find my kisses exquisite because I smoke Lucky Strike") and, another time, in a racy bathing suit, gave Kumaoka a chance to fulminate about Foujita's character: "All he wants is money and fame."

Kumaoka even went so far as to claim that French elementary schools taught tolerance by citing Foujita as a bad example. "[The teachers tell] students that activities like those undertaken by the Japanese Foujita are completely deserving of their contempt, but that the students must not be contemptuous of all Japanese because of him. It's all right for the students to be utterly contemptuous of Foujita alone." Although such appraisals today seem to choke on their spitefulness, they were taken seriously in certain Japanese circles.

This was only the beginning of the criticisms circulated during Foujita's visit. Deeply wounded by such treatment, Foujita was not the sort who could forget old slights, and his widow seems still not to have forgiven the Japanese for the cold reception accorded her husband in 1929. "Even in his old age, Foujita spoke with sadness about those days," Kondō comments, "and hearing the stories, his wife said that she, too, became extremely angry."

Foujita found a friendlier reception in Japan among the general public, which was not swayed by the disapproving newspapers and art world. Crowds of fans, eager to know every detail about the visiting luminary, did all they could to keep up with his doings. At Foujita's first exhibition in Tokyo, visitors thronged to see a collection of his oils, drawings, and prints. The second Tokyo exhibition was also packed, despite a steep entrance fee. Hayashi Yōko believes that Foujita's works sold well because increasing age and financial pressures had forced him to move away from the style that had made him famous in Europe—a style that had seemed too Japanese and unoriginal to his audience in Japan. On display in Tokyo in 1929 were works with more standard European looks and themes—notably muscular male and full-fleshed female nudes—and this matched Japanese notions of up-to-date Western art. But what pleased one audience could not, at the same time, satisfy the other. "As soon as Foujita sought a rather academic style and lost his originality," Hayashi writes, "he seemed a mediocre artist to Westerners."

When Foujita traveled around Japan by train, eager citizens waited to catch a glimpse of him at every stop and bombarded him with gifts. *Profile of Paris,* a collection of his writings published during the visit, sold out fast and was reprinted numerous times. For Foujita, the conclusion was clear: adulation in Japan was possible only if he could get beyond his critics and reach out to the admiring hordes. Kondō is not alone when he sees a connection between Foujita's desire to make contact with ordinary Japanese citizens and his later embrace of mass-market war art.

During this trip, Foujita's public pronouncements were not the sort that would be unanimously admired by his listeners, some of whom preferred much more modesty. But when he spoke, Foujita felt the need to get a few points across, and clearly could not resist seizing the chance. This was the kind of behavior that fortified both the supporters and detractors who battled throughout his life (and, in some cases, beyond). In his talks during his stay, Foujita could display a genuine nobility about his calling: "If you think that this year you will produce a masterpiece and surprise the world, you won't be able to produce a masterpiece. A masterpiece spontaneously emerges at some point in time, and this will surprise you afterward. You should not be thinking of the result when you start out." He was convincing about the lofty nature of his goals: "We must work magic on our easels."

Yet there was overreaching, too, in his presentation of his recent history. At times, Foujita seemed to follow in the tradition of those Japanese who have achieved the impossible—turned a bicycle-lamp business into an electronics empire, started a supermarket chain—and agreed to tell about their experiences. In such accounts, there must be travail, there must be despair bringing the protagonist to the brink, but through it all, there must remain an unassailable ability to stick to an unconventional path. Since these narratives are created for the Japanese, who like stories about the triumph of moral uprightness, success cannot come overnight, in the form of a stock sale or a lottery ticket, but must be accompanied by years of disciplined labor. Foujita's Tokyo lectures, "Seventeen Years in France" and "The Life of an Artist in Paris," describing his ups and downs, are models of this genre.

Foujita laid it on thick when he spoke of his experiences in Paris—the freedom, the operatic struggles, his hard-won success. He got in a few barbs about the uselessness of his artistic education in Japan, a questionable thing to do, since at least one former teacher was in the audience. Foujita not only conveyed a sense of Paris's wonders, he also offered himself as a living example of what that atmosphere had produced. Stern Japanese wanted to dismiss him as loud and vulgar, but he pounded home the idea that his behavior had led to verifiable achievement. This is where Foujita certainly had the right to gloat, for he had, without question, toiled long and achieved success: in an exhibition hall nearby, dozens of completed works offered proof of this. "Once I even painted for twenty-fours hours, from four in the afternoon until four the next afternoon. Then I went to sleep for five hours and again worked hard for eighteen hours . . . I have a very strong body, and in the seventeen years I have been away, I have never been sick. I've caught a cold every once in a while, but I've never had a headache even when I've only slept for two hours."

In other remarks, he also could not resist reminding his listeners about his courage and iconoclasm in making artistic decisions. "I decided to do just the opposite of what the others did. The trend of those days was to pile on the paints wildly and apply colors thickly. I decided to bring life to my works by using paints very sparingly and smoothly. I didn't use much color, mainly black and white. While others used a thick brush, I instead tried to create an oil painting by using a fine writing brush." When Foujita spoke these words, doubtless in a supremely assured manner, there was nothing that could have consoled his envious colleagues.

Foujita repeatedly counseled Japanese artists to remember their Japanese background, since they could not hope to produce anything new if they merely imitated the West. This principle was dear to this artist, who was constantly accused of abandoning his Japanese roots. Stick to Japanese traditions, he said; don't copy from the West; be fearless and original always. The stew he described was complicated, and while he seemed to offer suggestions, he left no doubt that only he could mix the ingredients properly. "When we Japanese express our individuality, we must not forget our nationality. A Japanese will not suddenly be able to become a Westerner even if he tries." When he visited an exhibition of Western-style Japanese artists, he underscored the hazards of not following his advice. "The influence of artists like Segonzac, Rouault, Chagall, Dufy, Braque was obvious. I started to wonder if I was back at the Salon d'Automne. That's how much Western-style artists in Japan long for the Parisian art world." And as Kondō points out, Foujita did not hesitate to go further, needling his audience about how they had misjudged a pioneer like himself.

> We artists must not think like ordinary people, but must in fact be a step ahead of everyone else. At first, when the artist does something eccentric, everyone invariably calls him crazy. Or people look down on him and consider him weird. So they call him crazy and feel for a time that they have analyzed the person, and this calms everyone down. But this person is not really crazy and comes forth with something great.

This trip home has attracted other commentaries, and Tanaka Jō, a Foujita biographer as disapproving as Kondō is appreciative, comes up with a very different view of those days. Throughout Tanaka's biography, Foujita is castigated for lacking sincerity, a prime Japanese virtue. Over and over, Tanaka blames Foujita for his calculating nature and even for possessing the savvy insights into the marketplace that contributed to his success. In Tanaka's mind, the superiority of the guileless, starving artist over one who succeeds is incontestable. No wonder that Foujita gets beaten up badly in Tanaka's book. For example, Tanaka did not have to look hard to find instances of Foujita's calculating approach to the 1929 visit home. He starts with Foujita's first appearance on the landing dock upon arrival, when this returning hero made sure he was the last passenger to disembark. For his grand entrance, Foujita appeared at last in his checked jacket and riding pants, with Youki on his arm. "Slowly he made his way down the center of the stage," Tanaka writes without veneration. "The heels of his riding boots made a distinctive sound as he walked down the smooth sloping gangplank, and this made a deep impression on everyone who came to meet him." And when not trying to monopolize the limelight, Foujita took pains to wheedle his way into the good graces of influential people in Japan. In

Tanaka's view, "He connected with the most powerful people in every realm and every field."

In those days, before there were many museums in Japan, one of Foujita's exhibitions took place at Mitsukoshi, the Tokyo department store. Foujita, alarmed that his works might be displayed among Mitsukoshi's underwear stalls, insisted on certain conditions, and Tanaka makes him sound arrogant when he tells the organizers, "You make sure that there are no loincloths or salted fish on sale near the exhibition hall." Despite the conflicts, the exhibit drew those enormous crowds, as Tanaka grudgingly concedes: "After about five months of vacation in his homeland, Foujita definitely enjoyed the pleasures of being a great actor onstage. At the same time, he was relieved to realize that he could easily make money in Japan any time."

In the end, Youki beats all her Japanese competitors by supplying the most droll account of their journey to Japan. Aside from trips to Belgium, she had never traveled outside of France and so her impressions are those of a European let off at the end of the world. As she later wrote in *Youki's Confessions*, "You really have to go to the Far East or to Slavic countries to know what a mob is." On the trip over, she found Foujita a buoyant travel companion at various ports of call, despite his financial problems. Not for him a gloomy retreat to his cabin to add up his remaining assets. Instead, he joined her in enjoying places like Hong Kong, where he posed for the camera in coolie attire. Youki fell in love with China, savoring the Peking duck and proclaiming both French and Chinese cuisines the best in the world.

At last they reached the Japanese port of Kobe, where Foujita's father received them. Youki writes that he immediately "kissed her on both cheeks," and if her account is true, this father—a military man and an upholder of traditions—would have had to overcome a lifetime's worth of training in restraint to achieve such a casual, alien mode of greeting. Since she could not understand the language being spoken around her, Youki was forced to depend on Foujita for interpretations of events. Perhaps she sensed a chill beneath the gracious welcomes, since he told her that his Japanese compatriots were proud of his success abroad but disturbed about his preference for France over his own country. "And Foujita adores France," she writes, unaware of how such a sentiment could upset the Japanese public.

I discovered that Youki made a lasting impression on at least one of Foujita's family members when I had tea with his nephew Ashihara Yoshinobu in Tokyo. The nephew, by then a very old man, put down his teacup as he thought about that 1929 visit. "Oh, that wife of his was so pretty!" he remembered almost seventy years later. "Foujita never found anyone better." When not charming the younger generation, Youki tried to take everything in. She was surprised by the ornamental role of large cabbages in flower gardens; the deer of Nara and Miyajima, slobbering and aggressive in their lurch for treats, tried to knock her down. Youki may have found Japanese people odd, but she quickly discerned that the Japanese, like "visitors to a zoo," looked upon her also as an alien specimen. "Foreign visitors [at the hotel] are at home there and are delighted because the Japanese fuss over them, invite them out, help them, guide them around. The Japanese don't do this out of kindness. The Japanese really want to observe your tics, count the number of cigarettes you smoke, the glasses you drink, try to get you to say something stupid, catch you making a mistake." Youki was also not enchanted when the waiter attempted to serve her a wine called "Bordo," which was supposedly direct from France. "Don't make a scene," the nondrinker Foujita told her testily. "What difference does it make whether you drink Bordo or Bordeaux? It's the same poison."

On a better day, some students who had dedicated themselves to fomenting revolution came to the hotel to seek her advice. Eager to be of help, she suggested that they assassinate the emperor as a start. When the students said that they had no problems with the imperial system and preferred to destroy the capitalists, she urged them to try blowing up the posh area where Foujita would be holding his exhibition. Ready to try anything, Youki composed a short poem comparing the red maple leaves of autumn to bloodied samurai and attended a Christmas fête in a very elaborate kimono, topped off by a formal Japanese wig weighing eleven pounds. While willing to don the wig, she could not abide other local customs: in her view, the Japanese bars closed too early. "Tokyo is very lively, but everything must close at 11 p.m. except the geisha houses." Finally, she found an octopus shop open late and was content to enjoy a late-night drink among the raw fish.

Youki's sightseeing tapered off as the weeks passed, and she longed for home. Although she found refuge in foreign embassies, where they served whiskey, her criticisms of Japanese society became more caustic in letters to friends in Paris. En route to visit Kumamoto, where Foujita had spent his early years, Youki's openness was tested when Foujita's father sat on the train in his long red underwear.

Still, Youki tried to concentrate on the positive sides of their trip in her memoir—the crowds who surged in to see Foujita's work, providing much-needed sales, and the banquet with visiting stars Douglas Fairbanks and Mary Pickford. When Foujita addressed the guests at this dinner, he declared with much emotion that he had come back to see his father and country for the last time. The audience, perhaps shocked at Foujita's public renunciation of his native land, received this announcement frostily. Again, Youki, who was more interested in Mary Pickford's wrinkles, did not sense the impact of such a statement.

TWENTY-TWO

STUFF OF DREAMS

Surrealism is the order of the day and Desnos is its prophet.
—*André Breton, 1924*

Until Foujita drew a picture of a lion and its naked female trainer, his admirers had expected him to produce less belligerent portraits of similar subjects. He had earned a reputation based on more saucy, but less confrontational cats, who looked out from the sitting room walls of his satisfied customers. Likewise, his nudes, reclining and white, might have been suggestive, but not of the kind of trouble implied by a woman cuddling a lion while clad only in black stockings. *The Trainer and the Lion,* a 1930 work completed after Foujita's return to Paris, introduced the revised version of his former favorite subjects. There is a very large and irate lion—mane and whiskers a much more hairy challenge than usual for Foujita—and a curvy, unapologetic redhead, who is tickling the lion while wearing only green shoes, black stockings, and pink garters.

In addition to more assertive subjects, the colors in the painting are fit for a circus, where, presumably, this duo make their home. In any other artist's works, the green-and-yellow-striped curtains would not startle, nor would there be anything surprising about the very red surface upon which the lion, in particular, makes a stand. With the gay, shiny pillar in the background and a sun trying to invade the night, the viewer has to search for any spots of Foujitean white. No sign either of the sinuous line, which Foujita had drawn and redrawn for salons and clients. Instead, a disembodied, black-gloved hand points a finger of accusation at the undressed female tamer, who looks unconcerned.

This work has called forth many interpretations, but the most obvious thought deserves first mention. Incorporating so many new features, *The Trainer and the Lion* does not appear to be an inconsequential side venture for Foujita, but more of a full-scale effort to renounce his old style. When he returned to Paris in 1929, he faced an art market destroyed by the worldwide financial crisis as well as his own diminished stardom. In considering how to revive his prospects, he could have turned to his old standbys—the cats and the naked women—but by then their vogue had passed. His old style had always had limited possibilities that, at his best, Foujita nurtured to intriguing effect. The line, the white, the naive quality, the Japanese elements—these created a lovely and peculiar surface charged with ambiguity. To the detriment of his standing in Europe, he could leave out the subtleties and easily reproduce facsimiles of those features. Such shortcuts were too tempting to an artist whose spendthrift ways and wife made him very much in need of money. "This is beautiful, this is fine," a friend once murmured as we passed one of Foujita's earlier works. "At least here he was still trying." When he wasn't trying, Foujita produced works that were careless and mannered, pallid and empty.

He could also have given his public more of Japan in his creations, since those effects had served him well in the past. At the height of his fame, Foujita had not been able to resist the profits offered by unadulterated *japonisme* and had accepted commissions on Japanese themes. As a book illustrator, he had been particularly active, and of the more than fifty titles that bear his name, many promised his French public a thoroughly Japanese experience: *Japanese Legends* (1923), *Geishas' Songs* (1926), and *Shizouka, Tranquil Princess* (1929). But for an artist aching to return to the spotlight, there was not much further he could go with exact representations of a legendary Japanese temple bell or the folk hero Urashima Tarō on his special turtle.

In this harried transitional period, Foujita at least deserves credit for trying to start a different kind of conversation with *The Trainer and the Lion*.

The black-gloved hand pointing at the lion tamer in *The Trainer and the Lion* is a detail that has been much discussed. That gloved finger could be finding fault with Youki, who served as the model for the tamer in the painting. If so, her misdeed can only be related to the tamer's cozy connection to the scowling lion at her side. Since Youki was never short of intimates, perhaps there's a clue to the lion's identity in the clash of objects in the painting, as surreal and perplexing as a dream: the poet Robert Desnos—who caused a lion's share of trouble in Foujita's life at this time—did some of his best-known work when he was half asleep.

"I met Desnos for the first time when I went to buy a pipe for my husband," Dominique Desanti told me in Paris, her great friend Desnos still in her thoughts. "It was at a pipe shop called Le Caïd on boulevard Saint-Michel. You can still find the shop there. I worked translating captions into French for Agence Photographique. This was in around 1938, when Desnos was known to a very narrow circle of people. He was my first living Surrealist poet. Desnos spoke to me when he saw me hesitating over a pipe. He liked to talk to people. I met him the second time at a scrap shop—they sold china and used items of all kinds—on rue de Buci. Desnos liked to collect such things and had an eye for them. He taught me what was good.

"We once went for a drink at a small café where he was well-known. Suddenly, outside there was a demonstration of hard, right-wing royalists selling *L'Action française*. Desnos jumped out of the café and shouted, "Vive l'Espagne républicaine!" I feared there would be a riot, but fortunately the mob turned a corner. The bartender said to Desnos, 'This time we had luck, Monsieur Robert. You are not bleeding.' He had apparently got involved in such things many times before. I was nineteen, and he was thirty-eight."

In Robert Desnos, Desanti had found herself a friend rare in many ways, a friend worthy of her sorrow even sixty years after his death. Desnos grew up around the lively Les Halles marketplace, where his father was a vendor of poultry and game. Desnos himself was a pure product of Les Halles: his parents had met when his mother was minding the cash register at her family's neighboring rotisserie. "His poetry was nourished in this district," Desanti writes in her biography, *Robert Desnos, Novel About a Life,*

> by the strong odors, by the vivid colors on the dirty gray soiling the old buildings, by the mysterious lights, the night, and down lanes at the bends of streams whose names sounded like songs: Lavandières-Sainte-Opportune, Coutures-Saint-Gervais, Juges-Consuls, Grande et Petite Truanderie, Passage du Grand-Cerf.

Desnos's beginnings contrasted with the more affluent backgrounds of the other Surrealists, and while he took pride in his rough upbringing, he was sensitive to slights from colleagues who came from more established families.

When Desnos first joined the Surrealists, however, his talents were quickly recognized. The Surrealists, seeking the most essential, uninhibited truths, were drawn to *écriture automatique* (automatic writing), the recording of words spoken in a trancelike state. More than the others, Desnos could enter into a trance easily and come forth with astounding utterances from those depths. "I remember vividly the pale eyes of Desnos," wrote the model Jacqueline Goddard, "eyes to look at another world." In a dream state, Desnos spewed forth metaphors, telepathic communications, and especially puns, which supposedly emerged from his unconscious. The poet Louis Aragon, who was another member of the Surrealist group, described the spectacle of Desnos creating in public:

> In a café, amid all the voices, the bright lights, and the bustle, Robert Desnos need only close his eyes, and he talks, and among the bocks, the saucers, the whole ocean collapses with its prophetic racket, its vapours decorated with long oriflammes. However little he is encouraged by those who interrogate him, prophecy, the tone of magic, the revelation, of the French Revolution, the tone of the fanatic and the apostle, immediately follow. Under other conditions, Desnos, were he to maintain this delirium, would become the leader of a religion, the founder of a city, the tribune of a people in revolt.

Desnos eventually ended his association with Breton and the rest of the Surrealists after a series of disputes, but he continued to write dreamlike Surrealist verse. Later on, he had a radio program that invited listeners to submit their dreams for dramatization and interpretation. "Who among us has not received in a dream the visit of unusual characters or famous people?" Desnos wrote, to encourage listeners to send in their dreams. "Who among us has not while asleep lived through comic or tragic adventures in odd countries?"

Not only were the dreams dramatized on his radio show, but Desnos also offered dream analysis, pointing out encouraging signs to the dreamer, no matter how alarming the dream might have been. To a woman who had dreamt about blood and a suicide, Desnos said that she "will see her secret desires come true, and furthermore she will learn of the marriage of a friend, but she must watch out for colds and the flu." In the 1930s, Desnos continued to reach out to the general public with his witty advertisements, which sang of such things as a cure for intestinal worms: "Le bon Vermifug' Lune."

Desnos's Surrealist work has long been out of fashion, but his later poetry retains its grandeur, direct as a dream in expressing his longings. Unsteady in certain matters, Desnos tended to adore women who were unattainable or treated him badly. For a long time, Desnos pined for the singer Yvonne George, who became "the star" (l'étoile) in his poems. "The star" was an apt nickname for George, since she was an impossible love object (a dope addict who did not care for men). Her health wrecked, George died young, and Desnos next turned to Youki, who became "the mermaid" (la sirène). Both women inspired him to write, with the precision of firsthand experience, of splendid and imperfect love:

> For so many long months, my dear, I have loved you . . .
> I am tired of struggling against a fate that keeps escaping me
> Tired of attempting to lose myself in forgetting, tired of remembering
> The least perfume emanating from your dress
> Tired of hating you and tired of blessing you . . .
> Call the mermaid and the star with loud cries
> If you cannot sleep with your mouth shut and your hands clasped

One of Desnos's most lasting poems of love and yearning was written in 1926 (another version is now inscribed upon the walls of the Memorial to the Martyrs of the Deportation in Paris):

> *I have dreamed so much of you, walked so much, talked, slept*
> *With your phantom, that all that is yet left to me perhaps*
> *is to be a phantom among phantoms and a hundred*
> *times more of a shadow than the shadow that walks and*
> *will continue to walk gaily on the sundial of your life*

Youki and Desnos met for the first time in 1928, soon after Foujita complained that he knew nothing about the publication *Révolution surréaliste*. Youki was in charge of Foujita's cultural education, and in this case, she had been lax. Quick to make up for her oversight, Youki went to pay a call at the Galerie surréaliste, where she bought a subscription to their journal and purchased all the back numbers. She made an impression on those present there, arriving in her chauffeur-driven car and definitely not dressed like a starving poet. She was soon joining her new Surrealist friends for nights out and had an initial, off-putting encounter with Desnos when he teased her with some paper spiders. The next time around, she revised her opinion: "I was struck by his eyes, which were the color of oysters, with large black rings under them, and his fine big mouth with its kind smile."

Gradually, Desnos became part of the Foujitas' intimate circle, and while Desnos definitely felt drawn to Youki, contemporaries also describe the men's genuine fondness for each other. Both had proven records for unrestrained behavior—Desnos had no difficulty creating poetry in public from his mind's dreamy fragments, and Foujita did not hesitate to make impromptu drawings, even on the eggs for sale at a market. Desnos had once released a briefcase full of mice to get back at a café owner, while for Foujita, front-page frolics were everyday events. In addition, the immigrant artist and the poet from the rowdy neighborhood were not snobbish about their connections to disreputable pursuits. When Foujita introduced Desnos to the Japanese art of the tattoo, the poet discerned the stuff of dreams in those designs:

"As touching as an inscription upon the wall of a cell, tattoos always carry the sign of emotional depressions and exaltations, and, like the initials engraved on the trunk of a tree, they commemorate an instant of sadness or tenderness."

In honor of his friend's oft-used symbols, Foujita tattooed a mermaid on Youki's thigh and a bear with stars—for Ursa Major—on Desnos's arm.

Foujita's surrealistic phase, which began in the Old World of Europe with his well-dressed wife's sashay across a gallery, ended in his flight to the New World with pretty much only the clothes on his back. Between those two events, Foujita fretted about his personal life and took the opportunity to learn from his new Surrealist friends. Among other things, Desnos taught him that Youki was more fickle than Foujita had admitted, and on his own, Foujita realized that he was getting old. The Surrealists also showed Foujita about the need to push beyond everyday perceptions in order to understand these and other facts. Having mulled over their lessons, Foujita came up with another surrealistic creation, the 1930 painting *The Victory of Life over Death*, which was as complicated as anything Desnos ever muttered in his sleep.

Foujita's painting features Diana, goddess of the hunt and the moon, floating across a nighttime sky on a crescent moon. Another woman, who may or may not be Diana's mother, stands with her womb exposed to reveal that she is pregnant with twins. They may or may not be Diana and her twin brother, Apollo, in utero. The pregnant woman has her foot on the ankle of a very animated skeleton, whose raised arms suggest that it is still alive. There's a guillotine looming outside the window and a furry white dog on the staircase who looks understandably worried about these goings-on. Once again, this is certainly not a typical Foujita creation, since the naked women, riding a moon or displaying an exposed uterus, are doing more than just showing off their skin, which is in any case more flesh-colored and defined than in earlier paintings.

The main features of Foujita's former style have vanished again, and in their place is a great deal of activity, from full-color figures alive and dead, partially dissected, canine and immortal. In this bewildering scene, the only certainty is that the artist has seized upon new ways to express his turbulent state of mind. The day after finishing the painting, Foujita had reason to believe in the resonance of his overwrought emotions. "The night that I painted this work about conception and death, Diana and the guillotine, [the artist Jules] Pascin hanged himself in his Montmartre studio and died. All my friends were surprised by this strange combination of coincidences."

Aside from the vibrations flowing between this painting and the suicide, *The Victory of Life over Death* shows Foujita's anxiety shooting off in many directions. The work makes vivid his concerns about living and dying, but he could not represent all his woes with the guillotine or the writhing skeleton. Foujita left out references to the tax troubles that had wrecked his finances and the wife who was falling in love with his friend.

In the end, it was left to Desnos to provide a picture of the situation. In 1931, the Foujitas moved into a new Paris apartment, but because of Foujita's financial difficulties, Desnos, then working in real estate, signed the lease for him. As a result, the leaseholder Desnos was torn between his loyalty to his friend Foujita and his love for Youki. Youki, for her part, was urged by both men to reform her habits, to cut down on her drinking and her nights away from her husband. To provide more complications, Desnos eventually moved in with the couple. Before these difficulties reached their boiling point, Foujita, Youki, Desnos, and Foujita's nephew Tomonobu decided to take a walking tour in Burgundy during the summer of 1930, and it is here that Desnos began his story.

"Au revoir, Vaugirard," wrote Desnos about departing from Paris, in his spirited account of the trip, "and you, charming restaurant 'Sheep Foot,' oasis of optimism built in front of the slaughterhouse; au revoir, Chinese restaurant 'Shanghai,' rue Cujas, the dance halls of Javel . . . au revoir, au revoir, see you soon!" With these words, Desnos tried to establish a cheerful setting, but anyone aware of the details he omits sees the nightmare that looms. The tour organizer was Desnos, the couturier Foujita, who spent two days and two nights before their departure at his sewing machine, tailoring the short pants and colorful knapsacks they used en route. Though all were nattily dressed for the outdoors, their travel arrangements told of a lack of funds. The group did not drive out to the countryside in a chauffeur-driven automobile, but instead fought for seats in third-class train cars. Desnos describes himself scolding a woman who has taken his seat—"You back off, Miss, you back off forty centimeters so that I can sit in the exact spot reserved for my rear, thanks to two francs fifty and the power of the rules."

In reporting on his group's progress, Desnos described the ups and downs faced by a band of city dwellers unaccustomed to long daily treks. He presents himself as an optimist in the face of any number of baleful omens. At his most merry here, Desnos admits that the group's interests varied, with Foujita more impressed by the relics spotted en route, and Desnos, Youki, and Tomonobu committed to sampling the local wine at every opportunity. Desnos's account, like a dream sequence, presents only fleeting images, but their significance cannot be missed. "Foujita wants to visit the village, its oddities, its marvelous hidden corners, its masterpieces of ancient art and other postcard subjects," Desnos wrote. "We will drink an aperitif at the biggest café." Foujita, who drank only water, made no attempt to compete with his fellow travelers in their consumption of liquid refreshments. Once, when Foujita and his nephew fell behind, Desnos and Youki consumed three bottles of wine ("the wine was a little stiff but in sum very agreeable") while waiting for the stragglers.

As the days passed, the sightseeing and the wine tasting continued. "Our short pants, Foujita's face, our appetite, and our thirst caused a sensation." But there are signs that not everyone was feeling jolly in the open air. After another extended wine tasting, Desnos confesses that he, Youki, and Tomonobu have become a "band of rowdies," while Foujita, "impassive," stares out at the scenery. At one stop, Youki rolled up her sleeves to give a local pig a massage, Foujita did his exercises in the middle of the square, and Desnos split some wood. The local people, Desnos reports, were vaguely revolted by this spectacle, but at the same time grateful for the unexpected diversion. Later on, Foujita gave a judo demonstration for the town's youth.

The dream at the end of Desnos's account was Foujita's. Before describing the contents, Desnos shows that even in a lighthearted essay like this one, he cannot stop himself from writing beautifully:

On nights like that, the prowler slips into the farmyard and steals the fat geese and precious hens, happy not to have been preceded by the fox, in fur-lined evening coat, who plants its white fangs into the trembling belly of the turkeys and rabbits, and sneezes hair and feathers . . . On nights like that, the young boy whose voice is cracking wakes up; he listens. Far away, in the forest, resounds the ululations of a night raptor and the piteous cry of the hare it slaughters. Damp with sweat, the boy dives back into nightmares.

On a night like that, Foujita dreamt that he was awakened from his sleep by Desnos and Youki. They forced him outside and up to a hilltop, where they tried to get him to down a glass of wine. When he protested that he drank only water, Youki insisted that he drink just one glass. The ensuing fight landed the three of them in a ravine filled with bottles "of all shapes and all colors and all dimensions," which broke as they fell. At the end, Foujita drowned in a sea of wine that penetrated his ears, nostrils, and eyes, while Youki and Desnos continued drinking together.

TWENTY-THREE

TRANSITIONS

Everybody has heard many stories about Foujita, the Japanese painter who lives in Paris, and who is here now for a visit while his pictures are on exhibition. You hear that he always wears bright red socks with evening dress; that he owns a great house in Paris and gives swimming parties (or is that Van Dongen?) in a glass lined pool; that the enamel texture of his pictures is one result of the fact that he paints sitting on the floor, holding the canvas with his bare feet, as Japanese painters used to do.
—Geoffrey T. Hellman, The New Yorker, November 22, 1930

Foujita's letters to Youki are now part of the Robert Desnos archives, a large collection of documents stored in a hushed Paris library. While reading through Foujita's correspondence, only the most single-minded biographer will be able to resist perusing Desnos's papers as well. That is because Desnos's writings, chronicling his involvement with twentieth-century French literature and politics, have the feel of sacred documents. A member of the Resistance during the German occupation of France, Desnos was arrested in 1944. He was deported to a concentration camp and eventually died as a figure of tragic commitment. The scraps of paper with his final notes bring back the suffering and poetic passion of Desnos's last days.

By the time of his arrest in 1944, Desnos had been living with Youki for thirteen years. (Her relationship with Foujita ended in 1931.) She insisted that her arrangement with Desnos remain free—that is, she would not give up her side liaisons—while he acquiesced and paid her many bills. Anguish over women was a sensation familiar to Desnos, and it served as an engine for his poetry, but as his letters show, the familiarity of the emotion did not lessen his pain. "Youki, my dear Youki," he wrote to complain on an average day. "You told me to come, that you would be there. I told you that I would come, but you do as you like. You were not there. I am very unhappy. But I don't reproach you for anything." True to his nature, Desnos remained devoted to her to the end. On the day in 1944 when the Gestapo came to arrest him for his underground activities, Desnos could have escaped, but he remained in their apartment for her sake. "Robert could have hidden in the building," Youki wrote, "but he did not want to do this because he feared that the Germans would take me away."

His terrible journey began that day and took him to rue des Saussaies for interrogation and then on to a transit camp in Compiègne, where he had reason to hope for his release. Youki did not fail him, as she begged influential officials to prevent his being shipped out to a concentration camp in Germany. She brought Desnos large packages that included fruit, roast beef, clothing, and even champagne, but when she finally was able to see him, she told him of having failed to stop his deportation. "But don't worry," he said to encourage her, "I will return." The poet of dreams and love rode on a train to Auschwitz-Birkenau and then to Buchenwald, Flossenbürg, and finally Flöha, near the border of Germany and Czechoslovakia. Fellow prisoners have told of his efforts to cheer them up by telling fortunes or analyzing their dreams. In April 1945, Desnos and other prisoners were forced to walk for three weeks to Terezin in Czechoslovakia, arriving the night before the end of the war in Europe on May 8. Weakened by illness, Desnos died a month later. In July 1944, he had written one of his last letters to Youki:

Our suffering would be intolerable if we could not consider it a momentary sentimental disease. Our reunion will beautify our life for at least thirty years. As for me, I take in a great gulp of youth; I will return filled with love and strength. While I was working, a birthday, my birthday caused me to think of you at length. Will this letter come in time for your birthday? I would have liked to offer you 100,000 American cigarettes, twelve dresses from the great couturiers, the apartment on the rue de Seine, a car, the small house in the Compiègne forest and the one in Belle-Isle, and a small bouquet for four sous. In my absence, always buy flowers; I will reimburse you. The remainder, I promise you later. But, first of all, drink a bottle of good wine and think of me . . . My love, I kiss you as tenderly as honor permits in a letter which will pass through the censors.

Youki's collection of her Foujita keepsakes, filling a small storage box, is only a minor part of Desnos's archives. An investigation soon reveals that she did not just save items dating from her years with Foujita; Youki also clipped articles about him long after they had separated. Youki retained possession of the scrapbook he made about his first exhibition in 1917 at the Galerie Chéron, and the excitement of a young artist starting out is evident in Foujita's careful preservation of tidbits from those days.

One wonders what Youki thought about Foujita's public letter to Picasso, which she clipped from the periodical *France-Japon* in 1938. This letter, written by Foujita after he had returned to live in Tokyo, was addressed to Picasso but actually attempted to reassure the French about Japan's peace-loving nature. By then Japan had invaded China—the savage Japanese occupation of Nanjing having taken place just a few months before—and these aggressions had soured European opinion of Foujita's native land. In his new role as apologist for his country's activities, Foujita wrote his open letter to Picasso and the French public about Japan's natural beauties and serenity, even throwing in some praise for the cherry blossoms and Mount Fuji: "[The cherry blossoms] are truly beautiful flowers which are comparable to the noble silhouette of Mount Fuji . . . Every year when the cherry trees are in bloom, I admire them with the heart of a child, and I turn my dazzled gaze toward majestic Mount Fuji." About the war in China, Foujita offered this balm to any who might doubt Japan's intentions:

"Everyone here in Japan is busy with their own daily needs, joyous and happy, in spite of the fact that Japan must fight to defend justice and peace." Youki's reaction to this unctuous piece of writing can only be imagined, but there's no question about what the anti-fascist Desnos would have thought if he had read Foujita's letter. During that period, Desnos was composing lines such as, "Fascism and all its bankers / They have gold, they have cannons / But we fight for the whole world."

Youki also saved a newspaper clipping from August 1946 that incorrectly reported Foujita's death in Japan in the bombing of Nagasaki. This bit of misinformation from *Le Figaro*, written a full year after the Nagasaki bombing, memorialized the supposedly dead Japanese artist: "His bangs and his large glasses singled him out in Montparnasse to those who sought out celebrities."

In her most revealing pile of Foujita memorabilia, Youki saved the letters Foujita wrote to her while they were still together. These communications, which date from 1923 to 1931, now sit for eternity in too close proximity to the writings of the French poet who was Foujita's rival. Desnos's letters resound with the majesty of the French language as he bears witness to his time. Words, of course, can also seduce, and in this regard, Foujita definitely came up short. Yet, in the end, there is no need to compare Desnos's letters to Foujita's, which tell the story of a sometimes lovesick, sometimes heartbroken, sometimes furious Japanese artist trying to keep control of his emotions. He also gets credit for linguistic effort, since he struggled to express strong feelings in his very fractured French. Many of these letters were written because Youki took trips on her own, leaving Foujita in Paris to work and pine for her.

In the early days of their relationship, Foujita did not complain much about Youki's need for these vacations. After all, he had seen Fernande's restlessness erupt into a search for a new man. Perhaps fearful of facing the same upheavals again, Foujita forced himself to tolerate Youki's travels. In a feeble show of bravery in 1923, he wrote about how much he trusted and loved her. But theirs was not a love to be constrained by vows of fidelity, and with good reason he went on to worry over the men who might also find her appealing. At the same time, he begged her to forgive him for his feelings of unease. *"Everyone in Paris is free,"* he said later to a group of Japanese, in full-blooded praise of French mores. *"You can blithely go around the park arm in arm with your friend's wife. The couple walking doesn't care about this, and the people looking don't think a thing about it."* Foujita's letters to Youki show him struggling to adopt this broad-minded frame of mind.

The money Youki often requested, together with Foujita's being left alone with the cat for long periods, may have been the cause of his gloom on another day. Calling himself an idiot, he writes that at forty years old, after nine years of struggle in Paris, he has achieved nothing. Though well-known and earning large sums, he has no fortune to show for it. By the end of this letter, he forces himself to perk up again because he does not wish to upset his beloved, who, after all, is busy trying to have a good time. *"In Paris, women . . . receive money from men,"* he also said later on. *"Then the woman spends more money than she has received. The woman goes around wearing the finest clothes. She becomes more attractive, and men flock to her. Then the main man in her life becomes jealous and feverishly does this and that to get money to give her . . ."* Here Foujita described his own situation well, but he still could not bring himself to bawl Youki out, impinge upon her freedom, or stop sending her funds.

While Youki was in Brittany visiting her cousin, Foujita had a disagreement with Georges Chéron, the dealer who had arranged his first shows. Chéron, eager to make money from other Japanese artists, had started selling the works of Koyanagi Sei, Fernande's new lover, and Bandō Toshio, whom Foujita accused of copying from him. In a memorable letter, Foujita wrote to Youki about the argument he'd had with Chéron over these new clients. According to Foujita, one of these artists (Koyanagi) had stolen his wife and the other (Bandō) had stolen his technique, his landscape style, his still lifes. Savoring his undeniable clout in the art world and his own (mixed up) verbal cleverness, Foujita roared at Chéron about how he refused to have anything to do with a gallery that represented two thieves.

In search of a certain kind of japonaiserie, Chéron had in fact commissioned Bandō to produce endless quantities of small paintings. Bandō was one of those lesser-known Japanese artists in Paris who had gone to Europe seeking artistic liberation but ended up subsisting on the crumbs of Foujita's success. With glee and execrable French grammar, Foujita wrote to Youki about the day he encountered Bandō in person. After yelling at Bandō, calling him a thief and an imbecile, Foujita departed, triumphant and happy.

Those first letters do not tell only of Foujita fulminating against rivals—there is also a more tender love story, about a Japanese artist who could not fully believe that he had won the heart of a stylish, literate European woman. But the letters resume again in 1930, after Youki and Foujita's trip to Tokyo, and these show a different frame of mind. By then, Foujita no longer found his love so perfect. In these later letters, Foujita was the one who was away from home, since he had gone by himself to the United States for three months to drum up sales. He had an exhibition at the Reinhardt Galleries in New York City, and although one newspaper reported that a private showing began "wowishly," the review in *The New Yorker* could not have helped Foujita's cause: ·

> Foujita, with his cats and his bangs, makes up the show at the Reinhardt Galleries. The artist himself has been at most of the seances, to add a personal touch to the proceedings. Foujita has many followers. He is a facile worker and brings to Western subjects the inborn sense of design that goes with the Oriental. This always produces a salable object, or one that catches the eye of the Westerner. We, however, have never been much moved by the stuff, thinking it workmanlike and tricky, but not very deep.

Foujita kept promising to send for Youki, but never earned enough for her transatlantic fare. He searched, often in vain, for business in the United States, while Youki became desperate about being abandoned in Paris with insufficient funds.

Meanwhile, nervousness about the future undermined Foujita's patience with his bored and fun-loving wife back in Paris. He writes Youki that he has smiled and pretended to be happy but his great financial burden has left him exhausted and at his wit's end. More precisely, he wants her to understand that he has to return to France with at least

500,000 francs. An exaspe   complaints
about Youki, achieving in   tensity and
specificity that he apparen   king to her
in person. Serious, respons   1ow he sees
himself, while she is attac   It was this
same fondness for "drinking, . . . gaiety, and . . . criticized to
the end of their marriage. The letters show that solitude has made him
edgy and the struggle to sell his works in Manhattan has added to the
strain. As a sign of his vexation, he asks Youki to do nothing less than
transform her character completely—to give up her friends, her late-
night escapades, her desire for total freedom.

In her memoir, Youki mentions the "pretty redhead," who became
Foujita's next companion after his return to Paris, but at the same time
she accepts some responsibility for the end of their marriage. Youki
admits that her relationship with Desnos had been a factor, and ever
philosophical, she faces this change of circumstances with aplomb:
"When the cycle of life starts to turn against you, one must let it make
its own evolution."

Since none of Youki's letters to Foujita have yet been discovered, we
are left to speculate about her side of the story. Offering assistance at
this juncture, some Japanese males do step forward to present a more
sympathetic view of her. In their accounts, Youki appears to have been
more than the frivolous creature who mistreated Foujita and spent his
money. Through the alcoholic vapors, she walks by uncertainly, a very
young woman who perhaps would have benefited from a husband not
so given—when they lived together—to silent reproach. The journalist
Matsuo Kuninosuke saw Youki's tempestuous side when Youki was
drunk, but sensed a lonely, poetic mood on sober days. He remembers
her perfectly white skin and beautiful voice, as well as the compelling
air about her. During visits to Foujita, he would find her still in her bed-
clothes in the afternoon, exuding a voluptuous charm and smoking
countless cigarettes. Youki, a great reader of Rimbaud, Aragon, and
Apollinaire, could also return home late at night inebriated and in the
company of another man. "I only drank a little. Just a little. Twelve or
thirteen cocktails," she said on one of these occasions to Foujita, who
did not utter a word in response. Matsuo later discovered Youki in bed

with a young man who ran a hat shop, but again, Foujita left the house to go horseback riding without a murmur of protest.

Many years after Foujita and Youki's alliance had ended, Foujita's nephew Ashihara Eiryō visited her in Paris, where she was in bed with a cold. Youki had earned Ashihara's affection years before, when she had given him pointers in romance and French literature. Feverish that day, she blamed herself for the break with Foujita and then went on to give her unmarried nephew more advice:

> What I resent about your uncle is that he never advised a woman about what she should do. Just think about it. I was seventeen when my relationship with Foujita began. What does a seventeen-year-old girl from the countryside know? . . . Why didn't he tell me to stop drinking? Why didn't he tell me to be more careful about money?

In his colossal desire to avoid confrontations, Foujita walked out on Youki one day in 1931 without saying a word. As a French acquaintance, Théodore Fraenkel, said, "Foujita went out to buy cigarettes and he left for Japan, from which he returned only for a brief visit several years later." After a few days, a Japanese friend told Youki about a note Foujita had left for her in a drawer. ". . . Don't go looking for me. Have pity on me. I am leaving forever," Foujita wrote. In a long letter that surfaced later, he went into more detail about his discontents, reviewing one last time those points he had tried to drum into her before. Her drinking, her friends, her taste for good times did not go well with his sober character and his need for quiet to do his work. "My life is finished. I am tired and old and I do not have the strength left to fight on in Paris . . . You were not born for me."

In a very Japanese burst of good manners, Foujita also took the time to send Desnos a hastily written message that is now preserved on a very crumpled piece of paper. "Thank you for everything you have done for me . . . It is your destiny to take care of Youki."

TWENTY-FOUR

ADRIFT IN THE WIDE WORLD

They had never seen the rumba danced, or heard "The Sausage Vendor" . . . They hadn't even seen rum drunk from coffee cups.
—José Antonio Fernández de Castro, "On Foujita in Havana"

The question asked in 1931 was, Where should a ruined Japanese artist go to improve his financial picture and his mental health? The answer—not long in coming—was, As far away as possible. Already Foujita had shown signs of plotting an escape while he was struggling to earn money in the United States. Perhaps he had drawn too many cats too quickly en route to his next exhibition because, in a weary mood, he had written to Youki from New York, suggesting that they drop everything and take to the road like vagabonds. As it turned out, Youki probably would have hated the rugged journey that Foujita had in mind. Tokyo had already strained her tolerance for an environment less comfortable than Paris, and in comparison with the stops on Foujita's projected trip, Japan was the height of civilization.

But Foujita found a woman who would prove to be intrepid on the ground, aboard a ship in the middle of nowhere, and on hikes up to high altitudes, as well as in traveling through revolutions. She was Madeleine Lequeux, a former dancer at the Casino de Paris, and although her idiosyncrasies invited more surveillance by authorities than was desirable, the couple did not get themselves into serious trouble. (A Cuban journalist noted that she created "more conflicts than a cross-eyed traffic cop.") According to an excellent story that is hard to confirm, Madeleine had been the mistress of a shady American businessman. Well taken care of, but terrified under this man's patronage, she wanted to leave him and sought Foujita's help. The large stash of gold and diamonds that Madeleine had received from this boyfriend came in handy after she and Foujita left together for Latin America. Madeleine, whose red hair went well with her blazing temperament, was an impulsive character from the outset, prone to histrionics and excessive drinking. But Foujita never tired of using "The Pantheress"— her nickname—as a model.

Foujita wrote at length about his two years of traveling in Brazil, Argentina, Bolivia, Peru, and Cuba—he skipped Chile because of an ongoing revolution—before he headed north to the United States, stopping first in New Mexico and then going west toward California. Foujita must have toiled long on his essays, perhaps when he was trapped in his room at siesta time, since he would have needed an extended period to come up with such evasive communiqués about his fast-moving adventure. His travel accounts, aimed at Japanese publications, stuck to such matters as Peruvian pelicans and the number of Japanese immigrants in a given vicinity. He of course mentioned nothing about how Madeleine left him for a while to go to Acapulco with some Mexican singers, nor did he discuss her growing appetite for cocaine. He also omitted telling about the night he toured Rio de Janeiro's red-light district in a kind of eye-catching outfit—culottes, vest, sandals, topped off by his earrings—that was not often seen in those parts. The prostitutes, responding to his fashion statement, howled in appreciation as he strolled down the street.

Most important, Foujita wrote almost nothing about why he decided on the New World as his destination in the first place, but at least we know from other sources that the artist Jules Pascin had long urged him to make the trip. Pascin, renowned for a more nervous type of line and nude than Foujita's, had sailed off to the United States in 1914 to escape from the First World War in Europe. "Even if all Europe became one dungeon," the poet Heinrich Heine had once said, "there would be still another hole for escape: this is America, and thank God!, that hole is even bigger than the dungeon itself." Pascin settled down in New York for a while and even became a citizen of the United States. After New York, Pascin had headed south to make the first of his visits to Cuba. "I want some nice, quiet country," he wrote, "with pleasant gaie [sic], not gloomy people where I could do lots of work or have a nice time if I should have the means to feel lazy or preferably do both at a time." In his works, Pascin expressed a European's amazement at Cuba's languid, sunlit life under the palm trees. He caught the mood of a society at once oppressed and untouched. Like Foujita, Pascin had the restless soul of the permanent expatriate. Unlike Foujita, Pascin gave in to his despair and committed suicide in 1930.

Robert Desnos may also have been influential in getting Foujita to make his journey. Urged on by his many Latin American friends, Desnos had also traveled to Cuba, in 1928. Once there, Desnos found himself enraptured by the "beautiful black women," "precious sky," and "smell of darkness." Desnos brought back to Paris not only the Cuban writer and musicologist Alejo Carpentier—whom he hid in his cabin on the ship—but also his discovery of Latin American politics and music. Youki claimed that Desnos introduced rumba records to Paris. "I will never forget this humble village close to Havana," Desnos wrote, "that they call *las fritas* and more often *la playa* . . . I will never forget the black musicians whom I must see again, dockworkers by day at the port and at night magnificent and obscene dancers." Back in Paris, Desnos kept on about his days and nights in the tropics, and Foujita, who was frequently in his company—whether he wanted to be or not—responded to the promise of those stories.

"Among those who have lived since the beginning of history, whom would you most like to be?" reporters asked Foujita soon after his ship landed in Rio de Janeiro in 1931. His reply reflected his disgust with the current world: "I would like to have been the first man Adam, who had no falsity about him. I'd have Eve as my lover and would be able to live by myself without the worry of politics, war, machine-driven civilization, in a natural paradise full of animals and plants, and empty of all other humanity." When the reporters next inquired about what he most detested in this world, Madeleine was pleased to inform them that Foujita most disliked the journalists. At this press conference and others, Foujita benefited from the slow exchange of information from the Old World to the New. Word about his declining renown and financial stability had not yet registered in Brazil, and so for the residents there and in countries beyond, Foujita still had the luster of a Parisian artistic celebrity. Soon enough, he would have to reckon with his faded reputation, but that would come later and in another place. For a time, in Latin America, Foujita could still delight in the privileges of a none-too-certain fame.

Almost immediately, Foujita started to earn his keep among the well-heeled citizens of Brazil. He received commissions for portraits, and the income went to pay for expenses along the way. If one of his Latin American works, *Portrait of a Family* (1932), is any indication, flattery was not part of Foujita's appeal. The portrait, in pencil and pastel, depicts a scowling mother staring off to her right. Perhaps fresh from a domestic quarrel, she seems to be practicing her next furious retort as she sits with her three listless children. Though the clothing and hairdos give Foujita adequate chance to flourish his line, the cat in the middle is the portrait's only agreeable feature.

In other works drawn during his stay in Latin America, Foujita abandoned this bloodless version of his characteristic style. He whole-heartedly turned to red-striped trousers, circus stars, and human drama. This was clearly an artist who had traveled a long way in order to find a new way to paint. Set in the festival's aftermath, *Carnival at Rio de Janeiro* (1932) has two men sleeping off the effects of the party, while in front, a dazed, barely conscious carnival-goer embraces a woman as he peers off into the distance, trying to fathom what exactly has left him in this predicament. Despite Foujita's only qualified endorsement of carousing, colors galore brighten the patterned clothing and discarded confetti. The work shows off his psychological insights and his flair for such realistic effects as two dirty bare feet. Similarly, *The Two Women* (1932) juxtaposes a still life of a cluttered tabletop with hanging clothes and what look like two partially dressed prostitutes, resigned to their futures.

Foujita wrote of being impressed by Brazil's vast size, the magnanimity of its population, and the large flowers and fruits. The empty stretches of land impressed this visitor who was accustomed to the more cramped conditions of Japan and Europe. In his imagination, space meant an existence bigger in every way; Foujita was stirred to consider the wildness that such lands could accommodate. "It's the kind of huge country where people think nothing of taking a long trip on horseback, and while going through a forest, pulling out a big knife to cut down a big tree with two thousand bananas. They can eat just half of one and then go on, leaving behind the remaining two thousand bananas." Brazil, with its open immigration policy, had been particularly welcoming to the Japanese, and in his role as the well-prepared tour guide, Foujita informed the Japanese readers of his travel articles that 150,000 to 160,000 had settled there. He also provided assurances that these Japanese immigrants had become accustomed to local conditions and rarely succumbed to disease.

Foujita did not write about the mixed reactions of Brazilian reviewers to the works he exhibited while in their country. These critics appreciated his predictable female nudes—in particular those of Madeleine—and the cats. The well-known critic Mário de Andrade praised "the extreme silence, the deep emptiness of Foujita's paintings and drawings" as well as the "sharp lines, the wide flat surfaces . . . the relative coldness or placidity of expression" which produce a "state of astonishment." At the same time, there were protests about his works on Brazilian themes, which announced changes in Foujita's style and subject matter. "Is this the same Foujita that we have come to know?" "He is here in these works, but then again, he is not." The Brazilian critics believed that Foujita had gone well beyond his field of competence, demonstrating ignorance of the carnival spirit and Brazil in general. They were further piqued because the people he drew looked more Asian than Brazilian.

According to witnesses, Foujita—with his usual stoicism—maintained an amiable demeanor. Camaraderie came easily to him on a continent where the twinkle of Montparnasse, however diminished, still meant much, and he was a sought-after guest in Brazilian social circles. In particular, he renewed his friendship with the Brazilian artist Candido Portinari, which had started in Paris. Influenced by Foujita's artistic advice, Portinari adopted a starker, whiter style, which was immediately labeled "Fouji-nari." Foujita paid no heed to the regime of Getúlio Vargas, who had seized control of the Brazilian government in 1930. Vargas forced austerity upon the Brazilian population, constraining the lives of the artists as well. In such an atmosphere, Foujita seemed like a miraculous vision of freedom as he made his way through Rio and São Paulo—where he disliked the beggars, the badly paved roads, the constant rain—in his striped trousers, sleeveless shirt, and, as always, the earrings.

The next stop was Argentina (5,000–6,000 Japanese residents), where Foujita and Madeleine spent five months. He found Buenos Aires just like Paris in many ways and especially noted the high cultural level evidenced by the Rodin bronze in a park; sixty thousand excited art fans thronged to his exhibition and forced him to hide out in the art gallery's storeroom. He went next to Bolivia (150 Japanese in residence), where also some kind of war had broken out. Nonetheless, he stayed for a while among the llamas and alpacas of the mountain capital, La Paz. From there, Foujita journeyed to Lake Titicaca: "It's 4,000 meters above sea level on a peak in the Andes, which would be like having a lake on top of our Mount Fuji." At Cuzco, he saw the remains of the Inca capital (and found three or four Japanese living there) and went up to Machu Picchu (150 Japanese).

In these travels, often undertaken under taxing conditions, Foujita once again proved himself an excellent traveler, physically hardy and eager for surprises. He deserves credit for braving Latin America's changing altitudes and temperatures, undercooked food, and infrequent baths. Constantly painting or sketching, Foujita tells of standing alone one night on the deck of the ship that was crossing Lake Titicaca. Despite the freezing cold, he could not stop gazing at the snow-capped peaks rising in the darkness and felt the land of the dead floating upon the waters. Many ideas must have come to him then, since black and white were, after all, Foujita's colors.

Foujita left no detailed account about Cuba, but maybe that was because he did not want to let his Japanese readers know how much he had loved it. Others have written about the holiday mood he sustained throughout his stay, with the help of the bongo drums and a song called "The Sausage Vendor" ("Only one sausage really exists, only one . . ."). He benefited also from the conviviality of the artists and writers who took him touring. Apparently won over by the coconut milk and the rumba, he extended his stay from a week to a month. He was escorted to a local dance event by a Cuban writer who promised him an experience as "fresh as recently picked pineapple and juicy as our white sugar cane." A gregarious, generous spirit was much appreciated in Cuba, and the same writer paid Foujita a great Cuban compliment when he wrote of "the Japanese artist, who knows how to be a friend." On another fine day, Foujita drank mineral water at an outdoor café while a Guatemalan writer downed a coffee-cupful of rum and then composed a Havanaesque haiku in his honor.

Foujita did run into difficulties at his Havana exhibition of thirty-three watercolors, all of which had been painted on the spot; everything else had been sold in Brazil and Argentina. His response to this trouble left me with an agreeable impression, one that flickered back into my mind again later, when I considered Foujita's more bellicose war years. The exhibit started well, since Foujita was introduced as an artist who "represents an example of how it is possible to adapt to a foreign culture without abandoning one's own, how to create one's own international mode of expression without renouncing the native elements of one's nature and culture."

On display were Foujita's dogs, cats, Parisian scenes, and also *The Burial of Christ*, a work much admired—and unfortunately stolen the first day. The burglary was gravely described in newspaper accounts, down to how the thief tore the painting from its frame in the exhibition hall's bathroom. The theft was seen as a dishonorable blot on all of Cuban society, and since the robber eluded capture, the mortified exhibition organizers insisted upon reimbursing Foujita for the loss. It was an interchange where only character counted, since no international newspaper would publicize the negotiations. Gracious and sympathetic on an island where he played baseball with outsized grapefruits, Foujita insisted on donating a work before his departure.

At the time of Foujita's visit to Mexico, his old friend Diego Rivera was out of the country, busy painting murals up north in the United States—"Gringolandia," according to his wife, Frida Kahlo. About twenty years previously, in Paris, Rivera had painted Foujita and his friend Kawashima in their Greek outfits; at that time, Rivera had been dabbling in Cubism, and Foujita had been studying Greek statuary and dance techniques. Since then, Rivera had gone home to Mexico, where he was swept up in revolutionary activities, in which his art played a major role. He placed his formidable physical self at the forefront of Mexico's mural movement, battling for control of major walls in official buildings and, usually victorious, painting frescoes on such subjects as Aztec history, land reform, and the revolutionary Zapata's white horse. Rivera offended his capitalist patrons in New York City, when, contrary to plan, he included the face of Lenin in his Rockefeller Center fresco *Man at the Crossroads* (1934). The ensuing fiasco culminated in the destruction of Lenin's likeness and the remainder of the work.

Impressed by his friend's frescoes at the Ministry of Education and elsewhere, Foujita seems to have realized that Rivera's audacity far exceeded his own more modest acts of daring. There were Rivera's large size, sexual escapades, and sprawling, tempestuous works of art—all ideally suited to the hot weather and chili-peppered cuisine of Mexico. "Rivera keeps two pistols at his hip," Foujita wrote in admiration, "and each time he mounts the scaffolding to start painting, he fires a shot from each one. He says that he does this every day because it calms him down and also scares off the journalists who might criticize him." Returning to an old theme, Foujita especially praised Mexican artists like Rivera and José Clemente Orozco for emphasizing their national traditions, unlike most artists elsewhere who slavishly duplicated the styles current in France.

Although Foujita wrote about Mexico and Rivera, he skipped over his own encounter with the Latin revolutionary spirit. This had started during his visit to Cuba, when there had been some student unrest and

Foujita, unaware of these upheavals, made remarks to a Cuban newspaper that were misinterpreted as hostile to the revolt. When Mexican artists heard about these counterrevolutionary statements, they tried to prevent Foujita from entering their country.

At this point, the Mexican artists sought the help of the Japanese artist Kitagawa Tamiji. In the annals of Japanese expatriate life, Kitagawa deserves his own chapter, for he perfected a peripatetic existence every inch as distinctive as Foujita's, but one that set off an entirely different kind of fireworks. Kitagawa went to the United States in 1914 and eventually studied at the Art Students League in New York City (which he found "overwrought, dried up, dreary"). He next traveled to the American South and Cuba before settling in Mexico in 1923. Carelessly native where Foujita was dapper, inept at accumulating money where Foujita was expert, Kitagawa gravitated toward the downtrodden in his itinerant artistic life. This earned him the trust of the Mexican poor, whom he often portrayed in his work.

It is hard to imagine Foujita fitting as comfortably as Kitagawa did into a Mexican Indian's home in a village, where he had gone to paint. Kitagawa slept on the floor with the rest of the family, next to the pigs and the chickens. Likewise, it's hard to picture Foujita being offered, as Kitagawa was, the hand of their son's widow, along with forty head of cattle and fifty acres of land. Kitagawa did consider this proposal for a little while, but then fled for his life after an unnerving encounter with the inhabitants of another village. Eventually, Kitagawa married Ninomiya Tetsuko, a Japanese woman he met in Mexico. In contrast again to Foujita, Kitagawa's revolutionary credentials were impeccable. At the time of Foujita's visit to Mexico, Kitagawa was running an open-air painting school in Taxco. Such government-supported schools encouraged children and ordinary people to draw from nature outdoors, thus bringing the inclusive principles of the Mexican Revolution to the world of art.

"It's not only that we won't welcome Foujita here," one Mexican artist told Kitagawa. "We are completely opposed to his visit. Does Mexico have any use for his kind of bourgeois art?" Another artist said: "Don't we already have the Japanese Kitagawa in Mexico? One Japanese is enough. We don't need Foujita." The artists urged Kitagawa to go to the Japanese legation to tell of their opposition to Foujita. Once at the legation, Kitagawa learned of Foujita's other problems. Since Madeleine had no papers to prove that she was legally married to Foujita, the Mexican government considered her a prostitute and refused to allow her into the country. Eventually, Mexican officials relented, and soon after the couple reached Mexico, Foujita held an exhibition—as he had done at the other stops along the way—but this time, the venue was at the Ministry of Education, where Rivera's frescoes covered the walls.

Now it was Foujita's turn to be unhappy. "There wasn't a single decent person who came," he told Kitagawa. "The place was empty during the day. At night, finally a lot of people came but only laborers wearing work clothes covered with grease. I was speechless with surprise. It's not likely that I am going to be able to sell paintings to such people. On top of that, they had vulgar laughs and stared at me with sneering looks in their eyes. The Mexican Ministry of Education is not the kind of place that's popular with the rich." Kitagawa decided not to tell Foujita that the Mexican bourgeoisie, far from being ideal customers, knew next to nothing about modern art, while some of those "laborers" were sophisticated art connoisseurs who had adjourned to a coffee shop afterward to discuss Foujita's work. "Foujita's exhibition was a total failure," Kitagawa writes. "It was almost totally ignored by the press."

Later on, Foujita arrived unannounced at Kitagawa's crude mountain residence in Taxco and stayed for about a week. The home had little electricity, so they lived by candlelight—and without a radio or news of the outside world. It is said that Foujita went to Taxco alone because Madeleine had temporarily run off to Acapulco with some Mexican singers. "I was in Mexico then and thirty-nine years old," Kitagawa remembered later. "Foujita came to visit. He taught me many things. He demanded a great deal of himself and would have sacrificed everything for art. I suppose this came from his view of an artist's responsibility. To put it in extreme terms, he wanted to live his art even if he had to sacrifice his human side. I'm different. For me, art was not really the issue. I just wished to be able to live fully like a human being. I don't think you can give a strictly objective opinion about which way of life is correct."

Like many before him, Kitagawa was bowled over by Foujita's social skills. Taxco's foreign residents and sightseers immediately recognized Foujita, and since multitudes wished to meet him, he was the honored guest at nightly social functions. "Even though he doesn't touch a drop of alcohol," Kitagawa wrote, "he was truly adept at socializing. He was very sought after no matter where he went."

One moment during the visit merited a picture, preferably in the artistic manner of Kitagawa. His paintings, with their straightforward colors and intense emotions, often showed the close human connections among Mexicans in humble surroundings. Kitagawa, who was already married by then, could have created a fine painting from the nights he cooked meals for Foujita over the charcoal fire in his Taxco home. The two Japanese men had evenings when they sat together eating the spicy tortillas with their hands, and on one occasion, Foujita felt moved to speak about himself: "Your family life seems harmonious. I envy your happiness. Compared with you, I'm unlucky. I have no luck with women. I really don't know what it is to have a home."

Foujita and Madeleine left Mexico in 1933 and toured the American Southwest. They surfaced in California, where newspapers described his exhibitions in Los Angeles and San Francisco. "Paris may be the world center for ideas," Foujita diplomatically declared in the *Los Angeles Times*, "but Hollywood is the world's fashion center. The sun tan and the long dresses of Hollywood origin are now universal." Madeleine spoke of a film she and Foujita had made about Mexican bullfights. On her own, she said, she had collected her experiences in a memoir, "Mexico Without a Revolver," which unfortunately was never published.

They sailed from Los Angeles, and on November 16, 1933, Foujita and Madeleine arrived in Japan.

TWENTY-FIVE

NEW START AT HOME

But it had been necessary to go home, for she was very attached to the soil of her own land, and could not be away from her native place for so long. All that traveling also had put a great burden on their finances and Issaku had to go back to work. They had been able at least to leave their son behind as their keepsake, their tie to Paris. Each year for as long as her son was there, the chestnut trees would blossom in their abundant loveliness on the Paris streets.

—Okamoto Kanoko

After his long trip to Latin America, Foujita returned to Tokyo in 1933, this time for a long stay. His broken relationship with Youki and ongoing financial troubles were certainly important reasons for his change of residence, but other developments also drove Foujita in this direction. He had long cherished France for receiving him with generosity. The friends, the masquerade balls, the notoriety—these had matched Foujita's personality and ambitions. When asked in 1929 what he found most attractive in France, he answered, "Freedom," without hesitation. At other times, he had been fascinated by other aspects of French life—the art world, the parks, the staircases, the police, the women. For a long period, he was so delighted at having made his escape from Japan that he did not miss an opportunity to rejoice in the superiority of life abroad.

But gradually Foujita's elation seemed to ebb. He ventured to suggest that all had not been so delightful while he was living in France and even allowed himself to express negative opinions. "[In France] they quickly bury Japanese art by saying that in the past and in the present, there's no originality," he wrote in 1937. "I have often become furious and indignant about such statements." A biographer who knows what is going to happen later on must pause over each of these remarks. The discontents Foujita allowed himself to utter during the 1930s grew into more forceful expressions of anti-Western feeling and pro-Japanese patriotism not many years later.

According to the Japanese poet Kaneko Mitsuharu, Foujita never had illusions about his role in French cultural life. In the square de Montsouris house in Paris that Foujita had shared with Youki, Kaneko was surprised to find on display the kind of portable shrine used in Japanese festivals, which, along with piles of Japanese "junk," advertised the resident's nationality. "Foujita is supposed to be a Japanese completely imbued with the French temperament," Kaneko wrote, "but that was not the French temperament I had imagined up to that time. He taught me about many things. To live shrewdly in Paris, he said, I should always emphasize my Japanese origins. The French have no interest in Japanese who try to be French. I listened to his opinions very seriously." When Kaneko was hard up for cash, Foujita stuck to this position, counseling his friend to earn his fortune by selling Japanese parasols decorated with birds and flowers on the beach at Deauville. Foujita even went so far as to introduce Kaneko to a Deauville casino owner who might help.*

On the way back from Latin America, Foujita would have recognized the other difficulties he faced in going back to France. Amidst the reports of Japanese aggression in China, artworks by Foujita of Japan would not have attracted great numbers of eager buyers. In general, France had become a less hospitable home not only for the Japanese but for all the bands of foreigners who had flocked there after the First World War. The worldwide depression fostered an unwillingness on the part of the French to offer refuge to those who might take jobs away from the country's citizens. Then there was the ever-present nationalism, which grew more intense as France felt increasingly threatened by such

---

*While Kaneko did set to work drawing the birds and flowers on the parasols, there is no report about the outcome of this undertaking.

political events as Hitler's rise in Germany. The standing of the foreigner in France was also not improved by the story of Serge Stavisky, a Russian Jew whose huge swindle started a deadly riot in 1934 and brought down two French governments.

About his return to Japan, Foujita, as usual, preferred to hide his own private feelings. Adaptability and good cheer came more naturally to him when he stepped out, and this state of mind reigns over his autobiographical writings. There were fortunately other Japanese artists who were not so restrained, and when they returned to Japan from Paris, they described their reactions. "If I go back to Japan," the hero of the 1924 play *Old Toys* moaned, reflecting a common dread, "not a single person around me will understand how I feel. They will try to get in the way of everything I do . . . A society which threatens and restricts your freedom, will not, as a whole, let you fulfill yourself, no matter what outstanding qualities are hidden within you."

Once back home, such adjustments to the restrictions of Japanese society were galling, but only part of the problem. Artistically, too, the change was tremendous. In the most basic ways, Japan was not ideal for an artist who specialized in Western-style painting. With sliding paper screens for walls, Japanese homes had little room to hang the oil paintings of the returning artists, in contrast to Paris where even ordinary residences had much wall space. In addition, high-quality painting supplies were expensive or impossible to find.

To some returning artists, the scenery was another issue. France inspired them more than the Japanese vistas they now faced outside. As the artist Kume Keiichirō complained,

> Just looking at the landscape of Europe is enough to stimulate my sense of beauty. I felt that I wanted to paint what I saw as it really was. On the other hand, the colors in Japanese scenery are somehow difficult to render for the artist and one must make painstaking efforts to capture a scene. It isn't at all enjoyable. I am afraid that my degree of interest in the natural scenes of the two countries is simply different.

It is no surprise that Kume stopped painting entirely once his landscapes were limited to those of Japan. "When he was confronted with the unenjoyable scenery of Japan," one commentator observed, "his inspiration ceased and, naturally, so did his production of paintings."

More miserable still was Ogisu Takanori, who practically waited until the Second World War came to his front door in Paris before he forced himself back to Japan. Once home, he found all his apprehensions confirmed. In particular, various vapors unsettled him:

> The scenes featuring the misty climate of Japan, the indistinct hazy scenes with the thick veil of water vapors—these are really the scenes in Japanese-style painting often depicted by the Tosa school. It is my firm belief that such scenes actually spurred the development of ink painting.
>
> Since times long past, Japanese paintings have been composed of floating clouds and mist. But in Europe, I came to follow a style which presents a thoroughly clear view of things. Mist just does not suit my artistic work.

After the Second World War, Ogisu was the first Japanese artist to return to Paris.

On the other hand, Sakamoto Hanjirō had no such regrets about going home. He's the Japanese artist I mentioned earlier who could not digest the Western food during the boat ride over to France and nearly starved to death en route. No surprise that Sakamoto was absolutely ecstatic about being back in Japan. "Just as they say, Paris is indeed a city of flowers. But it is a flower without any scent. The moon glows, the snow falls. But those are just natural phenomena. One can draw nothing that speaks to a person's heart . . . And especially when it comes to an abundance of natural beauty, no country is as blessed as Japan."

Upon his return to Japan, Foujita, like these others, had to adjust to the mist and the mores of his native country. After November 1933, when Foujita and Madeleine arrived in Yokohama, he also had to contend with Japanese evaluations of his artistic achievements, and this was a more daunting task. Foujita declared that he had come back for his father's eightieth birthday and was going to stay in Japan for just six months. This would give him time to exhibit the work he had done in Latin America, travel to the Philippines, Java, and Sumatra, and be back in Paris by summer. As the time passed, his itinerary underwent drastic alterations, and with the exception of a one-year stay in Paris, Foujita remained in Japan until 1949. During those years, Japanese opinions of him were crucial to his peace of mind and professional survival.

Once again, the Japanese public reacted to Foujita with much wariness. In a country where soy sauce was the much-preferred scent, Japanese who had lived long abroad were said to "smell of butter" because of all the foreign influences they had absorbed. Foujita, immersed in European ways for a long time, surely gave off an unfamiliar aroma. In addition, he did little to make his repatriation easier. Bravado had enabled Foujita to enter French society, and transformation into a modest figure more comforting to the Japanese was not possible. Inevitably, he stirred up talk in foreign diplomatic circles, where he often socialized, as well as in Japanese society. There are recognizable elements in the stories that made the rounds—for example, the one about Foujita arriving almost nude at an embassy costume ball with three souvenir shrunken heads from an Amazon Indian tribe. And by his side was the obstreperous and often tipsy Madeleine, who also did not easily harmonize with the decorous ways of Japan.

Even a stable, compliant Western woman would have felt her sanity being tested as she tried to settle down with a Japanese husband in his country, where she did not know the language or the customs. Madeleine, variously described by Japanese observers as totally drunk or walking around the house without any clothes on, might have been expected to have more difficulties than most. Before going on, we must mull over what Foujita anticipated when he brought her home with him. "His present wife is not Youki," his family optimistically told the press upon Foujita's return. "We think she will take to life in Japan." Madeleine spoke no Japanese and had a hot temper that, newspapers reported, vented itself in at least one physical assault upon Foujita. She showed no interest in pastimes the Japanese believed suitable for women, such as the tea ceremony or flower arranging. Instead,

Madeleine entertained herself with sightseeing trips to the red-light district (where she struck up a conversation with a friendly prostitute) and by trying to establish a career in Japan as an authentic singer of French chansons. Later on, she joined the dancers of the all-female Takarazuka theater troupe for a brief engagement.

Madeleine's career as a chanteuse showed promise for a while. There could not have been many former French showgirls looking for singing jobs in Tokyo in those days, and so she had the field to herself. Her habit of downing some beer before performances at the recording studio and radio station was alarming, but she assured observers that these liquids improved her voice. For their new residence, Foujita built a red-brick, Mexican-style studio in his sister's garden, and the couple seemed to be settling down, but within two years Madeleine's chansons about storm-tossed love began to seem ever more appropriate. Claiming that she missed her mother, she announced that she was returning to France. Foujita assured the inevitably curious journalists that she would soon be back in Tokyo and even offered them advice about how to keep romance alive: "Three years away makes her feel nostalgia for home. The reason marriages between Japanese men and foreign women don't work out is that the men don't send the women back home every once in a while."

Foujita, who had used Madeleine as his model hundreds of times, said she never looked the same twice. It was in Tokyo that he created his most telling portrait of her, *Madeleine in Mexico* (1934). Madeleine sits amidst the undisciplined landscape of Mexico, where she has no trouble fitting in. The giant cactuses twist their way forward, overpowering the civilized, turreted building in the back. Such scenery might have fazed a less spirited tourist, but the Madeleine of the portrait knows herself equal to this setting, and so she can will herself into a minute of calm. Her extreme stillness looks studied and temporary, offered as a favor to the artist. To show that he knows Madeleine better, Foujita splashed red onto her dress, the poppies of her big hat, and her hair.

A year after her departure in February 1935, Madeleine came back to Japan as unexpectedly as she had left. Although her arrival was sudden, she did not require advance publicity to make her presence felt. It was said that she returned in haste because a Japanese artist in Paris had told her about Foujita's attachment to a Japanese woman. Indeed, he had supposedly been spotted strolling arm in arm in Ginza with this new romantic interest. After Madeleine's ship arrived in Yokohama, Foujita took a launch out to meet her onboard. Undone by jealousy and the various substances she had imbibed, Madeleine went berserk. A magazine article said that she had walked around the deck nude. There was a row with the journalists, which culminated in her pitching a camera at a photographer. In her cabin, she raged at Foujita, slugging him and breaking his glasses. With this quarrel, Foujita once again gave occupation to those employed by the gossip sheets.

Despite this unpromising reunion, Madeleine did manage to pick up the pieces of her life with Foujita. Though she suffered from depression and fainting spells during this second sojourn in Japan, there were still her chansons to distract her. In high spirits at the end of June 1936, Madeleine went over to the Nichidō Gallery to give her new record to the owner's wife. But later that same day, Madeleine died at home. Her sudden death spawned such rumors as the one about her having died of drug withdrawal in her bathing suit while watering the lawn with Foujita. There was another tale that had Madeleine naked in the bathtub, where Foujita and a young artist discovered her corpse. At the time, reporters had their own theories about suicide, but most now believe that she died of a stroke.

Witnesses say that Foujita was devastated by her death, and when friends gathered at his studio to offer sympathy, they urged him to draw a sketch of the dead Madeleine's face. "Now I am truly alone," Foujita said, weeping. "Other people have families, but I don't even have any children." At the Christian funeral, held at home, Foujita stood beside Madeleine's coffin in a light gray tuxedo and purple necktie.

TWENTY-SIX

ART FOR THE PEOPLE

Foujita's art is rooted in a kind of homesickness. In literature and music also, homesickness is apt to appeal most readily to sentimental people.

—*Araki Sueo*

Through all this, Foujita had his professional life to consider. Here we see a very resourceful artist floundering about his next move. In Paris or Latin America, Foujita had been able to gauge the local atmosphere with sure instincts—he didn't have to think twice about what to do or say in a particular setting. Mauve suits and sword dances had been just right for Paris, and he had thrived there for a long time; in Latin America, he struck just the right balance between seasoned master and convivial celebrity. Now, back in Tokyo, the correct behavior and correct artistic approach did not come to him so fast. It is strange to see Foujita fumbling around in Japan, a land now foreign to him. His intuitions were less keen, and like the former fashion star who repeatedly turns up in the wrong outfit, he seemed bruised by the mishaps. All this while the Japanese art critics were working hard to shatter his reputation.

Within a few months of his return to Tokyo, Foujita had an exhibition at the Nichidō Gallery in Ginza. His seventy-seven works—mainly from his Latin American trip as well as paintings of cats and women—sold out quickly. The gallery owner, Hasegawa Jin, who had been

selling Western art in Japan for only five years, found the collaboration
with Foujita a learning experience. Hasegawa wrote,

> The evening of the vernissage [private showing before the ex-
> hibit opened], the fancy cars of the ambassadors from every
> country and of esteemed Japanese ladies and gentlemen pulled
> up at the gallery entrance one after another. The gallery was so
> crowded that there was no place to stand. With the gallery full
> of such guests, Foujita, who wore a chic checked jacket, greeted
> each and every person warmly. He went down on one knee and
> kissed the hands of the ornately dressed wives of foreign diplo-
> mats. Only Foujita could get away with such flashy behavior. He
> had all the right gestures and flourishes, just as in a painting.
> "So this is the way to open a big show" was the thought that
> made a deep impression on me.

Not only was the Nichidō show a commercial success, but some
critics even offered words of praise. Still, the burst of applause was
brief, and as Foujita's stay in Japan lengthened, other reviewers threw
themselves into sneering at his work. These critics became particularly
agitated when Foujita dared to exhibit—along with the usual nudes,
cats, Parisian landscapes, and Latin American scenes—works on such
subjects as Japanese *chindonya* (itinerant street performers) and sumo
wrestlers. These were snippets of local color that often caught the eye
of foreign sightseers to Japan. But while the French critics had been enchanted by Foujita's evocations of a bewitching and faraway Japan,
Japanese critics, who lived there, were not similarly moved. They accused Foujita of looking upon his homeland with an outsider's eye and
turning their culture into a collection of exotica. "Everyone was looking
forward to Foujita's works," went Araki Sueo's corrosive review of an exhibition later in 1934, "but if you make a scientific analysis of them,
they are nothing but modern versions of ukiyo-e prints and reflect a very
skillful kind of dilettantism. The bohemian Foujita has been away from
his native land for a long time. He has become enraptured by the sights
of Mexico, and with the same gaze he directs on foreign lands, he
chases his dreams about the old ways of his native country."

As the months passed, Foujita's position was also not helped by rumors of his declining reputation abroad. His allure had been based on his butter-scented overseas success, but since he had built a studio and showed no signs of leaving Japan, detractors began to suspect that he had come back to Japan because the market for his works had collapsed in Europe. To add to the difficulties, the insular Japanese art world had its own finely honed way of operating, and this included long years of deference to influential superiors as well as careful exchanges of favors between budding and established artists. Such a closed society did not offer a warm welcome to the likes of Foujita. Nor could Foujita's popularity have surged far and wide when he took a haughty tone toward Japanese colleagues: "You're from the countryside, and so it's understandable that you don't know much," Foujita told a rich Japanese collector who confessed a liking for another Japanese artist. "If you buy that kind of person's works, they'll all be worthless in the end . . . By contrast, my works will all become national treasures."

Eventually, Foujita turned to coffee to improve his situation. He received a commission to draw a mural for a Brazilian coffee showroom in Ginza. Central to this establishment was a coffee shop, which would not only promote imported Brazilian coffee but also confer the mark of modernity on all who enjoyed a cup. Who but Foujita could create a showy backdrop for such a place? The mural, with scenes from what Foujita called "cheerful, bright, warm, healthy, expansive" Brazil, measured a big sixty-six feet by thirteen feet. He worked very quickly, twelve hours a day, and finished the commission in just a month. "I did not make any preliminary sketches and drew each of the forty-eight people one by one from much of what was in my head. Afterward, I realized that coincidentally half were men and half were women. In working out the composition, I drew more than eighteen animals and afterward added items in the landscape . . . In addition to Brazilians, I drew Spaniards, Portuguese, Italians, and black slaves."

Though only sections of the mural have survived, a 1935 photograph shows the whole thickly populated mural spreading out on the walls of the ultra-stylish coffee parlor. The mural might have been large, but it was not large enough for Foujita, who evidently wanted to jam in every aspect of Brazilian life. A big star at the center, commemorating the proclamation of the Brazilian republic in 1889, shines above the many workers from the coffee fields spread out in the background. While coffee production is the theme of this work, there are also musicians, pieces of sculpture, a preacher, horses, and children. Hayashi Yōko, who has written mordantly about this period in Foujita's career, finds a naked woman resembling Madeleine at the far right. This version of Madeleine is pointing out Brazil on the large globe she carries with the help of an unfortunate local inhabitant who is apparently being crushed under its weight. Despite the great activity around them, some coffee workers take their siestas while a cow and a bull look on.

Foujita himself makes an appearance off to the other side, where he is depicted working at a canvas.* Next to him stands Madeleine again, fully clothed this time. The work is an obvious homage to artists like Diego Rivera whose monumental frescoes Foujita had seen in Mexico. Rivera, fired up by his own political ideas and general boldness, had filled the walls of places like the Ministry of Education in Mexico City with sprawling scenes from the lives of humble Mexicans. Rivera's frescoes, whether exalting miners lugging their shovels or slaves liberated by the revolution, were set ablaze by his own fiery spirit, including the fiery pleasure he took in offending those he despised.

It is painful to compare Foujita's coffee-shop mural and his others to come with Rivera's. Rivera covered his walls with powerful colors and symbols of his beliefs, while Foujita came up with only a conventional tourist's view of Brazil. Brazilians had scoffed at Foujita's depictions of their country during his visit and have questioned the verisimilitude of this mural: "If this is supposed to be a place where coffee is produced, what's that tropical rain forest doing in the picture?"

This flawed effort did not deter Foujita from transforming himself into an enthusiastic proponent of murals, which he began to promote

---

*Including the artist's likeness in a mural was a long-standing practice in Europe, but, as Hayashi notes, Japanese who were unaware of this custom saw Foujita's inclusion of his own likeness as more crass self-promotion.

as a way to bring art to the people. He did not advocate painting directly on walls, as Rivera had done, since Japan's moist climate and frequent earthquakes made this impractical. Instead, he recommended the use of large canvases to educate both Japanese citizens and foreign tourists about local customs. "We must get rid of our old ideas about murals in the manner of [Puvis de] Chavannes or reminiscent of the Tenpyō period or those with literary, philosophical, or symbolic overtones. Ours is an age which should welcome the birth of murals and their display of society's reality." At times, Foujita got carried away with his crusade to bring art to the masses. If you closed your eyes and did not know who was talking, you might think that a champion of the downtrodden had seized the floor. "I would like to advise artists to take to the streets. Artists do not only serve the individual pet whims of distinguished wealthy families; they must also think about serving the masses. We must work for all the people in this country to make opportunities to love and appreciate art available to all."

Though such pronouncements had some impact, politically minded artists had reason to question Foujita's touting of revolutionary principles. Hayashi, too, has little patience for his new stance: "In the first place, the bourgeois Foujita had no connection to proletarian ideas or antiwar ideas. His mural technique may have reflected the temper of the 1930s, but in fact his was basically bourgeois art for a small number of rich people." She shows that Foujita did not follow his own instructions and move his work out into those public spaces where the poor could be enlightened. He accepted commissions at locations where the well-fed and well-clad gathered to enjoy their comfortable stations in life—a department store, another coffee shop, a center promoting French-Japanese amity. For the entertainment of those well placed in life, Foujita drew bland scenes of places like Normandy. As fashionably dressed beauties lolled upon sunlit fields, there was no reference to the exploitation of the underclass.

TWENTY-SEVEN

JAPAN'S ALLURE

It has been said of Japanese food that it is a cuisine to be looked at rather than eaten. I would go further and say that it is to be meditated upon, a kind of silent music evoked by the combination of lacquerware and the light of a candle flickering in the dark.
—*Tanizaki Jun'ichirō*

Madeleine's death can be seen as an important turning point in Foujita's life for more than the obvious reason. After she died, he distanced himself from his old life in Europe and focused upon a new existence in Japan. He suddenly began to profess a new rapture for Japan and Japanese ways:

Since my return to Japan, the sight of European things on Japanese soil doesn't excite me at all. After my childhood and youth, I traveled to the West and stayed there for a long time. As a result, my familiarity with Japan was not complete nor was I able to live to the full in Japan. Now this once I would like to recover what I lost.

The most concrete evidence of his affection for Japan was Horiuchi Kimiyo, who would become his next wife. The Japanese Kimiyo, who worked at a Japanese-style restaurant in Tokyo, had the long face of a classical beauty and was about twenty-five years younger than Foujita.

Like most Japanese women of her times, she was accomplished in the traditional female arts of the tea ceremony, flower arrangement, and koto (a stringed musical instrument). She also demonstrated a fierce devotion to Foujita that continues to this day.

With Madeleine dead, Foujita declared that he could not bear to remain in the Mexican-style studio, which had been decorated according to her wishes, and decided to begin again by building something purely Japanese. While waiting for the completion of his new residence, Foujita rented temporary quarters near a lumber dealer and sushi shop. In a gushing essay, he describes his joy at finding himself living in a neighborhood filled with the sights and sounds of an almost-bygone Japan. A teacher of an old singing style was on one side of him, and a koto instructor on the other. In the early mornings, he heard the horn of the tofu vendor and watched the sun rise over the clothes-drying racks on the roofs. Throughout the day, he savored the cries of the other street vendors, hawking brooms and goldfish and bonsai. Looking out his window at the persimmon and gingko trees, he soaked in an ambiance removed from Western influences:

> Rather than paint at an easel, I find it more convenient to do my work seated upon a red rug spread out on the floor. When I pour water into a bowl with a design of plums and wet my horsehair brush, the long time I spent living in a foreign country recedes far, far away.

He had been back home for three years, but he said that Japan still felt new to him, and he never tired of taking in the sights. "Every day I wake up with the realization, 'Oh, I am in Japan,' and again a smile, full of fondness for the land of my birth, spreads over my face."

A critic might (and did) say that this kind of thinking was behind his recent works on Japan, which reflected little more than a tourist's superficial impressions. Others might have said that he was in the midst of an identity crisis, since he could not figure out exactly where he belonged. Whether one called it an identity crisis or not, Foujita's problem was no different from that of anyone who had to choose between the coziness of being home and the liberation of being far away. For him, there were the real pulls of Japan—he was not wrong about the charm of the tofu vendor—but questions remained about whether he could enjoy those delights in his place of birth while tolerating everything that went with them: intrusive relatives, backbiting colleagues, the discomfort of being too well understood.

By 1937, around the time Foujita was enjoying the sounds of the tofu vendor, the Japanese army had set up a puppet state in Manchuria, and in Japan, there had been assassinations of government officials who tried to restrain the military's ambitions. On February 26, 1936, army officers in Tokyo attempted a coup, in the course of which they occupied the Diet and other official buildings and murdered prominent politicians. After a few days, on the emperor's orders, the revolt was quelled, but the army's power nonetheless grew. In July 1937, using an incident at the Marco Polo Bridge near Beijing as a pretext, Japan launched a full-scale war with China. By the end of the year, the Japanese were in control of Shanghai, Beijing, and Nanjing. That same year, in Spain, the Germans, who supported Franco, bombed the small town of Guernica on market day, destroying the city and killing many civilians. Several months later, *Guernica*, Picasso's monumental protest, was exhibited at the Spanish Pavilion during the World's Fair in Paris.

In 1937, Foujita began to offer his reaction to world events, though on a smaller scale than Picasso and from a different point of view. "I would like people to know that artists also are very much aware of the times," Foujita said upon completion of *Thousand-Stitch Sash*, which showed women stitching *senninbari*, a good-luck sash made with one thousand French knots of red thread on a white cloth. Worn around the waist of soldiers going off to war, the sashes were also supposed to ward off bullets. Foujita said that if the painting sold, he would contribute the money to the war effort, but this did not mollify those who thought poorly of the work. "I don't think that *Thousand-Stitch Sash* has been drawn from anything like a love for Japan" was one response that appeared in an art magazine. "This is just a painting of Japanese customs seen through the eye of a foreigner . . . If a Japanese artist had painted this work, he would have made all the women beautiful, I think. It's all right not to do that. But the painting is too much like a 'study of folk customs.'" Foujita followed *Thousand-*

Stitch Sash with other works that depicted the war's impact on the home front.

In the early months of 1937, however, Foujita had more than the war in China on his mind. He was increasingly ruffled by a commission for Hirano Masakichi that he had not yet fulfilled. He kept putting this task off, since the work involved traveling north to Akita during the cold, snowy winter. In 1937, Hirano, a wealthy landowner and art collector from Akita, also did not seem consumed by the rising influence of the military—in fact, his interests generally led him far from such concerns. Years before, he had bought himself an airplane and become its pilot, but he had to give up this hobby after he crashed into Tokyo Bay and was barely rescued in time by a fishing boat. In other ventures, Hirano acquired a Harley-Davidson motorcycle and a fancy automobile. His habits were no secret in Akita. "My father would take a boat out on the river here," Hirano's son told me, "and entertain geishas on it. You have to think of my father as a man of the Meiji era. He was a landlord. He just had to wait for the autumn harvest when all the money would come in. Other than waiting for autumn, he really had nothing to do. People don't live like that anymore."

As a collector of Foujita's works, Hirano also stood apart from all the others, since he purchased twelve items for very considerable sums. The income was most welcome to Foujita, who offered him thanks during a 1936 stopover in Akita. In the course of this visit, the two men talked about building a Foujita museum in the vicinity. "I'd like it to be in the pure Japanese style," Foujita declared, showing himself Hirano's peer when it came to grandiose plans. "I'd like to start with something small, but then make it something on the order of Sanjūsangendō." (About 390 feet long, Sanjūsangendō, a Kyoto temple, is bigger than a football field.)

The most significant words in the 1936 visit were still to come. At a dinner in his honor, Foujita stood up to speak:

Foujita: "I take pride in believing that I am the world's number one artist. Even the pope in Rome invited me to have an audience with him."

Hirano (moving into position in front of Foujita's seat): "If you say you're the world's number one artist, I'd like you to prove it by creating the world's number one painting."

Foujita: "All right, if you're determined and willing to supply what's necessary . . ."

Although Foujita had made this public announcement about his willingness to create the best, and preferably the biggest, piece of art in the world, he took his time getting started. He deigned to travel north to Akita later to sketch a summer festival, and during a press conference, Hirano promised that this artist's creation would rival the murals of the Golden Hall in Nara's Hōryūji Temple. After Hirano boasted about bringing the radiance of Nara to Akita, Foujita returned to Tokyo and stayed put. There were the construction of his new studio to consider, his new life with Kimiyo, and the pleasures of Tokyo itself. Hirano made a trip to urge haste upon his artist, but Foujita would not be rushed. Although he might appear to be doing nothing, Foujita said, he was really hard at work planning the details in his head. Hirano, who had already dispensed enough cash to Foujita to "easily buy two or three houses," returned home without a definite pledge about a starting date. The citizens of Akita, who had been promised Foujita's imminent appearance, became upset at the delay, and some disappointed fans stoned Hirano's house. Faced with a small uprising, Hirano went to see Foujita again and this time received the assurances he sought. Finally, he could return to Akita to buy the necessary supplies.

Not only were there difficulties with the canvases for a work that would measure about sixty-seven feet by twelve feet, Hirano also could not locate a suitable building for Foujita to spread out and work in. Hirano rejected a restaurant banquet room, a school auditorium, and a large factory, before deciding to convert an old family rice storehouse into a studio. Once Foujita got himself to return to Akita, little time could be wasted. He believed that the distinction of creating the world's biggest painting would be easily surpassed, and so he aimed at setting a harder-to-beat record for speed in painting a work of that size. Foujita took walks around the city of Akita to get ideas before he began his project. Confident about his visual memory, he said that he required just one look at some Akita dogs fighting in the square or at the clothing on passersby to reproduce them on his canvas.

Rough sketches would only slow him down, and so Foujita painted directly on the canvas, toiling in the rice storehouse for twelve hours a day. He felt lonely without Kimiyo, who had decided to remain behind in Tokyo, where she did not have to face freezing temperatures. She was summoned, but soon after her arrival in Akita, she got bored and wanted to leave. Despite Foujita's pleading, she would not change her mind, so he asked for time off to escort her back home. Hirano became more incensed and appealed to Foujita's honor as a gentleman, his promise to complete his work. At one point, Hirano pulled out a dagger, requesting that Foujita commit suicide to atone for not finishing the job. "Foujita turned pale," biographer Tanaka Jō writes. In the end, Foujita (and Kimiyo) were forced to remain where they were.

Smoking many cigarettes, Foujita made his way across the huge canvas, and as an indication of the public nature of this project, he allowed visitors into the rice storehouse to observe his progress. He asked some to pose for him and drew cats and shrimp on colored paper as gifts. Hirano, desperate to keep him happy, entertained Foujita by playing records of regional ballads—Hirano also played one of Madeleine's hit chansons, which did not amuse Kimiyo.

At last, Foujita completed *Seasonal Events in Akita* on March 7, 1937. Hirano had timed the whole painting marathon and declared that, in total, Foujita had worked for 174 hours.

Because wartime restrictions on supplies stopped construction plans, many years passed before a proper home was built for Foujita's painting. Now visitors can see Foujita's *Seasonal Events in Akita* at the Hirano Masakichi Museum of Fine Art in Akita City, where it has occupied a very wide wall since 1967. As the title promises, the enormous painting presents Akita's most famous yearly happenings: the snow festival (with children making rice cakes inside igloo-like huts of compacted snow), the raucous lantern festival of summer, the competing teams at the January shrine offering, the shrine festival in autumn. Among the dogs depicted are Akita's famed breed, known for their fidelity and reliability as guards. Hirano's son proudly told me that three family dogs are in the painting as well.

The dramas jostling for space in the work have no distinct beginning or end, and so they all blend, one into the other, presenting a very long thoroughfare jammed with what looks like much of the population throwing themselves into the vibrant, crowded celebrations. The effect, both close up and from the distance, lies somewhere between crazy and spectacular, with crazy getting the edge. It takes discipline for the viewer to focus on a single section when besieged by this color-drenched outpouring of drum, gong, banners, and vendors, as well as energetic celebrants hauling in long, decorated poles for shrine offerings and candle-lit paper lanterns. The action views of the young men—one appears to be expertly balancing a long lantern pole with his buttocks—are fabulous in their accuracy, recording every tensed muscle and every costume detail. The many varieties of fastidiously rendered clothing fabric—leaf designs on the *yukata* robes, guild crests on the *happi* coats, *kasuri* weaves on the kimonos—demand very careful scrutiny, since their intricate patterns prove an artistic ambition that cannot be contained in a painting several thousand times bigger than this one.

Seasonal Events in Akita brings to mind equally crowded and exuberant scenes from the old Japanese screens and woodblock prints—sumo ceremonies, historical pageants, Kabuki plays—created by Japanese masters who had also focused on the lives of the common people. Although Foujita obviously felt more at ease in presenting the activities of the Japanese than those of Brazilians, *Seasonal Events in Akita* satisfies only as an extravaganza of densely painted objects. When it comes to expressions of emotion, the painting asks for and receives nothing. Foujita would have to wait for his wartime contributions to solve that artistic problem, but he had in the meantime honed his skills in speedily creating large, dramatic works packed with human figures. These talents, developed under duress in Akita, ensured Foujita's later prominence as a war artist.

And so, before the Japanese military campaigns of the late 1930s drew him in, Foujita made these efforts to diversify and to bring himself in closer contact with the lives of the general population. For a man beleaguered in so many ways, he deserves credit for an unflagging spirit as he lurched around trying to establish himself at home. Perhaps nothing better sums up the insecure nature of Foujita's situation than his most ill-advised endeavor during these years. In this one episode are combined the gall, the light-headedness, and the comedy of his free-falling state, which ended when he landed upon firm and war-stained ground.

In 1935, Foujita took on a project not heretofore associated with his area of expertise. Like many a celebrity looking for a wider audience, he decided to go into the movies.

While Foujita's technical competence was subject to debate, at least he once again got himself more involved in current events. His film career started because the Japanese government hoped to host the Olympics, but the country's reputation abroad had been greatly tarnished by the war in China. To repair Japan's international reputation, the Ministry of Foreign Affairs commissioned a series of films about contemporary Japanese culture that were to be distributed throughout the world. Foujita, already a genial Japanese face to foreigners, was selected as one of the directors. In case anyone questioned his credentials, he had a retort ready: "Up to now, only Japan's scenery and cities have been filmed, and so the foreigners have been sadly disappointed and don't feel any interest in Japan. I have spent a long time living abroad, and so I thoroughly understand how to get foreigners' attention. Now I will direct from the script I have written myself, and so I will be recognized in Japan as well."

In 1937, after viewing Foujita's completed film, *Japanese Customs*, some Japanese were appalled. The production was lambasted in certain quarters for "portraying Japan in a shameful light," and this was a blow to Foujita's blossoming moviemaking career. Only one section of Foujita's directorial debut has survived, "Sons and Daughters of the Rising Sun," and this seems uncontroversial enough at first, with its scenes of country youths at play. No one minded the part where the children happily run around the countryside together. The problem starts when the children get into a mock swordfight and one boy pretends to commit hara-kiri with a toy sword.

This was an outrage, according to those critics who charged Foujita with ignoring the modern, Westernized aspects of Japan and purposely focusing on backward old customs. According to them, he had portrayed Japan as poor and uncultured, and worse yet, with the swordfight and the ritual suicide, he had reinforced the idea of Japan as a war-mad nation. The argument expanded, as so many such arguments tended to do, into a general condemnation of the creator, his life, his work, and his general character. Commentators declared the film a dismal result of his having spent too many years in France, where he had catered to the Europeans' fantasy of Japan. Again there was the charge that once back home, he still looked with a tourist's eye upon the quaint customs of his native land. "I have depicted the simple feelings of the Japanese," Foujita stated in his own defense, "which I have known since my youth. Westerners, tired of their machine-driven civilizations, are seeking this kind of Japan."

The plans to show Foujita's film abroad never materialized.

Around this time, Foujita moved into his new residence, another milestone in his immersion into Japanese culture. The structure's pure Japanese design further fueled the contention that he looked at Japan like a dotty sightseer who swooned over antique chests and the samisen's twang. Water flowed by the bamboos planted at the entrance while the construction featured beams from Kyoto with some bark left on—for a more rustic look—as well as smooth Kitayama cedar. Inside was a traditional-style sunken brazier with an old-fashioned teapot suspended above, lighting fixtures of bamboo and Japanese paper, decorative curtains, tatami floors, and sliding paper-screen doors. According to one frequent visitor, the house had the feel of a fashionable Ginza restaurant making an extra effort to look authentically Japanese.

As he proceeded deeper into this Japanese phase, Foujita did not lose his sense of humor. In a 1936 self-portrait, he offers an ironic look at himself spread out on the tatami of another residence that is also packed with Japanese things. Painted with much care and color are the patterned kimono hanging on the wall, remnants of a Japanese meal on a low table, a strictly Japanese sliding door, teacups, a decorative curtain, a hibachi stove, and scattered floor pillows. Surrounded by this clutter, Foujita displays himself as a Japanese who has gone native without any regard for economy or common sense. As a cat nestles in the folds of his disheveled Japanese robe, Foujita smokes a cigarette and does not look absolutely comfortable in the new setting.

His face, so familiar from other self-portraits created in Paris, seems to ask the viewer about whether he's going to get away with his new disguise.

TWENTY-EIGHT

A MATTER OF COMMITMENT

Many artists were dying to be part of the war painting effort. That way, you could get materials for painting. But you had to be able to draw human figures. So the military would have gatherings of artists and see if they could paint people. Sometimes the military would bring in soldiers to pose for the pictures—create a kind of mise-en-scène. Sometimes the artists were taken out to the front. If you were an artist doing war paintings, you were well taken care of. But if you were a soldier, oh, it was bad; you had a miserable rank.

—*Suenaga Taneo*

Every time I go to your room, I always find empty rice bowls lying around in front of your door," Foujita berated his nephew Ashihara Eiryō:

There's no point in treating that young group of yours to good meals. They know how to flatter you, but it's only to get you to buy them food. Running a magazine and cultivating a bunch of young followers is a waste of time. Magazines like *Chūō kōron* or *Kaizō* may have influence, but a lightweight magazine like yours won't get you anywhere. Rather than running a magazine, it's better to cultivate your potential on your own and push ahead. A person who can't do anything by himself is a weakling.

Only the weaklings have to join forces with others to get something done. Just look at me. Just look at me.

As this snippet of dialogue shows, Ashihara required fortitude to survive conversations with his famous uncle. When he was a young man, he lived almost next door to Foujita's Japanese-style home. Estranged from his own parents, Ashihara came to depend upon his uncle for affection, free meals, clothing, and a red necktie he borrowed for jaunts around town. Aquiver with the hopes and miseries of the freelance, Ashihara wrote articles on many topics—movies, music, plays—and also taught and gave lectures. In addition, Ashihara was the sole staff member of a dance magazine. He says that he aimed to become an *honnête homme*, in the old tradition of a cultivated Frenchman, but to some Japanese, he may have seemed more like a man in need of steady employment.

The story has a happy ending because Ashihara did go on to become a respected contributor to Japanese culture. Sharing his uncle's affinity for France, he had a special interest in Western performing arts and did much to bring the chanson to Japan. But recognition only came later, after much struggle. When Ashihara was living close to his uncle, he appears to have spent a lot of his time sighing about his own unrecognized abilities, the world's coldness, and his lack of funds. Such moping did not go down well with Foujita, who believed in discipline and proper nutrition.

According to Ashihara, Foujita was in the midst of a slump at that time and had his own reasons to sulk. Since his works did not sell in Japan, he had to churn out ink paintings of fish, shrimp, and shellfish on colored paper for customers in the countryside. He also accepted commissions to do magazine illustrations. In Ashihara's eyes, his uncle had once strutted all over Europe in style but now was reduced to a constricted life in Japan, with a Japanese house and Japanese wife.

The nephew may have fretted over his uncle's diminished circumstances, but brooding did not come naturally to Foujita. "Japan is really a strange place," Foujita reflected. "Even if you can't make money in large quantities, you can earn dribbles of money here and there which eventually add up to a large sum." In fact, when he thought it over, he concluded that Japan offered artists too many side opportunities, and this impeded their development. Literary people could write for commercial outlets; serious dancers could become teachers. "That's why Japan doesn't produce great artists," he told his nephew. As usual, Foujita took a look around and concluded that only he had proceeded through life correctly. After all, when he had been desperate for money in Paris, he had done distasteful jobs: cleaned bathrooms, pushed around a mover's cart, worked as a model. While toiling at these unpleasant jobs, he had always longed to be working on his paintings, and as a result, his love of painting grew even stronger. In Japan, the situation was different. Artists could undertake pleasant work related to their specialties and make money. The artists were not particularly repulsed by these side jobs and even took some satisfaction from them. That decreased their commitment to their real work. "The youngsters here lose their original sense of purpose," Foujita said.

Such certainty in all things helped Foujita ride out the rough spots. A nimble mind allowed him to adapt his views to the moment, while insisting that his current view, though perhaps contradicting an earlier one, was absolutely correct. This trait kept Foujita from dwelling overlong on his mistakes, but Ashihara—to whom dwelling came as naturally as breathing—could not dream of such aplomb, and his confidence was jolted by his elder's changing positions. "Foujita always had the ability to make people believe that what he was doing now was the very best thing to do," wrote Ashihara in his autobiography, *Chronicle of Half My Life*. Foujita advocated marrying a Frenchwoman while he was married to one, dismissing Japanese women as emotionless and dull. He stuck to this point of view until he himself married a Japanese woman. Another time he asserted that no iconoclastic artist ("Look at Picasso and Matisse!") would dream of joining an art organization, since this would stifle originality. When he became a member of the art group Nikakai, he just as surely avowed that survival was impossible without group support. After all, his Nikakai comrades had defended him against criticisms and rallied to his side at the time of Madeleine's death. "Paris is different from Japan. That's why Picasso and Matisse could make it alone."

A coffee shop caused Ashihara great consternation. For a while, Foujita met people at the simple neighborhood coffee shop Brazileiro, since, he declared, receiving guests at home was an outdated waste of time. He objected to the Japanese who visited him at home at any time of day without an appointment or real purpose, their endless chatter interrupting his work: "An artist has to protect his time better than that." Next he repeated a remark that could not have earned him adoration among the locals: "That's why Japan doesn't produce any great artists."

To get around this problem, Foujita held court in Brazileiro, which he praised handsomely. Ashihara, quick to accept the recommendation of his sophisticated uncle, soon became convinced that the world's best coffee was served there. "This coffee is delicious, isn't it?" his uncle would effuse. "That's because this is real Brazilian coffee. I've been to Brazil, and so I know. You can't get such good coffee even in Brazil. This place is better than I can say and quieter than Ginza. It's absolutely amazing that you can find such a first-class spot in Tokyo." Ashihara became a regular at the coffee shop and even invited friends to join him.

As soon as his new house was completed, Foujita changed his mind. All of a sudden, meeting people at home did not seem like an outdated custom, and he no longer frequented the coffee shop. Staggered by this reversal, Ashihara could not make up for his uncle's absence. Foujita's magic had gone elsewhere, and Brazileiro now seemed dirty, the coffee bad. In his autobiography, Ashihara takes a dark lesson from these episodes, which he presents as a prelude to Foujita's shifting attitudes toward the Second World War: "I came to believe whatever Foujita said, and the exact opposite of what he said. That is, I came to believe everything he said and then again disbelieve everything he said." At the same time, Ashihara's dismay did not dampen his devotion and awe. He could not help admiring this uncle who moved through life with so many contradictions, so many defects, so much charm. His memoir gives off the true smell of a family quarrel, with affection and estrangement existing side by side. Ashihara also shows how his meddling, doting uncle evolved from a has-been who drew shrimp on colored paper to the dynamic leader of Japan's war artists.

That transformation took some time, since Foujita did not immediately throw himself into the job that would, to many people, overshadow everything he had done before. He zigzagged along the way, thereby disconcerting almost everyone. He kept on traveling, no matter what, and drew more cats to keep up his income. Yet in the end, he was telling everyone that he had offered up his painting arm in service to the nation.

It was in 1938 that Foujita began his official work for the military, but even so, he spent the spring of that year, as he had many others, going on a private trip, this time to Okinawa, where he enjoyed the scenery, the food, the friendliness of the inhabitants. Okinawans took pride in the distinct features of their language and culture, which set them apart from other Japanese, and Foujita was favorably compared with other Japanese artists who had tried to convey that essence. "All the subjects [in artist Mitsutani Kunishirō's works]," wrote the Okinawan poet Yamanokuchi Baku, "seem to be about to speak in Japanese. But in Foujita's case, his subjects seem to be able to speak, though haltingly, the language of the Ryukyu Islands. Among the works I have seen up to now, Foujita has created people who most look as if they actually come from the Ryukyu Islands."

Not every artist could arrive in a new locale and swiftly produce high-quality, true-to-life works. Foujita's talents, spanning a wide range of subjects, did not escape the notice of the Japanese military, which sought to memorialize its victories in China. Later in 1938, the Japanese navy asked Foujita to join a group of artists traveling to central China to create pictures of the war. Once he agreed, Foujita transformed himself into an earnest representative of the state just as easily as he had changed coffee shops. In no time, he mustered the correct phrases and attitude. "I look forward to the day when Hankou falls," Foujita told reporters upon leaving Tokyo for this assignment. "Let our band of artists be the first to travel there." The next day, at a stop at Fukuoka in southern Japan, he continued to praise the group's ambitions to the local newspaper: "There are now about one hundred artists who are accompanying the military in their operations, and some of those artists have created exceptional works. Our group also will see the fighting firsthand and hopes to create scenes of the imperial army's heart-wrenching fighting that will move viewers. The First World War in Europe was behind the birth of splendid war paintings, and so we must strive to create better works than those."

Lest such patriotic zeal lead to the conclusion that Foujita had undergone a complete conversion before he took off, his preparations prove that the old priorities remained in place. Before he departed, Foujita attended to his wardrobe. The military had supplied him with assorted items, including gaiters, binoculars, and a canteen, but Foujita, not yet satisfied, had his tailor make him a military cap. When that creation came out looking like the cap worn by the enemy Chinese soldiers, some feared that Foujita might be mowed down by his own side. He chucked the cap but stuck an imperial navy button on his chest and wore an official army hat with star insignia. The hodgepodge of military adornments amused a Western correspondent from *Life* magazine, who said that he looked like "an army and navy cocktail."

There were other signs that Foujita had become perhaps overly caught up in the theatrics of his trip. Before he left, he placed a lock of his gray hair in his writing box, "in case I vanish in the dust of China's yellow earth or drown in the Yangtze River." His wife, Kimiyo, known for her thorough housecleaning habits, quickly discovered the keepsake and called him, frantic, from Tokyo: "Is that what you were thinking about when you left?" she asked over a crude phone line to Fukuoka. "I don't intend to die," Foujita solemnly replied, ". . . but you never know your fate."

At his ease once he reached occupied Shanghai, Foujita met with other well-known artists and writers—Hayashi Fumiko, Kikuchi Kan, Ishii Hakutei—who were also on assignment for the military. Trundling off with a group to an Italian restaurant in Shanghai's French concession (where he found a photograph of himself in Argentina on the wall), Foujita could once again feel part of a community of eminent people involved in the central events of the day. This must have boosted the spirits of an artist who had lately been feeling neglected.

Along with reporters from American publications like *Time* magazine, Foujita, who had not demonstrated a love of flying under ordinary conditions, much less when a war was under way below, flew over the Yangtze River and, mindful of his artistic duties, tried to memorize the colors of the sky, the water, and the land as the plane swooped over the terrain. He spent the night in the war-torn town of Jiujiang, noting the flowers and grasses flourishing in the ruins. Sweating profusely in the heat, he heard the sound of gunfire in the distance for the first time. He finally got to fly up to the front, but not close enough to see an actual battle. Though he was too far away to hear the sounds of war, he could see the repeated flares of light and the enemy bullets falling into the waters: "This is my first experience of real war, and nervously, I sketch."

Next he was taken by boat toward the battleground and, disembarking nearby, drew a watercolor against the noise of exploding land mines. The soldiers protecting him soon blocked his view, but still he "joyfully" continued to work. On other days, from a battleship a short distance from the action, Foujita got as near to the war as he ever would, taking in the pillbox fortifications smoldering in a bamboo grove, enemy bullets whizzing overhead, and bombs exploding near the ship. He later lamented the state of modern warfare, which prevented him from drawing the enemy. Nonetheless, Foujita—adaptable in peace and war—knew that he could fill in the gaps. "At least I have developed the confidence to produce war paintings."

As the days passed, Foujita felt increasingly drawn in by the bravery of the Japanese troops and wanted to record events "to show to the youth of Japan." His memoir, which recounts his training for his new job as documentary artist, tells of his disappointment when he arrived too late to see Hankou (Wuhan) taken by the Japanese. He had to rely on an eyewitness, who assured him that the drizzle and the cloudiness on the night of his arrival were identical to weather conditions during the battle, as was the color of the Yangtze. Forced to accept this secondhand information, Foujita reproduced those hues for future reference. At a banquet to celebrate the Hankou victory, he definitely hit the proper note when he joined in expressing his deep gratitude for "the heart-wrenching hardships endured by the officers and men of the army and navy, their passionate patriotism, and courageous, loyal martial spirit, burning like fire."

While Foujita rejoiced in the Japanese victory, he also noted the shivering, hungry Chinese refugees walking half-crazed down the streets with their ragged bedding, the dead enemy soldiers on the ground, the split trees stripped bare. He felt it was as if they had been simultaneously hit by the natural calamities of earthquake, fire, flood,

Portrait of Mrs. Emily Crane Chadbourne, 1922. Tempera and silver leaf on canvas, 89.5 × 146.1 cm. Emily Crane Chadbourne was an heiress to the Chicago-based Crane Company fortune. This is the only major Foujita work in an American museum. (Courtesy of the Art Institute of Chicago, Gift of Emily Crane Chadbourne)

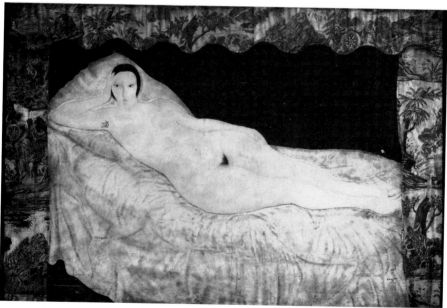

Nude with a Jouy Fabric, 1922. Oil on canvas, 130 × 195 cm. This nude of Kiki, the well-known Montparnasse personality, is notable for the white color of the model's skin and for the very detailed rendering of the patterned fabric. (Courtesy of Réunion des Musées Nationaux/Art Resource, New York; Musée d'Art Moderne de la Ville de Paris)

My Room, Still Life with Alarm Clock, 1921. Oil on canvas, 130 × 97 cm. One of Foujita's personal favorites, this still life was admired in France, but scorned in Japan for being too imitative of traditional Japanese works. (Courtesy of CNAC/MNAM/Dist. Réunion des Musées Nationaux/Art Resource, New York; Musée National d'Art Moderne, Centre Georges Pompidou, Paris)

Before the Ball, 1925. Oil on canvas, 168.5 × 199.5 cm. This very white painting, with its ambiguous emotional content, looks especially striking when exhibited among more colorful works by Foujita's contemporaries. (Courtesy of Ōhara Museum of Art, Kurashiki, Japan)

The Two Friends, 1926. Oil on canvas, 92 × 73 cm. Foujita did a number of paintings of two female nudes in this period, and this one is a good example of his expertise with his special white color. (Courtesy of Erich Lessing/Art Resource, New York; Petit Palais, Musée d'Art Moderne, Geneva)

Three drawings of cats, 1929. From *A Book of Cats* (New York: Covici-Friede, 1930). Cats became Foujita's specialty, and he drew them in many moods and poses. (Courtesy of the Rare Book & Manuscript Library, Columbia University)

Study of a Man Wearing a Sombrero, 1933. Pen, black ink, and brown, blue, and gray wash on tan wove paper, 35.72 × 30.64 cm. During his long journey through Latin America in the 1930s, Foujita created many works on the spot and sold them at the exhibitions he held along the way. He completed this drawing while in Mexico. (Courtesy of the Minneapolis Institute of Arts, Bequest of Mrs. Margaret B. Hawks)

Sumo Wrestler, Portrait of Yoshinoyama Yōjirō, 1934. Hanging scroll, ink and color on paper, 156.9 × 72.4 cm. After returning to Japan in 1933, Foujita did a number of works on Japanese themes, including this painting of a sumo wrestler. (Courtesy of Shuzo Uemoto/The Salmon Collection)

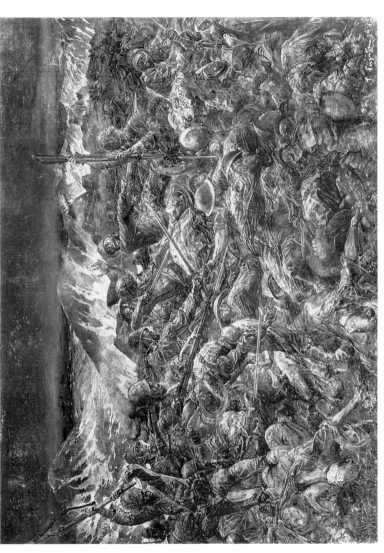

Last Stand at Attu, 1943. Oil on canvas, 193.5 × 259.5 cm. In their brutal treatment of war, Foujita's war paintings continue to stir up debate since they can be viewed as more than propaganda paintings. This one is a particularly gruesome depiction of a battle in the Aleutians. (Courtesy of the Collection of the National Museum of Modern Art, Tokyo [indefinite loan])

Compatriots on Saipan Island Remain Loyal to the End, 1945. Oil on canvas, 181 × 362 cm. This large painting, showing the mass suicide of soldiers and civilians on Marpi Point, was exhibited four months before the end of the war. The nobility of those facing death is movingly conveyed. (Courtesy of the Collection of the National Museum of Modern Art, Tokyo [indefinite loan])

a great storm, and then a war, with all the misery this implied. When he finally returned to Japan after thirty-three days, Foujita took pleasure in the sight of his country's intact natural beauties. (He also liked seeing the hundreds of schoolchildren waving flags of farewell to the Hitler Youth group returning to Germany.) A bowl of white rice seemed a great luxury.

Foujita may have summoned sufficient enthusiasm for the war in his public statements, but his artwork casts doubt upon the wholeheartedness of his commitment and the versatility of his painting skills. *Attack on Wuhan* (1938–40) and *Burning of the Nanchang Airfield* (1938–39), two paintings Foujita executed after his trip to China, do not presage a stellar future for him as a war artist. *Attack on Wuhan* is particularly unimpressive, showing two battleships crossing a very wide swath of the Yangtze under a stormy sky. Since Foujita had gone out of his way to find out about the weather and lay of the land that day of Hankou's fall, his clouds and river no doubt duplicate the actual conditions. But getting the sky and water right was a small part of the job. No matter how much some may praise the technical excellence of this river scene, Foujita's failure to include any combat seems a serious omission in a war painting. In years to come, when he had much less information about a battle scene, Foujita fared much better, for then he was free to improvise his way toward unforgettable images of Japan at war.

In a blatant sign of ambivalence, Foujita, along with Kimiyo, suddenly left for Paris five months after his return from covering the ongoing war in China. Foujita hastened to explain his motives to the Japanese public, who had reason to question his recent ardent support of the military's goals. "Now, three years after the sudden occurrence of the China incident, I am not leaving in an idle wish to continue my artwork," Foujita wrote in a newspaper article upon his departure. "Rather, the task which suits me best is to spread the truth about the righteousness of the true Japanese spirit to the thousands of friends I have scattered everywhere in foreign lands and to inform people there about the nature of the Japanese spirit. Using art as a medium, I hope to further the cause of international friendship. That is the motivation for this trip abroad."

Struggling to convince those who might suspect that he was delighted to escape his country—in the middle of a war—for life in Paris,
Foujita went on to detail the extent of his sacrifice:

> I, who have lived abroad for twenty years, returned to Japan
> after a long absence and have been here for six years. I have
> worked hard to inform myself about the East, have traveled
> by foot throughout Japan and even climbed sacred Mount
> Takachiho . . . I went to Korea, Manchuria and also spent two
> months in Beijing, where the level of development was aston-
> ishing. I had wood brought from Kyoto to build myself a house
> in the style of a traditional Japanese teahouse. I collected tradi-
> tional furnishings and garments from all over Japan. I married
> a Japanese woman . . . I was at the front for a month and saw
> with my own eyes the courage of our soldiers and was filled with
> deep emotion and gratitude, and this is why I made this sud-
> den decision. Now I will discard it all. I will forget about every-
> thing—the teahouse, the antiques, and the garden—and as a
> man stripped bare, I will travel to all the countries that have
> mistaken ideas about Japan and harbor unfriendly feelings to-
> ward Japan. I will meet face to face with the public there and
> spread the word about Japan's true intentions . . . There is no
> other road that I can take.

Since he professed his dedication to his country as he hurried away,
this is another of those moments in Foujita's life that have attracted
various theories. It is easy to see why many remain skeptical about the
reasons he offered for this abrupt decision. His nephew Ashihara believes that Foujita was actually shaken by a Parisian art magazine he
had read at the Belgian Embassy in Tokyo and left Japan because
he feared being forgotten by the Western art world. After reading the
magazine, Foujita realized that artists who had started out much after
him were producing good works, and his inferiors had surged ahead of
him also. "If I continue like this, I'll be finished," he told his nephew.
"I'm going to change my life. I'm going to Paris." Then again, Sasaki
Shigeo cannot rule out the possibility that Japanese military officials,

who had established ties with Foujita during his China trip, sent him abroad on some kind of mission.

Perhaps most credible are those who assert that Foujita left for Europe in April 1939 to avoid being swept up into the war. If he remained in Tokyo, his time would have been taken up collecting facts about weather conditions, the shape of tanks, and the uniforms of military heroes. Far off in Paris, he would have the freedom he had always found there—or so he hoped.

TWENTY-NINE

WARTIME CHOICES

When women sense that their chastity is in danger, they fight to the death to preserve it. Artists are weaklings in certain respects, but like those women fighting to the death, they, too, must hold on to their principles to the very end . . . Maybe we artists made some attempts to escape from doing war paintings and other things we didn't like. But even someone trying to look at us in a good light would not be able to say that we behaved as if we were holding on to our principles to the very end. In that sense, I have no choice but to say that I succumbed to the mood of the country at that time and am one of those who bear responsibility for the actions of Japan's art world.

—Abe Nobuya

With rare exceptions—among them the writers Tanizaki Jun'ichirō and Nagai Kafū, and the visual artists Maruki Iri and Maruki Toshi—most of Japan's artists actively supported the Japanese military's efforts during the Second World War. Many did not think twice, since they were in agreement with the government's drive to establish the Greater East Asia Co-Prosperity Sphere, bringing Japanese military might and Japanese civilization to the rest of Asia. Writers, painters, journalists, film directors, whether at home or stationed abroad, created works in praise of the valor of Japanese soldiers, the invincibility of the Japanese spirit, and the need to teach Japanese to citizens of occupied lands.

Though the vast majority of the creative elite did not have to be coerced, anyone who did resist could face severe harassment, imprisonment, or worse. "Don't you remember the man with the saber," reminisced artist Maruki Iri, one of the holdouts, "who came to suggest to us that we'd be better off if we painted war paintings? His saber clanked along. 'Don't be hesitant. Don't delay. Paint war pictures.' That was how he talked to us . . . It was difficult not to paint under such circumstances, with such 'encouragement.'"

The role of visual artists in the war effort was considered crucial, as an army officer affirmed in 1941:

Artists must be aware of the fact that their profession is a luxury . . . But once it is understood that art transmits contemporary Japanese culture to posterity, then art is no longer a luxury, but, I think, an endeavor of the highest importance. Even at a time when Japan is engaged in a war where life and death hang in the balance, art alone must be encouraged. Thus, for example, if the munitions factories need more workers, the artist who is true to his calling must take up his brush and continue to transmit the message of true art to many future generations even if bombs are falling all around him.

After the Japanese attacked Pearl Harbor in December 1941, the United States was brought into what became the Second World War. With this, the military solicited war paintings with more determination. Officials believed that powerful works would not only be a gift to posterity, but would also educate the public about the bravery of the troops and thereby increase devotion to the war effort. "In their intensity and colors," an army manual for artists stated, "outstanding artistic works created at the hands of a master can have a truly large emotional impact on people. Above all else, only a painting has the special ability to make us hear sounds without making a sound, convey emotions, and appeal to ideas." Eventually, all art supplies were controlled by the government and only approved exhibitions allowed.

Later, in the wake of Japan's defeat, the furor began over which artist had done what for the military and how much. Were these artists genuine patriots, understandably working on behalf of their homeland, or an unprincipled bunch ready to offer their skills to anyone who would give them a canvas and adequate living conditions? Did they participate because they had no other choice? Had their paintings been moving enough to prolong the war? Were these artists then responsible for inspiring many to die for the nation? After the war, excuses about past behavior were plentiful, and forgiveness was bestowed erratically. The debate is still far from over and, in fact, seems to gain strength with each new attempt to set the record straight. In the disarray of postwar Japan, officials from both Japanese and American organizations reviewed the evidence, but uncertainty was everywhere, and this included matters of war responsibility.

An English-language work, Kazuo Ishiguro's novel *An Artist of the Floating World*, captures the postwar dilemma of one Japanese artist who cooperated with the military. Ishiguro, who was born in Japan but educated in Britain, writes in his most Japanese manner here, his plot wandering back and forth like many a discursive Japanese-language tale. There is also Ishiguro's English itself, particularly the conversations, which, with their odd, slightly off quality, sometimes lull the reader into the belief that this is a Japanese novel that has been translated into English. Masuji Ono, the protagonist of *An Artist of the Floating World*, lives amidst the mess of defeated Japan. Respected during the war as a patriotic artist who labored for the nation, he faces the postwar hostility of his vanquished compatriots. "All I can say is that at the time I acted in good faith," Ono declares. "I believed in all sincerity I was achieving good for my fellow countrymen."

Ono may be burdened with extraordinary conflicts, but at the same time he is faced with the most commonplace of novelistic problems: he must get his daughter married. Novelists have long focused on premarital tussles to introduce more weighty issues, and here Ishiguro adds the Second World War to this old scenario. As in other such plots, there is much fretting in *An Artist of the Floating World* about the family flaws that might scare away a groom, especially since Ono's contributions to the war effort are the greatest barrier to his daughter's marriage. He encounters antagonism even at a tram stop, where he talks with one of his daughter's prospects.

"Sometimes I think" [the potential groom declares,] "there are many who should be giving their lives in apology who are too cowardly to face up to their responsibilities . . . There are plenty of men already back in positions they held during the war. Some of them are no better than war criminals . . ."

"But" [Ono says] "those who fought and worked loyally for our country during the war cannot be called war criminals. I fear that's an expression used too freely these days."

". . . But these are the men who led the country astray, sir. Surely, it's only right they should acknowledge their responsibility. It's a cowardice that these men refuse to admit their mistakes. And when these mistakes were made on behalf of the whole country, why then it must be the greatest cowardice of all."

Such debates about war responsibility are not, of course, limited to Japan, but for real-life Japanese war artists, the situation had its own peculiarities. In 1951, U.S. occupation authorities confiscated the 153 Japanese war paintings that had been recovered after the war—a very small fraction of the total created—and shipped them all to the United States. Stashed far away from Japan, in such places as Wright-Patterson Air Force Base in Ohio, the paintings stayed out of the news for a while. But in 1970, as a result of pressure from the Japanese, these paintings were finally returned to Japan on "permanent loan" and are now stored in the National Museum of Modern Art in Tokyo. Once the war paintings were returned, the controversy about the role played by Japanese artists during the Second World War began once more, many years after the war had ended. In 1977 the museum planned a large exhibition of war art, but at the last moment the show was canceled, with concerns about the likely criticism from formerly occupied Asian nations given as the official reason. The 153 war paintings remain in the Tokyo museum, away from public view, and are only shown piecemeal in occasional exhibits.

To my surprise, I discovered echoes of these controversies far from the source, in Concord, Massachusetts, just thirty minutes from my home.

Ihara Michio, the son of the prominent Japanese artist Ihara Usaburō, now lives in a spacious, shingled New England house that is down the street from Ralph Waldo Emerson's former residence. Michio has been in the United States since the 1970s, pursuing a career as an architectural sculptor. His metallic sculptures seem to take flight across ceilings, climb up walls, or rise from the ground of public spaces, in the United States and abroad. I visited Michio in his large studio on a perfect summer day when the hollyhocks were in bloom outside. At seventy-five, this white-haired artist has the self-contained air of a man just getting started on his life's projects, and as we talked just beside his shimmering sculptures in progress, he appeared pleased at having established a life, among his stainless steel frames and cubes, far from the ramifications of his father's fame. "My father objected to my becoming an artist, but I was stubborn. He did attend a group show in Japan where my works were exhibited."

Michio's father, Usaburō, who called his years in Paris "the most sparkling time of my life" and greatly admired Picasso, became an enthusiastic supporter of the war. A close associate of Foujita, Usaburō was at ease drawing groups of people and unafraid of high emotion. The military wanted no part of fancy styles such as Surrealism and Dadaism, "which ordinary people find difficult to understand," and instead demanded realism, human figures, good crowd scenes, and precise draftsmanship. Usaburō provided what they needed in *Triumphal Entry into Mandalay and the Cooperation of the Burmese People* (1942), showing grateful Burmese offering water and assistance to weary conquering Japanese soldiers. Though such scenes no doubt took place at the beginning, the Japanese occupation of Burma was hardly benign, and so the work now seems like a depressing illustration of Burmese naiveté.

Usaburō mustered more subtlety in his 1943 portrait of Ba Maw, Burma's head of state during the Japanese occupation, who posed in resplendent native attire with his Order of the Rising Sun medal conspicuously displayed. Though Usaburō's reproduction of the intricate design on the clothing fabric is noteworthy, a viewer's attention remains on Ba Maw's eyes, which tell much about his uncertain grip on authority. "My father was good at portraits, and I like this one," Michio told me that sunny day in Concord. "It's among his best." His father's situation became more insecure later on: "Many artists were scared after the war. They feared prosecution. In 1945 or 1946, a U.S. jeep came to our house. My father was scared, but it was really just a courtesy visit. I think that my father struggled after the war. He refused to be part of the artistic establishment. He wanted to be alone. He threw himself into working for an association that tried to help poor artists. Then he and my mother split up, and my father felt the need to concentrate on something. So the organization work was good for him, helped him during that difficult period. There were constant meetings. This was in the 1950s. He regained his confidence."

Not only did Ihara Usaburō commit himself to the war effort with his artworks, he issued statements that were scrutinized after the defeat. "Following the imperial will," he had proclaimed at the time of Japan's attack on Pearl Harbor,

> and heedless of the great sacrifices involved, overcoming an unprecedented, pitiful history and advancing despite many difficulties, the brave soldiers of our Imperial army have given us this great joy. And now indeed we have in truth been able to envision the glorious and radiant, endlessly expanding future of Japan, a land which traces its origins back to the gods.

Writing much later, a Japanese artist reviewed these words in shock: "When I was transcribing Ihara's sentences, I started thinking that maybe there was a soldier armed with a pistol standing behind him. As Ihara announces his total belief in the land of the gods in his stilted, exaggerated manner, I cannot believe that these sentences came out of a man who spent four and a half years in Paris and was enchanted by Picasso."

When the war ended, Usaburō, like so many others, felt obliged to defend himself: "It is inaccurate to say that the artists who created the war paintings were militarists. Before the war, no one in the art world held such beliefs. Therefore, the artists selected and given orders at the beginning were, above all else, those able to paint human figures and especially soldiers. Afterward, almost all those who had confidence in their ability to create figure paintings joined in. So you can't generalize and say that only those artists who didn't create war paintings were pure artists." While such statements may have exonerated those artists who participated with reluctance, art historian Michael Lucken concludes that they could not be applied to Ihara Usaburō, whose artistic contributions and strident words made him a leading figure among war artists.

Back in Concord, Ihara Usaburō's son Michio lives at quite a distance, in many ways, from this kind of discussion. He has also moved far from the steadfast realism of his father's wartime works, which left nothing unsaid. Michio has managed to avoid such bluntness by scattering his insights among the metal balls and squares that hang from public buildings.

Before I left for home, Michio brought out a memento he had found in his father's studio after his death. It was a doll of a postwar Japanese beggar that had been made by Foujita in 1946. Such beggars scrounging for food were numerous after the war, and this one, dressed in rags sewn by the expert tailor Foujita, carried a DDT pail and firewood on his back. "The occupation soldiers used such pails to spray the Japanese," Michio told me, "disinfecting them constantly. The beggars would pick up the discarded pails and use them to carry their cooking oil."

When he made the doll, Foujita was reeling from the effects of the defeat even more than Michio's father. His former artistic comrades had deserted him, and he complained bitterly about this ostracism. As he sought ways to escape from Japan, Foujita faced condemnation from many quarters and the possibility of being declared a war criminal. It is safe to assume that a measure of wrath went into every stitch of the beggar doll's rags. "My father helped Foujita when he wanted to leave Japan after the war," Michio recalled. "I think that Foujita's suitcase was hidden in our house while Foujita himself hid elsewhere before he left."

THIRTY

FACING REALITY

*I read only dispatches from England and France about the Euro-
pean War, and ignore everything from Germany . . . Day and night
I pray for a French victory. It is at such times that a Joan of Arc
should appear.*

—Nagai Kafū

Foujita and Kimiyo arrived in Paris in May 1939. Upon reaching
the Gare de Lyon, he was questioned by journalists curious
about where he'd been since 1931, when he had last set foot in
France. He deflected such questions in his own way, by taking off his
trousers and doing a dance in his long Japanese underpants. Without a
doubt, Foujita was back in town.

He and Kimiyo moved to Montmartre, where he raved about his
view of the city from the top floor of an eight-story building. "*Zekkei—
zekkei* (What a splendid sight—what a splendid sight)," he exclaimed,
quoting a famous line from a Kabuki play. At one point, Foujita revisited the Dordogne region, where he had found shelter during the First
World War; it is not known if he went by the musty chateau he had frequented back then. Again in Paris, he went to the Comédie-Française
and tried to learn about the latest women's clothing fashions. His daily
schedule was packed, and if his writings are any indication, he flour-
ished. Only his cats showed that he had come back to Paris in fearsome times. Foujita's *Cats (Battle)*, an alarming 1940 oil painting,

teems with cats who are doing more this time than just striking the usual fetching pose. On the contrary, the cats strewn across this canvas are vicious, baring tongues and teeth as they claw at one another in a quarrel with no beginning or end. Condemning the base instincts waiting to be let loose in even small domestic animals is one thing, but Foujita did not stop there. The painting considers each flexed muscle and arch of fur as the animals set about destroying one another. Again, in the dramatic *Still Life with Cat* (1939–40), which presents superbly drawn fruits, vegetables, and fish, Foujita disrupts the vista of plenty with a lone bird flying across the black wall in the background. To the side lurks a sly cat, caught in the middle of deciding between two ways to wreak havoc—by gobbling down the food or the bird.

After the Germans invaded Poland in September 1939, Foujita became increasingly used to the sight of gas masks and bomb shelters in his neighborhood. Yet he did not seem alarmed about his situation even after the Japanese Embassy advised its nationals to return home. In fact, when Foujita and his Japanese friends gathered in a café to discuss this development, they displayed such good cheer that they were scolded by French draftees seated nearby. During his strolls around Paris, he frequented the flea markets and took pleasure in finding unusual bargains like an Empire clock, which he proudly repaired himself. This was not a man in any rush to leave Paris.

Unlike in Foujita's previous stays, his social life revolved around expatriate Japanese, perhaps because his Japanese wife could not speak French. The Japanese artists Ogisu Takanori and Kōno Misao lived close by, and Foujita tells of a festive evening when he prepared a mackerel dish, Kōno prepared rice curry, and Ogisu, macaroni, while everyone argued away as if they'd forgotten all about the war in Europe. During those tense days, the men did not feel inclined to continue their usual work and so took up frame making as an alternative. It should come as no surprise that Foujita involved himself totally in his ongoing project, purchasing a frame-making machine, wood, and other supplies. He nailed, painted, and decorated the frames himself, toiling out on his terrace in the sun until his body ached. Kōno, who lived diagonally across from him, also made his frames on his terrace, and during the day, the two men conferred from their outdoor perches about their progress.

The interlude soon came to an end. Foujita wrote that on May 9, 1940, Paris did not seem to be at war as he kept constantly on the move with work or social engagements. Rarely alone, he had future exhibitions to consider and a large fee to be paid for a Japanese group show in June. He could still beam at proof of his celebrity, such as when the man painting the apartment next door ventured to declare kinship with him as a fellow painter. Overhearing this conversation by the elevator, the concierge broke in: "This *monsieur* is a *grand maître*, and you're just some worker. I'm shocked to hear you say that you're both artists. It's like the difference between the palm of your hand and the sole of your foot."

On May 10, Foujita was awakened by the sirens warning of an imminent German attack. The glass in his studio shook from the vibrations made by the anti-aircraft planes just before he and Kimiyo fled with their gas masks and folding chairs to the bomb shelter below. On May 17, when a bomb was dropped in a place ten minutes from his home, Foujita still could not get himself to depart for Japan. This, despite the fact that French authorities closely monitored Japanese artists as citizens of a quasi-enemy country. Ogisu tells of being kept under strict surveillance and harassed by the police when he tried to paint outdoors.

Only after the Germans occupied Belgium did Foujita at last decide to go back to Japan. Acting fast, he managed to secure reservations for Kimiyo and himself on a Japanese ship embarking from Marseilles and packed his belongings at night, using his flashlight against the blackness of Paris at war. "My friends advised me not to stay in the capital. In any case, I almost have no friends remaining there. Pascin is dead. Apollinaire is dead, Modigliani is dead, Soutine has fled to the Midi, and Kisling is dead also. I take my leave again, asking myself if I will ever return."

Ogisu, even slower to leave Paris, describes his surprise at coming upon Foujita suddenly packing up. Once Foujita changed his mind and decided to go, he, as always, developed great confidence in his choice and exhorted everyone else to follow suit. Ogisu pitied Kōno, who had been planning to spend the rest of his life in Paris but was beaten down by Foujita's urgings. Ogisu soon came upon Kōno preparing to go home also. "[Kōno] had to close down a house he and his family had been living in for more than ten years, and he definitely could not manage as skillfully as Foujita."

Though Paris was in an uproar over the German onslaught, Foujita and Kimiyo succeeded in getting to Marseilles and boarding the *Fushimi-maru*, which was the last Japanese passenger ship to get through the Suez Canal until the end of the war. When they were out on the Indian Ocean, he received a telegram from a Japanese newspaper announcing the German takeover of Paris: ON 14TH GERMAN FORCES MAKE BLOODLESS ENTRY INTO PARIS. QUICKLY TELEGRAPH AN ARTICLE ABOUT THE PARIS OF YOUR MEMORIES. Foujita kept in his cabin some peonies he had taken from Cézanne's garden, so perhaps he read this cable amidst those wilted souvenirs from his old life. The skies had been clear for many days, and Foujita attributed a large part of the German success to the good weather. That night, after informing the others about the city's surrender, he went out to stand on the deck and surveyed the black, stormy waters. "The memories of my long years in Paris filled me with overpowering emotions, and these, mingling with the mad rush of thousands of waves, seemed to toy with me. I spent a lonely night, absolutely wide awake and unable to sleep."

Cézanne's peonies and the sleepless night show one side of Foujita's response to the fall of Paris. There was another aspect, and Foujita shifted into that second mode with ease. On the voyage home, his friend Kōno saw evidence of this other state of mind: "Of course, Foujita had more than an ordinary person's need to be the center of attention. A part of him needed to have people saying, 'Foujita! Foujita!' all the time. When the Second World War broke out, my wife and I went back to Japan on the *Fushimi-maru* along with Foujita and his wife. In the ship's dining hall, he used to do things like sing military songs with great gusto, becoming as usual the focus of everyone's attention."

Not only did he sing Japanese military songs during the journey home, Foujita also started to express negative opinions of the French whom he had just left behind. From his new vantage point, those hours lounging around the cafés started to seem less attractive, and he did not have to look hard to find reasons for the French collapse. He believed that since the end of the First World War, the victorious French had taken life easy while the Germans had steeled themselves for a new conflict, hardening themselves against luxuries to avenge their loss. Sounding very much like the stern scion of a military family, he expressed disdain for the French populace's blasé attitude toward war, which, he claimed, had weakened their ability to resist. He held up for particular derision a report about French primary schoolchildren's replies to questions about the war. These children said that they disliked Hitler and felt that wars, such tragic events, should definitely be avoided. Attached to their families, they wanted to live in peace and freedom. How—went Foujita's reasoning—could a country hope to achieve victory if it imbued its children with such flaccid pacifist sentiments? "The reasons for France's defeat can be clearly seen in the children's answers."

On July 7, 1940, Foujita and Kimiyo arrived back in Japan. He said that he looked forward to feeling tatami beneath his feet after a long absence, and getting further into the spirit of things, he expressed pleasure at returning to the "land of the gods." Foujita and Kimiyo did not look like a couple who had narrowly escaped the trauma of a vanquished European capital. On the contrary, they stepped off the boat in Japan looking positively gorgeous, the very essence of Parisian chic. In a newspaper photograph, Kimiyo wears part of the gleanings from her first journey to Europe—a smart Western dress, complete with pearls and saucy hat. Foujita is in a debonair jacket, black shirt, and dotted necktie. He has carefully arranged his gray kappa hairstyle so that the bangs sit atop soon-to-be controversial eyeglasses with large, expensive tortoiseshell frames.

The Foujitas brought a whiff of glamour to the Japanese, who were facing the deprivations caused by an ongoing war. The couple was fêted warmly upon arrival, but tortoiseshell eyeglasses and well-coiffed hair would not remain popular in a country where sacrifice and service were the reigning virtues. A Japanese woman, returning in her finery from ten years in Paris, similarly recognized that her old life was over as soon as she got off the boat. A representative of Japan's Women's Patriotic Association handed her a flyer: "Let's give up all luxuries."

Foujita had most of his hair cut off a month later. The kappa hairstyle—his trademark for twenty-five years—was replaced by a very short crew cut much more in keeping with the austere atmosphere of those days. Commentators past and present have much to say about his visit to the barbershop, since the haircut signaled the end of his bangs and the beginning of his submission to reality. (According to one account, he realized that he must cut his hair when his dandified European appearance prompted a local journalist to accuse him of being a spy.) Never one to miss an opportunity to publicize his activities, Foujita informed a friendly reporter about his haircut, and a photograph of the newly cropped artist appeared in the newspaper. Looking far more serious with his forehead exposed, he also had his tortoiseshell eyeglass frames cut down to more modest dimensions.

So momentous was this event that he visited his father to inform him about his new coiffure. Afterward, Foujita talked about his hair with a reporter:

My kappa has seemed strange to some people and has led to misunderstandings. Actually, my long hair was a souvenir of the days in Paris when I was poor and didn't have the money to go to the barber. Every time I used to look at my hair, I would scold myself and say, "Work hard and don't forget the past." After that, strangely enough, the kappa became fashionable in the art world, and I found it unpleasant to see the excessive posturing of the young who would say, "Artists must have a kappa." Under present conditions, the kappa is especially useless and harmful, and so I have made a definite decision. It will be good if this has an effect on even a small number of our young people.

Ogisu Takanori, who had remained behind in France after Foujita left, remembers being sent a Japanese newspaper around that time. He was astonished to see a photograph of the shorn Foujita, whom he had just recently seen off in Paris with his kappa intact. "He was a man with a big talent for understanding the temper of the times," Ogisu observed.

THIRTY-ONE

TO TOIL
FOR THE NATION

For someone waging war, the bloodless seizure of a place is truly wonderful, something to be grateful for. But for an artist, this causes problems. While it's important to make a documentary record of a seizure that amounts to merely taking over a place easily without any drama, it's difficult for an artist to create such a work, due to problems of subject matter and other things.

—*Foujita*

So why did Foujita do what he did next? Why did he not only cut his hair, but also move to the forefront of the military artists? Yes, he was a patriot, proud of his Japanese origins, and yes, as a Japanese, he wanted his side to win. But for a man who had lived outside of Japan for so long, wasn't his involvement excessive? A recent study calculates that Foujita's war art consisted of at least 150 oil paintings, plus about 50 watercolors and drawings. Although only about two dozen of these have survived to the present day, the scale gives a clear idea of Foujita's astounding diligence during the war years. This is unlike the image of Foujita himself during wartime, which remains an out-of-focus impression, jiggled around by his fame, the content of his paintings, his public statements, and not least, the everlasting high dudgeon of his defenders and enemies. Few who have pored over the facts can resist guessing about Foujita's state of mind during the war. Speculations abound, especially since there is little concrete evidence to back up any theory.

"Foujita came back to Japan more Japanese than the Japanese," says the writer Donald Richie, a longtime resident of Japan. "This is a definite cultural trait. This happened in some way to Kawabata, Mishima, Tanizaki. It is a known cultural pattern. He reveled in the freedom abroad. That's a pattern—to revel in the freedom and at the same time to resent all those things."

And then there is the role of the Foujita family, whose military connections cannot be overestimated in his rise to eminence. Since his father had been a general in the army medical corps, military figures were commonplace in Foujita's circle. Foujita's familiarity with important officers eased his way upwards; his talent for the job, of course, ensured that he reached the top. A little filial piety could be added to this mix. Wasn't it true that his military assignments didn't just put him back on the front pages of newspapers—his preferred spot—but also gave him the extra pleasure of pleasing his relatives?

Entering these disputes, Ashihara takes his uncle's side, asserting that Foujita had no other choice but to join the war artists. This was the only way of life possible for Foujita if he wanted to get through the war. Had he not acted as he did, he could not have gone on living in Japan. Ashihara is a proponent of the idea that Foujita looked on his war work as an artisan who was just doing a job and had no particular attachment to the subject matter: "In the same way that Foujita believed that women were merely 'flesh,' so a gun or a flower was all the same to Foujita."

One dissenting opinion brushes all these others aside. Artist and critic Monden Hideo cites Foujita's writings during the early part of the war, at the time of his 1938 trip to China, when he eagerly supported the militarists' activities: "The 'widely believed theory' that Foujita did not go along with what was happening at first but was pressured by those around him . . . is wholly at odds with the real Foujita . . . Rather, Foujita stayed ahead of developing events, took the lead, depicted the situation, and created his war art."

The artist Nomiyama Gyōji presents a more ambiguous picture of Foujita in those days, and I find his blurred portrayal easier to accept than the other, more sharply defined views. Nomiyama mixes much sadness with much amazement when considering Foujita in wartime and beyond. As he speaks, he also chuckles here and there in appreciation of his own jokes. Nearing eighty when I met him in his sleek Tokyo studio in 2000, Nomiyama was preparing for an exhibition, and so the space was full of his large abstract canvases. Ageless octogenarians are not a rarity in Japan these days, but Nomiyama has an urbane, rock-star charm that sets him apart. In his oil paintings, rich colors fight across giant canvases, and soon after the death of his wife, he used angry whirling shapes to protest this private calamity. There's often a calligraphic stroke to make a point. Nomiyama, the author of a number of books, has written about Foujita, too, in his sometimes biting, sometimes tender prose style.

As he reviewed his impressions of Foujita in his animated Japanese, Nomiyama darted forward to offer a delicious anecdote, then sat back to muse upon what he had just said. "You know, I have a personal connection to a big Foujita mural in the Maison du Japon in Paris, where I used to live as a student. I really liked to play Ping-Pong in the room where the mural was displayed, and I am afraid that my balls did a lot of damage to the painting."

Nomiyama was at art school in Tokyo during the war when he first encountered Foujita. "He came to our school and gave a talk—he had graduated from our school. All Foujita talked about was physical fitness. In order to paint, he used to say, you have to be physically fit. And how should you do this? You should wake up early in the morning and strip yourself naked. Then take a towel, twist it to wring out all the extra water, and give yourself a rubdown with it. That's the only kind of lecture he gave. I was hoping he would talk about art, but there was hardly any of that. He was very proud of his body, very good at judo. Really, he was a child in certain ways, kind of innocent."

Nomiyama next saw a solemn side of Foujita at the Tokyo Metropolitan Art Museum. The year was 1943, and Foujita stood ramrod straight beside his big, much admired war painting *Last Stand at Attu*, which depicted the remnants of the Yamazaki brigade making its final suicidal charge in defense of Attu Island in the Aleutians. Though the savage faces of the soldiers charging over the dead bodies tell the epic tale of war's barbarity, the public also saw a nobility in those who were dying for the cause. People gathered in front of the work to weep and pray.

"One day, when I was still in art school, a friend of mine said to me, 'If you go next door to the museum and donate some money, Foujita will bow to you!'" Nomiyama went to the museum right away and found not only *Last Stand at Attu*, but to the side its creator, Foujita, who gravely bowed each time a visitor put money for the war effort into the offering box. "Foujita was standing at attention beside that painting, wearing his wartime clothes. In those days, there was the danger of air raids, so everyone had to carry a canteen. Foujita didn't wear his like everyone else; instead, he slung it very stylishly over his back. His helmet, too. Ordinary people wore regulation clothes, with things like gaiters, but Foujita was different. He had on grand leather boots. I watched him bow each time people put money in the box beside the painting. I wanted to see if he really would bow to me also, and so I threw in some money. He did bow to me! At that time, I thought he looked tremendously serious, as if he truly believed that Japan was the land of the gods."

Nomiyama's opinion shifted yet again when a woman friend, also an art student, moved into Foujita's home to help out with chores in the studio. This friend told Nomiyama of strange goings-on in that household, like the eerie events on the night *Last Stand at Attu* was completed. "My friend told me that Foujita signed the painting at night," Nomiyama said, "showing that he was finished. Then he called in his wife and my friend, and said to them, 'Let's say a prayer.' This was to honor the men in this painting who had died. They put up candles and performed a small ceremony in front of the painting. Then— my friend insisted—the dead soldiers in the painting came to life for a moment and actually smiled at them. For just a moment, she said, they really smiled. An article about this incident, with a photograph, appeared in the newspaper the next day. I asked my friend if the story was true, and she said yes, she saw it with her own eyes."

Here Nomiyama settled back to reflect upon this episode, seeming to sink into one of those ruminative spaces found in his paintings. "I started to think about it, and really, somehow or other, I smelled a lie.

There had to have been some preparations made for this publicity. Foujita claimed later that only the three of them were present, but he must have also called over a reporter and a photographer, in order for them to be at his house in the middle of the night to capture the scene. Foujita had really tried to concoct a little drama. 'The soldiers in the painting moved! They moved,' he must have shouted and got the newspaper to report it. But you know, if you study his nature, Foujita seems to have been the kind of person who actually felt that he could be the vessel through which otherworldly spirits communicated with this world. Really, he believed in such things."

Nomiyama laughed in great happiness as he launched into telling about another time Foujita made contact with the dead, an episode recounted in Ashihara's autobiography. "Foujita did not reject palm reading or fortune telling completely," Ashihara writes. "He wouldn't go out of his way to have such an experience, but if a chance presented itself, he liked to have his fortune read." Foujita then accepted what he'd heard. Ashihara tells about the time he escorted Foujita to a séance with two female mediums where communication with the world beyond produced spotty results. The first visitor from the dead was reported to be, not Foujita's ancestor, but Ashihara's, from his father's side of the family. Hearing of this, Ashihara was aghast, since he had come as a mere companion for his uncle and had no wish to communicate with anyone, dead or otherwise. His revulsion intensified when he was instructed to embrace the grimy woman writhing upon the floor who was supposed to be a manifestation of some dead family member. "I am susceptible to various allergies and have many likes and dislikes. I started shivering throughout my body and felt that I was going to break out in hives."

That was not the end of it. The next visitor from the world of the dead supposedly arrived on horseback and claimed to be one of Foujita's samurai ancestors. This spirit came equipped with a helmet for Foujita, a treasure invisible to the naked eye, but capable of making him invincible. Since Ashihara had seen his uncle playacting on other occasions, he was not surprised by Foujita's skill in performing his part, taking the phantom helmet and then prostrating himself reverently on the floor in gratitude. Once outside in the sunshine, Ashihara was

ready to debunk the whole experience, but stopped himself because
his uncle was busy flexing his muscles. "I have become stronger," Foujita told the shocked Ashihara. "Because I received that helmet, definitely no one can beat me . . . I'm not the same Foujita as before."

Aside from being enchanted by this tale, Nomiyama saw the connection to his own anecdote. "You see, Foujita really felt he had seen
the faces of the dead smiling at them in the *Attu* painting. And because
he believed in it, he had the power to convince my woman friend. So
she believed it, too. Foujita could in some ways play the medium's role.
He had that side to him."

After completing his art studies in Tokyo in 1943, Nomiyama was
drafted and eventually sent to Manchuria. Just before he went off to
war, his woman friend invited him for a farewell feast, at Foujita's
house. "In those days ordinary people could not get food for a feast, but
Foujita had a lot of such items in his house. That's because many of the
artists who painted for the military had received their assignments at
Foujita's recommendation. He was the most important of those artists,
after all. So the artists would go abroad to paint and when they came
back, they'd visit to pay him their respects, bringing him gifts of butter
and cheese. Ordinary people couldn't get those sorts of things then.
When I arrived there for my feast, all that food was like a dream. After
dinner I went to meet Foujita in his studio to have tea. That was the
first time I ever spoke to Foujita directly."

For Nomiyama, the next scene did not accord with his impression
of the Foujita who had bowed so earnestly at the Tokyo museum. In
the studio, Nomiyama was confronted with the unforgettable sight of
Foujita's extensive wartime wardrobe hanging about everywhere. There
were clothes to wear in air raids and clothes for going out. He had a
white hood and jacket just like the outfits worn by Edo-period Japanese firefighters, as well as touches of Cossack fashion in a green dou-
ble vest and a pair of red boots. "When I went into his studio and saw
all those clothes, I was really taken aback. 'What on earth is this?' I said
to myself. 'What kind of person is this?' Then I thought, Well, I guess
that he's just amusing himself with this war. War for him is only a
source of entertainment."

The night of Nomiyama's visit, Foujita peeled an apple for his nervous guest and seemed somber, aware that this young man would fight

in his place. Nomiyama remembers the moment: "In a very small voice, like a child's, he said to me, 'Please go and fight for the nation.'" Nomiyama developed a lung ailment while serving and was in a hospital at the time of Japan's defeat.

"When I think about Foujita, it all seems strange. He painted *Attu* and many other war paintings, and that night he said to me in a very serious voice, 'Please go out and fight for the nation.' But you know, even if Japan had won the war, no one would have been able to look back and find a single one of his paintings that shows war as something wonderful. When you look at his paintings you feel, 'War is really terrible.' None of the other war paintings by other artists have that feeling to me. In the other war paintings, the artists show the soldiers fighting, and even if they fall, they seem sublime. In Foujita's paintings, you don't feel that there is any difference between the enemy dying and Japanese dying. Everyone looks so sad. You look at his works and feel the awfulness of it. So I definitely would like to know about Foujita's state of mind when he painted his war paintings. I always wanted to ask him about that . . .

"I have always wondered about the two sides of Foujita's character. There was the very serious person who created such war paintings, and then there was the man who fooled around, doing things like collecting that clothing he had arranged in his studio. I have a lot of friends who are artists. And often the impression you get of the artist as a person is very different from the paintings they create. Which is true? I think that the painting is the real thing."

THIRTY-TWO

TALENT FOR THE JOB

The Pacific War started on December 8, [1941,] and that night I unexpectedly met [the artist] Ebihara Kinosuke on a street in Ginza. I remember that we ate beef in Suehirotei. Ebihara had one of his children with him. Beef had become a coveted item by then, and though what we ate was called sukiyaki, it was half beef and half fish. "Look, Ogisu," [Ebihara said,] "everything's going to be fine. If Japan takes over the Philippines, we won't have to worry about getting cloth for our canvases anymore. They've got a lot of jute there." Those days it had become hard for artists to obtain cloth for their canvases. But later on I heard that the jute from Manila was coarse, good for making bags, but that it couldn't be made into the fine variety artists needed for their canvases.

—*Ogisu Takanori*

After returning from Paris in the summer of 1940, Foujita settled back into Tokyo life. At first, he kept busy socializing with the other artists who had also just come back from France, but since he could never have enough company, he often urged Ashihara to stay on late into the night after the last guest had left. Always smoking a cigarette, Foujita left behind a trail of ashes and advice during these late-night sessions when he took up topics like his nephew's nonexistent love life. The decor of Foujita's studio once again underwent a change of theme, this time to a Western style that perhaps reflected the inhabitants' nostalgia for Europe. Kimiyo also adopted a new look. To go with her Paris wardrobe, she favored French perfume, bright-red nail polish, and shiny lipstick. Housecleaning no longer uppermost on her mind, Kimiyo preferred to reminisce about the delicious bread in Paris.

The works of established artists were considered a stable investment in those uncertain financial times, and so Foujita, the fresh whiff of France enhancing his popularity, enjoyed excellent sales. Even so, an exhibition held less than two months after his return marked the last throes of his career as an artist unconnected to the widening war. *Interior, Dordogne* (1940), one of the works he created in France, resurrected the extensive use of his white color, after a long absence, for a study of a sitting room in the French countryside. The painting fondly recalled the living quarters in a land distant from Tokyo, where the citizens regularly went on recreational hunting forays and drank wine with their meals. With his informal reproduction of such a setting, Foujita made sure that everyone remembered his connection to this way of life.

Foujita's sojourn at the sidelines, never destined to last long, ended when Lieutenant General Ogisu Ryūhei visited his studio in September 1940. Ogisu, recently retired from active duty, was one of the officers whose careers had been ruined by a 1939 border dispute with the Soviet Union in Nomonhan, Manchuria. In that confrontation, the stupendously underequipped Japanese troops had had about as much of a chance of success before the formidable Soviet tanks as did the region's swarms of mosquitoes. Something like twenty thousand Japanese troops died in that massacre. Fearful of the public response, the Japanese government at first tried to keep the death toll secret and made great efforts to silence survivors. In order to conceal the number of deaths, the boxes containing the ashes of the cremated victims were sent home in three separate shipments.

Ogisu was known for his brashness. Shortly before the slaughter of Japanese soldiers by the Soviet military, he had telegraphed army officials: "Kindly set your mind at ease." He also had a reputation for being too fond of the spotlight, and this perhaps accounted for his fast bond with Foujita. Ogisu would not concede that he had actually lost the border conflict, but instead considered his counterattack thwarted by the declaration of a truce. Stung by the abrupt end of his service, he commissioned Foujita to paint a work extolling the heroism of the soldiers who had perished at Nomonhan. To add further incentive to the offer, Ogisu used the funds he had received upon leaving active duty for the payment.

Ogisu also used his military connections for educational purposes. Once Foujita agreed to take on the assignment, the general hustled him off to Nomonhan to get a firsthand look at the terrain. Discussing his visit later, Foujita adhered to government policy when he ignored Japan's trouncing and perceived signs of the brave Japanese success over vastly superior Soviet equipment. Foujita described the limitless stretch of land and never-ending sky at Nomonhan where "the courageous, bold imperial troops achieved their military goals." After leaving the "darkness" of that earth, which held the spirits of those who had fallen in battle, Foujita went back to Tokyo and quickly set to work. He probably had not bargained on the frequent visits of Ogisu, his perfectionist patron, who haunted Foujita's studio and pointed out defects in the work in progress. Ogisu complained that soldiers were not holding their guns correctly in Foujita's drawings, or he found fault with the rendering of the belts. Soldiers requisitioned by Ogisu posed in the studio or simulated battles in full camouflage regalia—down to grasses and branches stuck into the helmet netting—in the small garden outside.

Although Ashihara believes that his uncle wavered at first in his dedication to war paintings, Ogisu's passion had its effect. After much practice, Foujita acquired expertise in drawing rifles, pistols, boots, and other military paraphernalia. At Ogisu's urging, Foujita visited a regiment outside Tokyo and took rides in tanks and fighter planes, whose details he noted in many drawings. Once, while he was a passenger, his military plane took part in a simulated air battle with a captured Soviet I-16 aircraft. Eager to study all the details, Foujita spent time reproducing the configurations of the clouds high up in the heavens.

Foujita's new taste for drawing tanks accurately and for experiencing somersaults in army planes was applauded by his outside supporters, but at home, he did not receive much encouragement, as Ashihara has chronicled:

"Listen," [his wife Kimiyo berated Foujita,] "you're old now. You've got to stop this flying around in army planes. If the plane crashes, you'll die, and then what will you do?"

"I'm not going to die." Foujita, with a cigarette stuck in his mouth, stared at Kimiyo straight on.

"How can you say that, 'I'm not going to die.' How silly can you be? That's not the kind of thing you can decide for yourself."

"I'll be all right. I don't ride in the dangerous ones."

"'Dangerous ones'? Can you tell which ones aren't dangerous? What are you talking about?"

Kimiyo especially resented his habit of ignoring her advice, while accepting all suggestions from other quarters.

"You don't pay the slightest attention to what I say—right?—but you listen to whatever General Ogisu tells you. He tells you that the way those soldiers are raising their hands doesn't look right or that they're wearing their hats wrong. I like the way you listen to him without a peep and then make those changes. You just do whatever he says. I don't understand why you don't get angry. I keep waiting, thinking, 'He's still not angry? He's still not angry?' But you don't get angry at all. Here we have a great artist like Foujita taking one order after another from some outsider, just listening and not saying a word . . ."

"There's no reason for you to talk like that. There's nothing to get angry about. I'm not taking orders at all. If he tells me that the position of the cap doesn't look right, I have to do what he wants, since I have an agreement with the army."

Foujita worked on the painting with a dispatch that would, until the end of the war, stun his public and patrons. Before Foujita joined them, Japanese war artists had been sent out to the front, but there had been little cheering about what they produced. Some artists complained that they were restricted by military secrecy or, though brought to the battlegrounds, could not figure out exactly where the war was taking place. One artist confessed to being overwhelmed: "I experienced the awfulness and power of war that cannot be captured by a brush or in a painting." When some artists were killed on assignments, the military allowed study of the battle sites only after the conflicts had ended; photographs, which increasingly replaced eyewitness experience, could not convey the whole tumultuous atmosphere.

Foujita, far from suffering artistic paralysis, was galvanized. His great passion for his war art is evident in descriptions of his life at that time. Early in 1941, Foujita was working on the Nomonhan painting when he received word of his father's death. It is reported that he wiped away tears and immediately returned to his canvas.

A very large oblong, *Battle on the Bank of the Halha, Nomonhan* (1941) spreads out like a giant scroll some fifteen feet wide and, as a contemporary newspaper headline proclaimed, shows the fight between a tank and humans, with the Japanese humans—on canvas at least—about to win. Foujita provides a battleground immense and mostly empty, with the sprawling field and a blue sky dipping down low to the horizon. Upon this stage, intrepid Japanese soldiers, with puny rifles their principal weapons, have seized a bulky Soviet tank. Elsewhere on the ground, the vulnerability of resolute Japanese soldiers is evident as they crawl forward, utterly exposed, through the grasses. Showing Foujita's fondness for small human vignettes, a soldier pauses to give his wounded comrade drinking water, while others rush toward another burning Soviet tank.

Foujita presented the Japanese during a very fleeting moment of triumph in the battle at Nomonhan. According to Mark H. Sandler, the painting illustrated the idea that the "Japanese spirit," saluted by the government as the nation's most potent weapon, gave their soldiers the ability to demolish a Soviet tank practically with their bare hands. Foujita left out the part about how the confrontation ended weeks later with the Japanese defeated and twenty thousand soldiers dead. None of the critics was inclined to point out the omission. "This painting depicts our brave troops fighting desperately with all their might . . . ," exulted a news story in the *Asahi*. "It is a moment when several of our soldiers, leaping upon an enemy tank in fury, have climbed up the tank."

With *Battle on the Bank of the Halha, Nomonhan*, Foujita sailed out ahead of his competitors among the war artists, a position he maintained until the end. "This oil painting, full to the brim with a special emotional impact," wrote one reviewer, "is a painting from a new era. And for the first time such a work has been produced by a Japanese." The painting now looks like Foujita's obeisance to the military, his job application as a war artist. In every category, he had met the requirements for the position and then some. He had demonstrated his expertise in drawing many human figures in an assortment of poses and could fill a big canvas with an action-packed, crowd-pleasing story. Such large-scale works served a crucial propaganda purpose, since they would be reprinted in publications and shown at exhibitions that traveled around Japan—all to rouse the public's martial spirit. Not only had Foujita chosen the correct images to convey the government's message to the masses, he had churned these out fast, without wasting time on sleep or misgivings.

But, like so many aspects of Foujita's wartime experiences, the story of this painting does not end with his passing off a picture that is both memorable and misleading. Other testimony stands in the way of firm conclusions about Foujita's feelings. In a recent television program, General Ogisu's son declared that, as a child, he had seen a second version of Foujita's *Battle on the Bank of the Halha, Nomonhan* in his family home; several other witnesses also claim to have seen this second *Nomonhan* in Foujita's studio. Since this second painting, never publicly exhibited, was lost during the war, whether it ever existed or not remains uncertain. Yet those who say they saw the second work provide enough vivid details—a velvet curtain, the artist's smirk—to make a tantalizing tale.

Foujita supposedly swore a few friends to secrecy and then unveiled for them this other, more gory picture of the Nomonhan battle scene. No blue skies to brighten the scenery in a painting that oozed death. Foujita had painted piles of dead Japanese soldiers, their bodies a feast for the flies and maggots. Through the flames of battle, Soviet tanks pressed forward unopposed, crushing the corpses underneath. "What do you think?" Foujita asked his friends, with a laugh that concealed much. "A masterpiece, isn't it? Just as long as you recognize my talent for painting in this realistic style, I'm satisfied." Since Foujita was later accused of being an unprincipled lackey of the military, his defenders have pointed to the second painting as evidence of his true, antiwar feelings.

Among Foujita's various experiences during the war years, a few definitely stand out. Such episodes do not help to clarify Foujita's state of mind but actually add to the mystery. His situation was admittedly more complex than that of other proud Japanese, since he had spent those many years as a resident of a foreign country. As soon as he came back to Tokyo, his loyalties were questioned, and gossips wondered if he was a spy for Japan's European enemies. It's certainly true that Foujita had to work harder than anyone else to prove his allegiance to Japan.

These issues make his 1941 visit to French Indochina especially thought-provoking. It was a controversial trip, too, one that caused him great trouble later. He arrived in Indochina so soon after the Japanese soldiers took over there that some people believed that he had been part of the invading force.

In July 1941, Vichy France, acceding to demands, allowed Japan to expand its occupation of French Indochina. This led to an American embargo on exports to Japan, and so began the series of events that would culminate in the attack on the U.S. naval base at Pearl Harbor. In the midst of these portentous political developments, Foujita joined a Japanese delegation bringing an art exhibition to Indochina in October. The exhibit, shown in Hanoi, Haiphong, Hue, and Saigon, was supposed to demonstrate that the Japanese would not only "liberate" conquered lands from Western rule, they would free them as well from the domination of Western culture. Asian artistic traditions would thrive instead—in particular, the traditions of Japan. The exhibition's Japanese-style works—scrolls, ink paintings, woodblock prints—by well-known contemporary masters backed up this Asian theme.

In one way, Foujita was the natural choice as a cultural liaison, since his French would be of use in this French colony. On the other hand, his renown as a Western-style artist strongly identified with imperialist France would seem to have undercut his suitability for the job. This was yet another problematical matter among the mix-ups and rainstorms buffeting Foujita during this tour.

The emancipation and uplift of an Asian population was not to be accomplished without a lot of aggravation. The energetic Japanese delegation tried to set up its exhibition in Hanoi, but its efficiency was no match for the Indochinese siesta. For four hours each day without fail, all of French Indochina, including all those setting up the exhibition, paused to take a rest. The Japanese, remembering that they were custodians of a wise, ancient culture, struggled to keep their tempers in check when the exhibition's opening was delayed six days. Because of a lack of wooden planks, they cut up logs and large rain forest timber for use in the construction. This freshly cut wood introduced a foul, fishy smell to the exhibition hall. The weather did not cooperate, either, since the unseasonable rain continued for forty days. Though nonplussed by the rampant thievery among the Vietnamese, Foujita did his best to hurry the preparations along. "At the entrance, we had them make a modern-style gate out of planks of wood and stick paper on it," he wrote. "I was struck dumb by their clumsy job."

It is impossible not to pause, once again, to consider Foujita's situation at that moment. He had transformed himself from a member of international society in Montparnasse into a stalwart promoter of Japan's military and cultural ambitions. Incredibly, while speaking French at an exhibition of Japanese art held after the Japanese military had muscled its way into French Indochina, he did not evince any strain about his new role. Others couldn't adjust as quickly, and this led to at least one moment of multicultural confusion. In Hanoi, he paid a call on Jean Decoux, the French governor-general of Indochina, who was then under Japanese military control. Decoux still had the idea that Foujita was something of a Parisian and looked forward to a relaxing conversation about life back home. This French official recognized his error when he reached out to shake his Japanese visitor's hand. Foujita, now an official representative of Japan, rejected the Western mode of greeting for the most formal of Japanese bows. The interchange got nowhere because Foujita, standing at attention, would only come forth with curt answers in French. Was he still painting cats? he was asked. "Yes, I do paint them, Your Excellency." Increasingly flustered, Decoux went on to inquire about his guest's current projects, and here Foujita apparently could not resist having some fun.

He answered very softly, "*Femmes nues* [Nude women], Your Excellency." Decoux, who could not understand exactly what had been said, repeated the sounds aloud in his own voice. He was exceedingly embarrassed when he understood the risqué words he had just uttered, and Decoux later declared that he'd never had such a comical experience.

Once the exhibition got organized, Foujita gave an introductory lecture in French about the principles of Japanese art. He urged his audience not to look for realism in the artworks on view, but instead to search the paintings for expressions of the artist's spirit. Savoring the pedagogue's role, he compared Japanese art to Japanese poetry, since both used spare images to express much feeling. A single branch of plum or a bamboo stalk, he declared, was all Japanese artists required. Here Foujita does not arouse skepticism, since his own painting style followed in this stark, suggestive tradition. You start to feel that he is going overboard when he praises Japanese artist Komuro Suiun, who follows the order of a tree's growth in his drawing, starting with the roots and working his way up to the leaves. Foujita compares this to the misguided Western artists' technique of beginning with the branches and working backward toward the earth, thus failing to make the connection between plant and ground.

There is more when a film is shown about Komuro's life and Foujita provides the commentary. "As you can see, this splendid house may be very big, but the taste is excellent. There is simplicity and, enhanced by Japanese refinement, the home has none of the showy extravagance of a grand Western house." Anyone reading this statement is at pains to stifle a hoot of dissent, since these words come out of a man whose residences, East and West, set a standard in excess.

The exhibition was most successful in Saigon, but attendance plummeted once Japan attacked Pearl Harbor. "The night before December 8,"* Foujita later wrote, "I was inside the mosquito net in a Saigon hotel and couldn't sleep at all because of the deafening roar from the airplanes sweeping one after another over the roof. My heart

---

*Because of the International Date Line, the attack on Pearl Harbor occurred on December 8, 1941, in Japan.

pounded because I knew something strange was going on. As I expected, early the next morning I saw the Chinese handbills announcing the declaration of war against the United States and Britain. I immediately ordered myself a uniform for my military duties in order to be ready to serve any time the summons came."

THIRTY-THREE

ARTIST AT WAR

When Foujita left to go abroad on research trips for his war paintings, my wife and I often went to Tokyo Station to see him off. He was given the status of a general, and he looked just like one, cutting a dashing figure in his quasi-military uniform. At one glance, you could see how pleased he was with himself. He seemed to be enjoying his little game of playing at being a soldier. This also was very much in character for Foujita.

—Hasegawa Jin

The author Ibuse Masuji was sent to Singapore as a member of an army propaganda unit the day after the Japanese seized the city from the British in February 1942.* Ibuse, renowned for humorous fictional works about the doings of ordinary Japanese, avoided direct assaults upon his characters' problems in his writing, preferring to take a more leisurely approach to grave issues. Postwar, Ibuse made plain his opposition to the war that had led the country to ruin, but he did so in writings that were warmly discursive and frequently heartbreaking. "Lieutenant Lookeast," a tale from 1950, took up the case of a former officer back home in his village after the defeat. This man is intermittently deranged, and when the psychosis takes

---

*This debacle is said to be either Britain's most humiliating defeat since Cornwallis's surrender at Yorktown in 1781 or simply its worst loss ever.

over, he can launch into military harangues or order his neighbors to bow to the east, toward the emperor's palace in Tokyo, as he demanded of his troops during the war. While poking fun at the officer's craziness, Ibuse also reveals the far less amusing reason for the lieutenant's mental disorder: he lost his mind after his authoritarian excesses caused the death of one of his soldiers. Going further in *Black Rain*, his bestselling 1966 novel about the atomic bombing of Hiroshima, Ibuse dared to combine horrors with digressions about the pleasures of fishing.

Ibuse never created fiction based on his encounters with Foujita, but he did write a reminiscence of their days together in Singapore. This essay, employing Ibuse's usual fictional techniques, takes a meandering route toward its destination, keeping outright polemics in the distance while stopping here and there to consider some human foibles. Foujita and Ibuse encountered each other when Foujita, leading a group of artists, was dispatched to Singapore to create paintings about the Japanese triumph.

Ibuse begins his essay in peacetime at the barbershop—one of his typical down-home settings—where he happens to see Foujita painting happily and singing a traditional Japanese song in a television program. The essay is Ibuse's elegy, since he writes not long after Foujita's death in 1968. From the barber's chair, Ibuse wends his way back to wartime Singapore and his memories of seeing Foujita painting and singing such a song. In no hurry, as always, Ibuse pauses to get a few laughs about another war artist who had his heart set on painting Japanese soldiers weary and covered in heavy fuel oil after their boat overturned during a river battle en route to Singapore. Exhausted soldiers filthy with black oil would not make the kind of uplifting tableau officials envisioned, and so a dispute broke out between this artist and his military handlers. Ibuse later spotted the artist's work at an exhibition and saw that the fuel oil idea had been replaced by a canvas almost completely covered with striking tropical foliage. A few spic-and-span young Japanese soldiers peered out from a small gap in the thick jungle leaves.

Foujita gave the military far less trouble, and Ibuse remembers him doing what was required with alacrity, singing and painting all the while. As editor of an English-language newspaper in Singapore, Ibuse regularly published illustrations from visiting artists, and he had heard reports about how Foujita drew swiftly on demand, polishing off a battle scene with ease. Later on, after they traveled together to Johor Bahru, Ibuse visited Foujita at an empty house that served as his studio. A soldier posed on the floor with his gun, and Foujita, to save time, drew his rough sketch directly on the canvas. During a break, he offered his tired model a cigarette and lit it for him. This kindness made an impression on the tenderhearted Ibuse, and in a scene that could have come out of one of his own stories, he observed Foujita attempting to get the young soldier to relax. The famous artist entertained his model by showing him how his own boots could be crumpled up easily into a compact shape. The young man, deadly serious about his assignment, remained standing at attention during the entire boot demonstration.

"This work is interesting, if you look closely," was Foujita's only remark to Ibuse about a painting, later known as *The Last Day of Singapore: Bukit Timah Highlands* (1942), which illustrates the city's imminent takeover by the approaching Japanese. In one corner is a Japanese soldier pointing out Singapore just ahead to a wounded comrade who will probably not live to see the triumphant entry into the city. There are other signs that Foujita, like Ibuse, preferred to present historical events as they swept across smaller and more touching human dramas. Barely visible in the distance, Foujita had drawn some Malaysians racing bicycles despite the battle in progress close by. "But Foujita did not explain any of this to me," Ibuse comments. "He just jokingly said, 'This work is interesting, if you look closely.' In a painting that presented a tension-filled story of war, he playfully inserted the bicycle race—and perhaps he was as delighted as a child?"

This painting and another of Foujita's Singapore works, *February 11: Bukit Timah Highlands* (1942), tell stories of bold, selfless exploits by Japanese soldiers, and so were just the kind of works the military sought. While they were intended for mass appeal, the paintings do not coddle the audience by prettifying the scenery. As such, both paintings have the look of war art for adults. Viewed from the distance, *February 11* also looks like the revenge of an artist who made his name on white. Mud-splashed is the overall impression from some distance away, but up closer, this very brown painting pushes the viewer into the gloomy facts of battle. The soldiers, hardly ennobled by their duties, try to press forward through a treacherous rubber tree forest, some grimly cutting through barbed wire and one bandaging a fallen man's wound. Foujita carried all his gifts into this bleakness and did not require flickers of light to guide him through. Rather, he moved across the dark landscape in his usual assured and meticulous manner, laboring over abandoned enemy vehicles, creases in uniforms, the damaged trees. In war paintings to come, Foujita returned to this congested, turgid style, as did other, less skilled war artists. The Japanese public responded to Foujita's gruesome but truthful scenes and swarmed in to see his work. (After the war, an American who saw the paintings of Foujita and others complained that the brown, jammed paintings had the look of tobacco juice.)

Ibuse ends his recollection of Foujita in Singapore affectionately, without any of the anger he directed toward Lieutenant Lookeast's fanatical nationalism. In remembering Foujita, Ibuse is in such a mild mood that he can get himself to recall war for its adventure, camaraderie, and artistic projects. The same mild frame of mind settles over some of the recollections of the artist Miyamoto Saburō, who also writes in memory of Foujita shortly after his death. Miyamoto describes the forty-five days he spent living in Singapore with Foujita, who invited him to share his luxurious living quarters, the former residence of a Dutch expatriate. His elder's dynamism sometimes alarmed Miyamoto, especially when Foujita lugged a large canvas out to the heights of Bukit Timah—the approach to Singapore crucial to the Japanese victory—in the daytime heat. Miyamoto need not have worried because Foujita had the whole canvas covered before heatstroke had any hope of overtaking him. "We would come back from our sketching," Miyamoto wrote, "take a shower and settle down for a siesta. When I went to visit Foujita after the siesta, I was often shocked to find amazing changes in a work I had seen just before."

In later years, Foujita always exclaimed to Miyamoto, "We really had a great time back then!" and there is every reason to believe he was indeed exhilarated during his Singapore stay as he rushed out in the midday tropical sun, painting, singing, collecting bomb fragments, and acquiring expertise in helmet shapes. Their residence came complete with rattan furniture, a second-floor terrace, and an Indian couple who saw to their every need. In an odd war painting, *A Soldier of the Imperial Army Arrives for the Rescue* (1944), Foujita called upon his experiences in those plush lodgings. At the left side of the painting, a Japanese soldier dashes into a colonial's home and finds a native servant tied up and gagged, presumably by her masters before they fled the conquering army. Foujita must have had every intention of conveying the required message about the cruel treatment of the native population by the Europeans and the liberation of the oppressed by the Japanese military. His sparkling depiction of the house, however, distracts attention from this main point. In wandering through the large, luxuriously appointed rooms with their European furnishings, Foujita neglected the end of Western imperialism to celebrate the joys of painting, which did not flag for him even in wartime Singapore. Seizing the chance to paint more than military boots, he lingered over the Western oil paintings on the walls (including a voluptuous reclining nude) and candleholders with sculpted cherubim, along with the former inhabitants' discarded underwear.

From Singapore, Foujita visited Phnom Penh with his group of artists, and curious crowds swarmed around them when they stopped to draw. The adulation constant, Foujita, as always, stood out from the other war artists perhaps because he wore a medal bestowed on him by Bao Dai, the emperor of Vietnam. Soldiers from that country presented arms when he passed.

Ibuse, seeking to avoid trouble, does not bring up any of the controversial aspects of Foujita's prominence. Miyamoto, too, saved his complaints about Foujita as roommate and competitor for other occasions. This time, after all, Ibuse and Miyamoto were writing in the aftermath of Foujita's death, and decorum required that they shun any derogatory observations. This is their polite way of overlooking the larger implications of Foujita's role in the war effort—and perhaps their own roles as well. Ibuse stopped midway, before he had to analyze the contents of Foujita's paintings, nor did he mention that the considerate, assiduous Foujita, who liked to stroll around in a military uniform, also drew attention to himself with shrill, nationalistic pronouncements worthy of the fictional Lieutenant Lookeast.

Ibuse's bemused way of viewing the world has much appeal, and once one is inside his consciousness, there is a temptation to linger there and assume his benign attitude—to say, in effect, everyone was caught up in the fever of the war, and artists know nothing about politics anyway. These are the excuses that one of Ibuse's narrators might offer in gentle rebuke of Foujita during wartime. In fact, such excuses are invoked by the real-life defenders of Foujita's war record, and certainly it takes little to make Foujita look uninformed and silly.

At the end of 1942, Foujita announced that he was breaking his ties with Western art. He was not alone among artists of those days in seeing the opportunity for more than military conquest in Japan's sweeping successes early in the war. In the days that followed the string of victories, not only did the end of the Western political dominance seem possible, but with it the end of Western dominance of the art world as well. "All ties with the French art world have been severed," wrote Foujita, aglow in December 1942. "From now on, the kind of art that people go to France to learn about will most likely die out. As a result, the innate dynamism of our own self-sufficient art has come to the fore." A few months later, he went even further in an astonishing article, "Farewell to the European Art World":

[Our film world] made *The War at Sea from Hawaii to Malaya*, a film which outdoes Hollywood. The Japanese film world turned away from Hollywood and was able to produce a triumph for the first time. Similarly, the Japanese art world cut off its communication with France, and with France forgotten for the first time, a great art reached perfection in wartime Japan. Following Rome and Madrid, Paris has turned into just a sightseeing spot where people go merely to enjoy famous works of art. It is no longer a place to go to learn one's craft. There's no question that the galleries owned by Jews have fallen on hard times. No longer will great artists dream about the past . . . In this great war, those who are teetering on the brink of ruin will die out, and those who stand head and shoulders above the rest will come to the fore. These are truly thrilling times when a battle to determine real ability is being waged.

Such avowals would have sounded more believable if Foujita had not, fairly recently, been practically dragged back home from France. He would have sounded more credible, too, if he had relinquished his own unbroken dependence upon European art or shown signs of moving off in a wholly new direction. But Foujita had learned much from the masterworks he had spent so much time studying in museums abroad, and those lessons remained with him, no matter what part of the world he inhabited. The Romantic artists, in particular, served his wartime needs, and their visions of historical events fired his imagination. One of Foujita's war paintings, *The Fate of American Soldiers on the Solomon Sea* (1943), looks as if it were lifted—boat shape, waves, and all—from Delacroix and Géricault.

As throngs of Japanese throughout the country flocked to see his prominently displayed war paintings, Foujita at last made the connection with the general public in his native country that he had sought for so long. Official circles also honored him. He received important prizes and assignments to paint momentous subjects—Pearl Harbor, Singapore, Saipan. He churned out these large canvases with superhuman speed. Perhaps, if so inclined, an observer might say that a glutton for publicity like Foujita should be forgiven for gobbling it all up, becoming so swollen with adulation that he put too much fervor into his war art and went to extremes in his public statements. There might also be the familiar refrain about his weakness for doing whatever needed to be done, saying whatever needed to be said, in order to remain at center stage.

Offering some of his reflections at the New Year in 1943, Foujita reported that a record-breaking one hundred thousand people had attended an exhibition of war paintings in Tokyo. He predicted that attendance would reach at least two million once the exhibit toured Japan. "Moreover, for many years to come, countless millions will inevitably be affected by these war paintings, and this must bring honor to our art world . . . We artists have all offered our right arms to the emperor. Our right arms must serve as guns, they must serve as swords." He goes on in a more exhortatory tone:

In the twentieth century, [Japanese artists] became more skilled at talking than at using their brush. Artworks were confined to limited topics. It became too easy to put food on the table just by drawing plums or peonies . . . Those were times when no hard work was required to become a big name . . . There are people now who cannot stand the sight of paintings associated with the war. Even among artists there are still many who completely ignore war paintings. Today, when the entire nation is at war, I would like as many artists as possible to paint war-related works, even if they do so all by themselves. These works will be a force in stirring up the people's belief in our inevitable victory and will be a great mission to leave to future generations.

Considered in still another way, Foujita's rhetoric might be understood as an expression of the fury he had stored up while in Paris. Perhaps he was unable to deny himself the chance to retaliate for the many racial slurs he had endured when he lived there. He had been stoned on the streets of Paris, assaulted by rowdies at a vegetable market, and called "Chinaman." Countless other incidents may have gone unrecorded. Contemplating Japanese victories, he might not have been able to stop himself from exulting in his revenge:

Years ago I was very proud to rank with the big names in French art. I used to think that French art was supreme . . . I have broken with France. I have burned my bridges and now must do some real hard work . . . It is not necessary to pay attention to France. It is not necessary for Paris to be Japan's teacher. Such a trend is emerging in our contemporary art. We don't feel a sense of gratitude when we look at art created before the war. I have the feeling that the artworks we are concerned with now, as well as the artworks that we will no doubt develop in the future, have all had their beginnings during this war. We

must throw away all art created up to now and begin our real
study . . .

Now I am working with only three or four of my fingers,
and I would like to create more, using my ten fingers. That is
how I feel . . .

As for modern French painting: the artists who drew works
inspired by French liberalism and individualism linked up with
Jewish gallery owners. Then strange international perverts from
all over the world got together and created modern art there.

In Foujita's overwrought harangues can be discerned as well the
signs of a man approaching old age and rushing, out of breath, toward
his last chance. In his late fifties, Foujita believed himself the most
gifted of the war artists. He had at hand a subject profound enough to
touch all Japanese, bring them to tears and prayer. He had disciples
who sought his counsel and firm ideas about how these young artists
should proceed. Fame already won, artistic immortality surely was at
hand:

> I feel that I now clearly understand what I have been working
> for in my more than forty years as an artist. It has become clear
> for the first time that I have worked for today. I feel deeply grate-
> ful that today I have the honor of being able to brandish my tal-
> ent and create documentary paintings which should live on for
> generations to come. I feel that I have offered my right arm to
> the nation.

By 1944, he had lifted himself into a euphoria he would never experience again:

> I want to paint perfect works which are correct in the details,
> are without mistakes in the realistic effects, and which look fine
> as a whole. I want to paint works which look good up close and
> from the distance. I want to achieve a technique which will
> make a deep impression on ordinary people and also satisfy
> artists . . . There is no one so fortunate as the Japanese artists of

today. Not only should we take pride in this, but we also must be struck deeply by the gravity of that responsibility.

There are many voices to choose from in rebuttal, but the artist Kikuhata Mokuma is unsurpassed when it comes to lambasting Foujita. Kikuhata made his mark in the art world with works thrust combatively at the establishment. Pugnacious in his writings, too, Kikuhata is not at all indulgent about Foujita painting and singing in Singapore. Nor does Kikuhata accept any psychological excuses for Foujita's behavior—the childishness, the love of attention, the memories of racial slurs, the worries about getting old. All these, Kikuhata—to put it mildly—rejects. Instead, Kikuhata pillories Foujita for failing to make the connection between his happy hours painting and the moral consequences of his finished product. For Kikuhata, there is no doubt that Foujita's excellent war paintings, painted with joy, promoted a catastrophic war.

"Ah, Paris," Kikuhata writes in *Artists and the War*, to set the stage:

For Foujita, Paris was truly his eternal lover. War is war, Paris is Paris. The capital of art, the capital of freedom, the capital of lovers—that's Paris. Foujita, who got mixed up with a bunch of incredibly optimistic French people, found himself suspended in midair, stuck in the middle of the World War. As long as Paris survived, he didn't care whether Hitler or Churchill was in power.

But not two years later, that Parisian guy "Foujita" seemed to be licking his lips in pleasure when he drew a war painting about the Japanese slaughter of French soldiers during the invasion of French Indochina.

Kikuhata has other things to say:

Foujita went mad. At age fifty-eight in 1943, he completely exploded . . . Faced with the sure signs of defeat, many artists felt deprived of their main theme and gave up war art. Foujita alone remained on the job, clinging sadistically to his subject matter without a pause. Absolutely delighted, he could paint and paint and never stop. He completed *The Last Day of Singapore* in twenty-six days, *February 11: Bukit Timah Highlands* in sixteen days . . .

And elsewhere:

They say that Foujita felt most confident about his painting *Fierce Fighting in Guadalcanal* (1944). When friends visited his studio, he was jubilant about the various poses he had drawn of the figures in the painting. They say he went to great lengths to point these out. He drew a real superman of a soldier who was stabbing someone with the military sword he had in his right hand, kicking someone else with his right foot, and, with his left hand, grabbing the chest of an enemy and throwing him around.

But, tell me, Foujita, do you know anything about war's sadness, which fills every inch of this soldier? It makes me shudder to imagine Foujita alone in his studio in his crazed state, thrashing himself about, brandishing the military sword, and studying the different moves that go into a slaughter.

About Foujita's postwar life in France, Kikuhata also has nothing but scorn:

At age seventy-three, Foujita was baptized as a Catholic. It was as if he wished to show himself immersed in repentance for his life, but even so, this can't make me feel anything for him. I don't care how much he devoted the remainder of his life to days of pious prayer. To me, it's as if Foujita, so like an empty shell of a human being, is taking pleasure in some frivolous playacting. After much debauchery and fooling around with women and fame, this smug man renounces worldly pleasure and, taking a well-worn path, appeals to Christ for forgiveness.

If such a Christ exists, then I, too, would like to have a word with him.

END IN SIGHT

After this war is over, let's start to paint pictures with the brightness of springtime.

—Foujita

I n those days, Foujita's studio was exceptionally lively," Foujita's nephew Ashihara writes of this brief period when his uncle was a leader of Japan's art world. "I can't forget those crowds of artists who used to come to ingratiate themselves with him." Ashihara admits appreciating the sausages and ham that the visitors brought back from their war journeys, but he was disgusted by those fawning throngs—Foujita's former detractors among them—and how much his uncle loved the attention:

> Around this time, an organization called Army Art Association was formed, and Foujita became the administrative head or something. He was definitely a big boss. All the artists had to belong to this group, or else they couldn't get painting supplies or canvases . . . The group decided which artists would go to the front and even where they would go. Since Foujita was the chief of this gang, he held the power of life and death in his hands and really lorded it over the artists . . .
>
> If you ask me, it was really too bad that Foujita became powerful. He liked power very much, longed for it. Once he became

powerful, he did not fear anything. He thought nothing of flaunt-
ing his status and went around saying that he'd offer his right
arm to the emperor. And further he thought nothing of harshly
criticizing famous artists who painted apples instead of war
paintings during this pivotal period.

Though his nephew disapproved of his activities, Foujita kept on
painting. He did not let up when the losses at Midway and Guadalcanal brought Japan closer to certain defeat. On the contrary, Foujita's
imagination, more overheated as Japan's situation worsened, was consumed by his ongoing projects and plans for future works. Military
calamities could not intrude upon his artistic ecstasy. "I am working on
two very large paintings of the Solomon Sea battle and the last stand at
Attu," Foujita wrote to an artist friend in 1943.

Nothing disturbs me—not the heat nor the summer showers
nor thunder. I haven't gone out since July 22. I'm pretending
to be away. Since everyone thinks I've gone on a trip to the
southern front, I'm happy to say that I don't get any letters or
phone calls or visits. I'm holed up in my studio and refuse all
invitations.

He worked fourteen hours a day and, according to his wife, rushed to
his studio while still chewing on his breakfast. He'd have finished
drawing an arm by the time she tidied up. Foujita was at first disturbed
when it became too dangerous to travel to the battlegrounds, but gradually he saw the benefits of staying put, especially at his age. He had
deprecated Western art in public, but in private, it remained his standard. "The old masters—Tintoretto, Delacroix, and Rubens—did not
go out to real battlefields to sketch. They never actually saw any war
where a horse and a naked woman descend from heaven, but humans
like them with powerful imaginations, great human beings like them,
gave the world those masterpieces." Cooped up at home, far from the
actual battles, Foujita came forth with the very brown and very passionate works that still tear at the hearts of Japanese. In case his in-
toxication needed to be confirmed, he added: "By creating these war

paintings, I feel that I have done work that has made my birth into this world worthwhile."

Last Stand at Attu is Foujita's vision of the ferocious May 1943 battle for Attu Island. Before the Americans reached the shore, their assaults from the sea and the air were so intense that the tundra broke up and flew about everywhere. The frozen cliffs were blown to bits; the island's whole topography was transformed in the process. During more than two weeks of fighting in cold and fog, most of the island's Japanese defenders were killed. Urged on by their commander, the remaining Japanese refused to surrender and vowed to fight to the last man. The men too weakened to participate in this final push committed suicide with hand grenades; Japanese army doctors killed the wounded. It is said that the surviving force, in their tattered uniforms and with their damaged rifles, looked like apparitions of death as they surged toward the Americans. "Every Japanese who could walk took part, some armed only with bayonets tied on the ends of sticks," the American side reported. At the end, only thirty or so Japanese were captured alive, out of an original force of at least 2,379. In Japanese, Foujita's painting is called *Attu Gyokusai*, and *gyokusai* (which literally means "shatter like a jewel") refers to the Japanese soldiers' suicidal fight to the death.

Fearful that the casualty figures would demoralize the Japanese public, this *gyokusai* was publicized instead as a magnificent manifestation of imperial military valor. The newspaper headlines urged citizens on: "Follow the example of the loyal souls who gave their lives at Attu!" "Get revenge for Attu!" "We hundred million together will launch an attack!" Purified and exalted, the deaths were used to inspire the public to fight even harder. Although Foujita's *Last Stand at Attu* was supposed to assist in this shoring up of fighting spirit, some Japanese took a different message from his landscape of hell. "We were preparing to fight off a possible American invasion, with brooms and such things," a Japanese professor once told me, "but when I saw this painting by Foujita, I did not feel the glory of battle but instead I smelled the horror of death. Look at the eyes—they are not looking at life on this earth." White waves beat against the harbor in the distance, but these are the only patches of light. The foreground is taken up with

the browns and blacks of the dead, the dying, and the combatants—
everything drawn with mad accuracy by Foujita. "This year I tried my
hand at the most difficult *chanbara*," he wrote to his friend, referring to
the Japanese sword-fighting bouts he had in mind when he created the
rapid hand-to-hand combat of the lunging, parrying combatants on
Attu. Those fighting in this painting, moments away from their own
deaths, have already renounced earthly dignity as they grapple amidst
the corpses.

Foujita witnessed for himself the Japanese public's reactions to the
painting:

> I saw old men and women down on their knees praying in
> front of *Last Stand at Attu* with their hands clasped together.
> I was surprised because this was the first time in my life that
> one of my works had affected people so much that they wor-
> shipped before it. I stood there by myself, amazed, as I watched
> the old people toss coins of offering in front of the painting
> and close their eyes as they said memorial prayers for those de-
> picted in the work. Of my many paintings, this one pleases me
> the most.

By the autumn of 1944, with the Japanese mainland in peril and food
shortages severe, Foujita and his wife evacuated to a country village.*
They rented the annex to the large home of the village's biggest landlord, and their bedroom also served as a studio. Kimiyo remembers that
the room, previously a storehouse for potatoes, smelled distinctly of
straw, but she also recalls her relief at escaping the hardships of Tokyo.
Foujita urged some other war artists to join him there and so established a small artistic colony. Since he had been accorded the status of
major general, he enjoyed strolling around the village in a military cape
with conspicuous golden epaulets. The villagers, much impressed by
the presence of this illustrious visitor from the city, bowed deeply as he
passed, and Foujita, inevitably, loved the attention.

*His two Tokyo studios were destroyed in 1945 bombing raids.

Their home was at the entrance to the village and so served as a central rest stop for the other artists and their families. Kimiyo recalls the nonstop guests—artists, villagers, military officials—as well as her shopping trips to the local black market outside of town. Because she had to keep these forays secret from local officials, she left at night, walking over dark mountain roads each way. She says that Foujita insisted that she also purchase goods for his colleagues. As she carried heavy bags home over the mountain paths, biographer Kondō reports, "She felt bitter about Foujita's loyalty to his friends."

The visiting photographer Domon Ken provides another view of Foujita's life in the countryside: "Their food was sumptuous," he remembers, since the villagers kept Foujita supplied with fresh vegetables and chickens. Foujita ate soups full of hearty ingredients, while the other artists subsisted on paltry fare. The village chickens nibbled at the millet and rice grains placed outside his house to dry, and the children didn't shoo the animals away. Foujita, content with his abundant supplies, merely laughed. He had no interest in rescuing food items that could feed hungry humans.

In the fall of 1944, Foujita and other leading war artists were summoned to a Tokyo meeting with the military's information bureau. Though the war news was ominous, officials insisted that new weapons would bring a change in Japan's fortunes. The defeat of Japanese troops on Saipan and Guam during the summer meant that the American troops were poised for major assaults on Japan itself. Despite such dire developments, officials called a meeting and urged the artists to continue painting works to encourage the nation to fight on.

"Miyamoto, this arm of yours is going to be important." Foujita spoke these words to Miyamoto Saburō when both men walked in the blackout darkness of a Tokyo street after the meeting and a steak dinner courtesy of the military. "The military is still telling us to paint war art, but I'm telling you now to beware. Beware! Better back off from that now." Although Miyamoto was fearful that such forbidden words would be overheard, Foujita continued: "Both of us will make use of our arms from now on . . . Yes, even if Japan is defeated, you and I won't have a problem . . . That's because we have our arms. We can draw. No matter where or when, that's all we need to be always able to put food on the table. We should be grateful that art has no borders."

And so we can assume that Foujita, in his country refuge, recognized that defeat was imminent. Although military officials at that meeting had not broached the subject, he had excellent sources of information among his family's military personnel. "Somehow once in my life," he had written to his friend in 1943, "I'd like to try to create even just one work, something which uses every last bit of my strength and tests my power to the very limit." *Compatriots on Saipan Island Remain Loyal to the End* (1945) bears the mark of an artist trying for such a masterpiece. Facing certain defeat on Saipan in 1944, the Japanese general ordered his men to fight to the last. He then committed suicide, but his outnumbered soldiers lived on to make their own suicide charges into American lines. Again, the death toll on both sides was very large. At the end, some surviving Japanese soldiers went on to their next task, gathering with Japanese residents of the island on Marpi Point, where a steep cliff looked out over the sea. Since everyone had been persuaded that death was preferable to the shame of capture by the Americans, both soldiers and civilians—some jumping, some blowing themselves up with grenades, some slashing the throats of their own children before killing themselves—perished in acts of collective suicide. In *Time* magazine, a distraught U.S. soldier described what he had witnessed:

> Down there, the sea is so congested with floating bodies we can't avoid running them down. There was one woman in khaki trousers and a white polka-dot blouse, with her black hair streaming in the water. I'm afraid every time I see that kind of a blouse, I'll think of that woman. There was another one, nude, who had drowned herself while giving birth to a baby. A small boy of four or five had drowned with his arm clenched around the neck of a soldier—the two bodies rocked crazily in the waves.

The influences of the artists Delacroix and Géricault can again be found in Foujita's *Compatriots on Saipan Island.* Delacroix had presented the plight of helpless Greeks facing slaughter by the Turks in

The Massacre at Chios (1824); in *The Raft of the Medusa* (1819), Géricault had exposed the desperation of survivors adrift on a raft off the African coast. Yet those French works had shown people in an instinctive, familiar struggle for life, while *Compatriots on Saipan Island*, with mass suicide as its theme, examines unknown emotions. Not for Foujita anymore the fury of a battle scene; this time he studies the crowd on Marpi Point as they prepare to die. His feelings thoroughly engaged, Foujita takes solace in their serenity, and his brush, too, finds its own quiet. One woman nurses her baby, another embraces her daughter in farewell, and yet another prays over the corpse of her child. The routines of life bring comfort to the last as still another figure bends over to comb her long hair. Behind her, a woman has just jumped off the cliff to tumble into the waters. The bedraggled soldiers are of little use, neither the one firing futile shots at the enemy nor the one getting ready to shoot himself. Allowing only a few outbursts to disrupt the resolve of these Japanese, Foujita shows a man staring in disbelief at the family member he has just killed. A single black-robed woman at the cliff's edge raises her arms, shrieking about a world that has brought them to this moment.

"We were about 200 meters from there," said an American soldier of Japanese ancestry after the war. He had witnessed the scene and later attested to the accuracy of Foujita's depiction. "Clutching the microphone and weeping, I shouted myself hoarse, 'Non-combatants, evacuate! Japanese soldiers, surrender like men of honor!' Thirty minutes would pass, then I'd repeat, and then another thirty minutes would pass. Nonetheless, from the trenches, Japanese soldiers wouldn't stop shooting down, one by one, those weeping children who were terrified about jumping off the cliff into the sea and were trying to run away from the arms of their pleading mothers. It was truly hell."

Because *Compatriots on Saipan Island* was exhibited just four months before the war ended, few Japanese saw it at the time. All supplies were scarce, and no photographs could be printed for mass distribution. The painting, with the determined, peaceful visages of those about to die, has been interpreted in very different ways. Some see this work as Foujita's unmistakable protest against the war; others see him adhering to official policy and showing the Japanese public that such a noble end was preferable to surrender, if mainland Japan was attacked.

Those who did see the painting in 1945 were moved to leave coins as sacred offerings. "The faces of the people who stand in front of the painting," an *Asahi* article reported, "are not looking at the painting with their eyes. Rather, they try to grasp the meaning with all the seriousness in their hearts. Some people stood before Fujita Tsuguharu's *Compatriots on Saipan Island Remain Loyal to the End* and could not stop their tears of indignation."

It was only decades after the defeat, when the war paintings that had been taken to the United States were returned to Japan, that more Japanese saw photos of Foujita's Saipan painting. By that time, opinion about Foujita and his connection to the war had swung back and forth several times. Those who felt that Foujita had been unfairly attacked after the war for collaboration with the military took this work and others as further proof that he had never supported the war's aims. "Foujita's war paintings *Attu* and *Saipan* do not whip up the war spirit, but instead tell of the misery of war," wrote the actress Nagaoka Teruko, Foujita's old friend. "Anyone who looks at those misery-filled paintings will pray that everlasting peace be granted to the people who died in the war."

There is, of course, no lack of other interpretations. The scholar Sasaki Shigeo, for one, emphasizes Foujita's status as a well-connected member of a military family, who knew quite early that Japan was not going to win. Sasaki feels that Foujita may have consciously tailored his artistic approach to suit this information, readying his reputation for conditions after the defeat. "Foujita had a sense that Japan would lose early on, and it is known that he whispered warnings about this to his artist friend. We can imagine that this played a part in the works he created at the end of the war (*Attu* and *Saipan*). Foujita skillfully made use of the requests from the military. He not only took up the heroic aspects of war, he drew works which stressed war's pain. And as time has passed, these works continue to elicit a complicated kind of sympathy from contemporary viewers."

THIRTY-FIVE

THE WRETCHEDNESS
OF DEFEAT

Ever since the China incident of 1937, eight long years of ceaseless hard work in wartime, with Japan's fate in the balance, have ended up in unconditional surrender. Every aspect of people's daily lives had been whipped into line on behalf of winning the war . . . What will happen to Japan now?

—Diary of Sutō Ryōsaku

On August 15, 1945, the Japanese emperor conceded defeat in a radio broadcast and urged his subjects to "endure the unendurable." More than 2.7 million Japanese had died in the war; additional millions were left injured, homeless, or hungry. Incendiary bombs had easily done their job, for fires engulfed whole neighborhoods of wooden structures. The atomic bombing of Hiroshima and Nagasaki brought unspeakable torments.

It took some time for normal life to resume in Tokyo, but since so many factories and buildings had been destroyed, even two years later the air was still clean and the view clear. One witness remembers standing in Ginza, where only two buildings remained, and being able to see across the "blackened plain" to Mount Fuji in the distance. In the weeks that followed the surrender, the devastated city could make no noise, leaving a stunning silence.

Although the Japanese have written again and again about the searing consequences of the emperor's words, no accounts describe

Foujita's personal reaction. It has, however, been reported that in early September he dug a hole in the garden of his country residence before the arrival of Allied occupation forces and burned materials relating to his wartime activities. He apparently had much to dispose of, since the fire continued long enough to alarm the neighbors. He advised other artists to destroy all the evidence in their possession, and at least one colleague, Ihara Usaburō, threw everything into a garden bonfire that his son can picture to this day. Foujita further readied himself for the Americans by making changes on the paintings he had stored in a trench outside his house during the war. He painted over his signature, dates of completion, and the subjects of the paintings—which had all been written in Japanese—and instead wrote "Foujita" in Western lettering. "Up to now these could only be shown to Japanese, but now I must show them to the world," he explained.

Kimiyo says that other artists began to shun Foujita immediately after the emperor's acknowledgment of defeat. Some living nearby in the countryside did not have radios, and so she and Foujita bicycled over to tell them the news. Her resentment of them began at this point, since she recalls that these artists—Foujita's close wartime associates—offered only cold greetings and refused to talk. According to Kimiyo, this group avoided Foujita from then on out of fear that his wartime eminence would get them into trouble with the Americans. The villagers, too, stepped back from Foujita, since his friendship had acquired a complicated element. This kind of treatment fed the great bitterness that Foujita came to harbor against the Japanese, a bitterness that took nourishment from many acts of treachery, real or imagined, and persisted until his death.

In October of that same year, Foujita agreed to work for the U.S. occupation.

Looking at the situation from the American point of view, as Michael Lucken writes, the recruitment of Foujita possessed a "certain logic." In cultural matters especially, Foujita's selection now seems inevitable. Settling down in a conquered land where the customs were none too clear, American occupation officials required assistance from the local population and understandably favored Japanese accustomed to Western ways. Almost immediately, the Americans decided to collect Japanese war art for a triumphal exhibition about the conquest of Japan, to be held at New York City's Metropolitan Museum of Art. They needed a Japanese to guide them around the art world and toward the paintings, some of which had reportedly been hidden in shrines and mountainsides. Americans who knew anything at all about art had heard of only one Japanese artist, and that was, of course, Foujita. His name came up, too, in the initial U.S. investigations into the whereabouts of the paintings. Soon a jeep carrying Captain Barse Miller, New York–born watercolorist and chief of the U.S. Combat Art Section, arrived at Foujita's country farmhouse.

Miller also rushed off to see Foujita because he was an old acquaintance. As a civilian, Miller had made a name for himself as a painter and muralist—his irreverent 1932 *Apparition over Los Angeles*, featuring the racy evangelist Aimee Semple McPherson, was removed from the Los Angeles County Museum of Art for being "too controversial for exhibition in a county institution." During better times, Miller had visited Foujita at his Paris studio; on a trip to California, Foujita had likewise looked up Miller and drawn some cats for his young daughter, who was appropriately named Kitty. War artists both, with ties to Paris and murals, the men had much to talk about on the day they met in the Japanese countryside. This dramatic scene cannot be imagined without seeing flushed, tense faces and the Foujitas' anxious hospitality. Miller had written in 1942 about his commitment to produce anything that would help win the war, but he apparently held no grudge against Foujita, an artist for the other side. Miller's widow told me that her husband was upset to find Foujita in "horrible circumstances" and supplied him with food and clothing. "They needed everything." For Foujita, once again, a talent for friendship proved crucial to his survival.

There are conflicting accounts about what exactly transpired that day in the farmhouse. Kimiyo says that it was the warmest of reunions between two old friends, but biographer Tanaka Jō claims that Miller closely questioned Foujita about his wartime cooperation with the Japanese military. It seems fairly certain that Miller drove back to Tokyo occupation headquarters with Foujita in the jeep and was instrumental in getting his Japanese friend official employment with the new American regime. Foujita was asked to collect Japanese war paintings for the exhibition in the United States. "This office has located and interviewed Mr. Tsuguji Fugita [sic] . . . ," reads an occupation document dated October 28, 1945, "who was head of the Japanese War Painters Society and he is considered the best qualified artist available for this mission. Mr. Fugita has indicated his enthusiasm for such a project and is anxious to undertake this mission." By the time Foujita returned to the countryside, rumors were circulating about his having been arrested for war crimes by the American soldier in the jeep. Instead, Foujita had again leapt out of the rubble to land on his feet at the center of current events.

Though the Metropolitan Museum of Art never held an exhibition of Japanese war art, a collection of 153 war paintings was eventually delivered to the Americans. There were more works by Foujita (fourteen) than by any other artist. The project, which started out with such promise, didn't keep him at the top of the heap for very long. Since Japan was abuzz with stories about American eagerness to prosecute war criminals in every field, some artists suspected that the occupation was collecting their war paintings, with the help of Foujita and others, to use as evidence against them at war crimes tribunals. More gossip had Foujita promising to undertake this job in exchange for not being prosecuted for war crimes himself.

In some quarters, there was furious reaction to this turn of events. Japan was in a state of ruin—defeated, destroyed, and occupied, with foodstuffs and other essentials scarce. And here was Foujita, who until just a moment ago had, from his well-fed and well-connected leadership position, exhorted artists to contribute war art for Japan, repeatedly writing of offering up his painting arm to the nation. This same Foujita was now waiting for official employment credentials from the American occupiers. He was sought after by the wives of U.S. military personnel who went to his studio to have their portraits painted; he also gave them painting lessons. Not lacking for food or comfortable accommodations during the war, courtesy of the Japanese military, he now was saved from scrounging because of American help.

It is true that most Japanese artists, if able, had created war art for the Japanese military. It is also true that after the war was over, very few came forward to express regret for what they had done. Yet no other artist had been so central, so productive, so passionate as Foujita. None had, like Foujita, achieved such renown for works so powerful that the public had stood in front of the canvases, weeping openly. And yes—as his defenders correctly emphasize—none had, like Foujita, inspired jealousy of the fire-breathing sort that contributed to the outcry against him. "You don't hear anything about a similar sort of hounding of people like [artist] Yokoyama Taikan, who was the head of the Patriotic Association of Japanese Art," the art critic Sawaragi Noi has said. "The acclaim and mass appeal enjoyed by Foujita, but not by others, proved to be his undoing."

In October, the artist Miyata Shigeo heard about plans for an exhibition to introduce Japanese art to the U.S. occupation. That's when the rage against Foujita hit the newspapers. Miyata had no quarrel with the exhibition itself, but found other details too much to bear. On October 14, 1945, Miyata described his state of mind in the *Asahi*:

Was I the only person completely amazed to see the names of the artists who would be assisting with the oil paintings? There they were, Fujita Tsuguji [Foujita's Japanese name], Inokuma Gen'ichirō, Tsuruta Gorō. Aren't these the very ones who, as people know, grabbed the leadership of the Army Art Association and were at the forefront in taking advantage of wartime fascism? It is not likely that artists will be declared war criminals, but if these men had any artistic conscience, this is the moment when they should be destroying their brushes and behaving in a circumspect manner for a while . . .

Who disparaged as traitors those artists who defended the sole bastion of the sacredness of art and did not create war paintings? Who were the toadying artists who twisted their own artistic natures, descended into vulgar academicism, fawned over the military, and had their pick of art supplies and other things?

And now that we have had a total shift of scene, this same bunch has the nerve to change their clothes and come dashing out at the opening curtain? When they behave like prostitutes, they not only bring shame on themselves, they disgrace all artists.

With this published complaint, Foujita, along with other war artists, understood that the transition to the new order would, at the very least, leave them battered and perhaps even sprawled upon the floor. Foujita's reply appeared in the same paper on October 25:

I refuse to accept the idea that artists, who by their natures are true lovers of freedom, are militarists. When the war broke out unexpectedly with the issuance of the imperial decree, the entire nation certainly all cooperated to bring about the war's successful completion, and along with them, many artists also carried out their obligations as citizens. Among those who made the greatest sacrifices were the artists . . . Now that all artists are also faced with the reality of the defeat, with profound humility and in good conscience, we must look squarely at the causes for the defeat and reflect. We must banish the world view constructed by the military government and the erroneous national policy taken under their leadership. We must thoroughly examine what constitutes world peace and genuine beauty, and then work with all our strength . . . Now especially, we artists must in good conscience do all we can to join together our love of Japan and our love of the world.

This was Foujita's view of his activities during the war, and he expanded upon these themes in the ensuing debates. The debates took place in public forums like newspapers, but were not forgotten at social events and on walks down the street. By any standard, Foujita's position represented a brazen turnabout. He claimed to have used his skills during the war merely as an artist toiling for his country. He had no ideological commitment to the wartime aims, the battles, the mass suicides; rather, he had been only trying to offer faithful service to his homeland. In short, he had created works of art, not political statements. It was a defense with a familiar sound, that of a technician just doing a job. Almost all Japanese, he noted, had similarly devoted themselves to the nation's military success. Now that the war was over, he should be permitted to do what all other Japanese were doing—adjust to a new state of affairs. Why blame him more than anyone else?

Indeed, Foujita had a lot of company when he completely changed his mind after the war. Overnight, much of Japan seemed to make that same transition. "The Americans arrived," John Dower writes in *Embracing Defeat*, "anticipating, many of them, a traumatic confrontation with fanatical emperor worshippers. They were accosted instead by women who called 'yoo hoo' to the first troops landing on the beaches in full battle gear, and men who bowed and asked what it was the conquerors wished." Artists, too, had no trouble adapting. "Those who just a month ago disavowed culture," the Japanese artist Uchida Iwao observed, "and wanted to organize attack battalions on our own soil are now going around yelling about culture, culture."

Foujita may have pointed to these others in his own defense, but—again—he did not in any way qualify as an ordinary Japanese. His celebrity had always set him apart, and he would not have wanted it any other way. He should not have expected to pass unnoticed into the next phase; he should not have expected to be ushered smoothly out of his country farmhouse and into the occupation's inner sanctums or over for teas with U.S. military wives. But that is precisely what he did expect. "I am the kind of technician known as an artist," he told a magazine that same October 1945, when the bitterness was already hot inside him. "Because I am an artist, I must paint everything. Like Hokusai, like Picasso, I must paint landscapes, still lifes, nudes, war paintings, and everything else . . . Japanese people are too fastidious, too timid; they think too much alike. They're good at finding fault with people, but never offer praise."

By contrast, there was the case of the poet and sculptor Takamura Kōtarō. Once Foujita's classmate at the Tokyo School of Fine Arts, Takamura had also gone to Paris, where he became enamored of Western life and art. During the war, he scuttled his admiration of Western culture for a jingoism so virulent that, after the war, a literary critic singled him out for condemnation: "Not only does Takamura Kōtarō, among many poets, bear the largest responsibility for what he personally did to the people of this country during the war, but he bears the greatest responsibility for the moral ruin of our poets as a group. That is the reason why he is a 'Class A' war criminal." By way of repentance, Takamura moved to a cabin in a snowy village in northern Japan, where he lived for seven years. Whether Takamura truly renounced his ideas cannot be determined, but he was willing to offer himself as a chastened figure in an isolated, primitive abode.

Though other artists did not choose to go to the extreme of exile to a snowy climate, most of them kept quiet and sequestered themselves at home, either remorseful about their wartime behavior or terrified by the occupation's ongoing roundups of war criminals. This was not for Foujita, whose temperament did not allow him to cower in the corner or utter words of apology. Sasaki Shigeo, scrupulous chronicler of Foujita's life, sorrowfully responds to this attitude: "Once the war ended, Foujita did not feel any guilt, and his characteristically aggressive attitude probably did not elicit sympathy from most of his artist friends who had, in their embarrassment, withdrawn from the world." Sasaki also finds fault with Foujita's detachment from his own paintings: "The patriotic sentiments expressed in Foujita's war paintings got many people involved in the war. Even though he may have been simply motivated by a desire to show off his painting skills, a work of art has an independent life apart from its creator, and that work of art itself contains ideas . . . This should have been made clear by Picasso's *Guernica*, which is also a war painting."

As official orders calling for the purge of wartime leaders were issued, the situation grew more perilous for Foujita. In June 1946, the newly formed (and all-Japanese) Japanese Art Association created a document titled "List of People in the Art World Who Should Bear Responsibility for the War." Foujita was one of the thirteen artists asked to examine their consciences and refrain from artistic activity for a while in acknowledgment of responsibility for wartime deeds. The association's charges against Foujita were particularly harsh:

> Fujita Tsuguji: In the creation of artworks, the most active, the most committed in his cooperation with the military. Also

played an active role though his writings, which argued in support of militaristic ideas. His fame in the art world and wider society lent great strength to the militaristic movement and exerted an extremely large influence upon the population at large.

The list had no actual punitive power, for it was the Americans who would finally select the individuals to be tried for war crimes. And furthermore, the list was withdrawn, for procedural reasons, a few days later. Still, even though its life was brief, this list could only alarm the artists cited and their associates. Retribution was in the air, and no one could predict the Americans' plans.

THIRTY-SIX

A VISIT IN JUNE

It happened toward evening. A servant was waiting for the rain to stop beneath the Rashōmon Gate.

—Akutagawa Ryūnosuke

This brings us to the rainy Tokyo evening and the tuna sashimi. Certain basic facts in this episode are generally accepted, and it is best to start with them. Foujita returned to Tokyo at the end of 1945 and set himself up in a new home. The artist Uchida Iwao visited him at this residence in June 1946. Uchida was the head secretary of the Japanese Art Association, the group that had just created the "List of People in the Art World Who Should Bear Responsibility for the War" with the damning accusations against Foujita. Uchida's visit most probably took place in the very brief period between the compilation of the list and its withdrawal. The two men knew each other well, and during the war, Uchida had produced paintings for the military. After the defeat, Uchida was one of the few artists who, in published articles, voluntarily expressed remorse for his wartime activities. He wrote to a friend of his disappointment with other artists who had swiftly and shamelessly adjusted to the new circumstances: "This reminds me of Dr. Koeber's comments about the Japanese as opportunists without beliefs, principles, ideas."*

---

*Raphael von Koeber (1848–1923) was a German-Russian teacher of philosophy at the University of Tokyo.

No one disputes that it was raining on the day of Uchida's visit, nor that Foujita served him sake and expertly sliced tuna sashimi.

After this, things get murky. In 1957, eleven years after the actual encounter, a journalist wrote about a conversation he'd had with a furious Kimiyo soon after Uchida's visit. She told the reporter that Uchida had visited in his official capacity as head secretary of the Japanese Art Association to declare Foujita a war criminal. Such an accusation would have incensed Foujita, who would have considered himself singled out for punishment by envious, fickle, narrow-minded colleagues. Like any person in similar circumstances, he would have realized that he was not going to get friendly treatment in Japan from then on. A logical solution would have been to escape to another country as soon as possible.

So arose the belief that Foujita had not really wanted to leave Japan after the war but that Uchida Iwao's visit left him with no other choice.

In 1968, soon after Foujita's death, Kimiyo returned to Japan from France, to bring a lock of her late husband's hair back to the land of his birth. Twenty-two years after the meeting with Uchida, Kimiyo added a new twist to her account of the two men's hours together. There was the rain and the tuna sashimi, but besides this, she claimed that Uchida had asked Foujita to declare himself the sole representative of all war artists, turn himself into authorities as a war criminal, and thus take the rap for the others.

That's where the "scapegoat" part of the incident got its start.

By 1968, Uchida had already died, and so his widow, Shizu, took up his defense. When her husband had returned home from the Foujitas' in 1946, Shizu remembered, he said nothing about any war crimes charges, nor did he allude to any scapegoat talk. He only seemed very cheerful and grateful for the excellent food he'd been served.

Kimiyo's version was accepted by some, but others strongly doubted her objectivity, her motives, her memory. The biographer Tanaka Jō wondered if Foujita had made up the whole scapegoat saga in order to present himself as a victim of the Japanese art world. That way, many Japanese would sympathize with his eagerness to leave Japan and would not blame him for abandoning his country for selfish reasons. Japanese public opinion was still important to Foujita; he never stopped caring about his reputation at home, whether he was in Tokyo or thousands of miles away.

In 1983, Uchida's biographer introduced another interpretation, temporarily dealing a setback to Kimiyo's testimony. This biographer rejected the notion that Uchida had gone over to hound Foujita out of the Japanese art world and out of Japan. "Uchida was not the kind of person who could pay a visit to Foujita with such a sense of self-importance," he confidently wrote.

Along the way, Uchida's lunch box entered the picture. Because food was not readily available in postwar Japan, anyone who took a trip away from home carried supplies along. Uchida brought his lunch box with him that day, and whether he was flustered by his errand or befuddled by the sake he'd consumed, he forgot it at the Foujitas'.

In 1999, Kimiyo's scapegoat story got a huge boost when NHK showed a television documentary on Foujita (directed by Kondō Fumito). The program definitely came out behind the idea that Foujita had been greatly influenced in his decision to leave Japan after an unnamed—though instantly identifiable—artist visited him one rainy day in Tokyo. The program promoted the notion that Foujita had been a victim, pure and simple, of his disloyal Japanese colleagues. Introducing Foujita's direct account of the story for the first time, the documentary quoted from his 1966 comments to a researcher that had never before been made public. Here Foujita categorically stated that he had been asked to assume the blame for war crimes, alone, on behalf of all his colleagues. Forty years later, he also remembered his stalwart words to the guest who made that request: "I didn't start the war, nor am I guilty of torturing prisoners of war. A fire got going in Japan and then the flames blazed up, and so I only tried my best to put this out. I don't know what is wrong with that. But if they want to call me a war criminal, that's fine. I'll submit."

"People spread the rumor that Foujita was no longer able to live in Japan because the Japanese Art Association wanted to get rid of him," artist Nagai Kiyoshi told me when I asked him about this episode. "We never ordered him to get out. Remember, it was not just Foujita's problem. All of us, to greater or lesser degrees, had cooperated with the war effort. In that way, the arts in Japan suffered a great deal. That's why I proposed that we reflect together on the whole idea of our responsibility for the war." Nagai had been thirty years old, the youngest member of the Japanese Art Association, when it was formed in 1946. He was eighty-four when I visited him at his Tokyo home to discuss his memories of the Uchida and Foujita affair. Nagai had recently undergone eye surgery, and melancholy about his vision tempered his annoyance at how the story had shifted over the decades. Still, once Nagai got started, he applied himself to the tenacious shredding of faulty arguments, a technique that he must have perfected in his activist days. We ate persimmons from his garden while he reviewed the evidence.

In an essay "Back Then and Now," Nagai has provided background details. While the Japanese Art Association did draw up a list of artists who bore responsibility for furthering the war, including suggestions for voluntary self-reflection, no official documents record a decision to declare Foujita or anyone else a war criminal, which was a far more serious offense. Nor is there anything in the records about sending Uchida, in his official capacity, to Foujita's house to convey such a charge. Also, in order to avoid misunderstandings, association members never went on formal visits by themselves, but with other members. So it is impossible, in Nagai's opinion, that Uchida went off, unauthorized and unescorted, on such a vital mission to Foujita's home.

For these reasons, Nagai at first did not even believe that Uchida had gone to see Foujita that rainy night, but the forgotten lunch box struck him as an undeniably real detail, and so he was persuaded that the two men had really met. This left Nagai to wonder, along with everyone else, about what the two artists had talked about. Perhaps Uchida went on his visit, as a personal friend, to request that Foujita publicly assume responsibility for his wartime activities, and so set an example for other artists? In the end, Nagai can, with the rest of us, only guess. "I cannot accept this idea that Uchida asked Foujita to become a scapegoat," Nagai told me. "Foujita himself made his own decision to leave Japan. He refused to play a part in the rebuilding of a democratic Japan, and so he left to live abroad."

The rain-and-tuna imbroglio developed out of the tremendous pain both Foujitas endured after the war. Friends abandoned them; he was excoriated in public forums. He believed that he alone had borne the blame for the art world's contributions to the war. To the end of his life, Foujita continued to defend his actions and his patriotism. "When faced with this terrible crisis, is there anyone among us who would not fight for our country, for our ancestors, for our descendants?" he wrote a few years before his death. "Wasn't it necessary to give up our own lives and fight with the same robust spirit as a common soldier, but in another capacity?"

The sense of betrayal festered even when he was safely out of Japan and settled in France. In his old age, Foujita continued to enumerate the wrongs done to him. For others, the facts may be hard to pin down, but for Foujita, the Uchida visit exemplified his "persecution" by the Japanese.

THIRTY-SEVEN

ENTER A NEW YORKER

I thought a great deal about revolution.
—*Harry Roskolenko*

From the Lower East Side of Manhattan (where he was born), from on board the *James Magee* (where as a young seaman he discovered Trotsky), and from New Guinea (where he served during the Second World War) came Harry Roskolenko, the next person to turn up on Foujita's doorstep. When Roskolenko arrived in 1947, Foujita probably had never been so happy to see anyone in his life.

Roskolenko, the son of a slaughterhouse worker, had joined others of his generation in the ideological skirmishes of the day. In the 1930s, he had posed as an American worker for Diego Rivera's Rockefeller Center fresco *Man at the Crossroads*, and he took to the streets to protest the destruction of the work when it was judged too radical for midtown Manhattan. Defying bourgeois convention, Roskolenko participated in a "small street insurrection" with Red Front Fighters in Hamburg and urinated into the Grand Canyon, saying, "It was a hole in the ground for rich tourists." Over the course of his international ramblings, Roskolenko had become a poet and a journalist. In 1947 he was just the sort of person Foujita needed.

Roskolenko, like so many others, knew Foujita from the old days in Paris. They had met at the Dôme when Roskolenko was fifteen and traveling around the world on a freighter. Foujita introduced the very young man to Kiki, who was, in Roskolenko's words, "comely, strident, Bohemian."

Now Roskolenko had a chance to return the favor. A full-fledged writer by 1947, he was able to visit Foujita at his Tokyo home. Roskolenko has provided a sprightly, though not completely reliable, account of the Tokyo encounter in his book *The Terrorized*. "When we arrived, Foujita was outside. His famous Parisian bangs were still there. Puckish, smiling, wiry, he had recently married his fifth wife. He purred like his celebrated cats. He looked at me, then said, 'You have grown many years since Le Dôme.'"

According to Roskolenko, Foujita had a specific task in mind. By the time of Roskolenko's visit, Foujita had been officially informed that he would not be charged with war crimes—no artists were charged— but this positive development did nothing to temper his urgent desire to leave Japan.

"I have sold only three paintings to the Americans," Foujita told Roskolenko. "They do not know of me. They do not come and so I am hungry. I want to leave. Can you get me a visa to America? Can you get me a big exhibition?"

Roskolenko had heard about some of Foujita's wartime activities, but was not fully informed about what had taken place. "During the war," Roskolenko writes, "Foujita had gone with the Japanese Imperial Army to various countries, arranging exhibitions in the occupied areas." He did inquire about whether Foujita had actually collaborated.

"Was art collaboration?" Foujita answered whimsically. "I exhibited cats, dogs, foxes—all ready to bite the enemy!" and he laughed. "But no one was eaten. They have the war trials, but they do not want me. I am not Tojo—yes? I am Foujita—no?"

Yes, he was Foujita. After all, he had taught soldiers how to paint. When they painted they did not fire bullets. And art softened the heart, we agreed. Now Foujita was asking me into his small studio, packed to the ceilings with gay canvases of his feline world.

The temperature inside the house was evidence of Japan's shortage of heating supplies. "It is very cold," Foujita said, leading the way to the studio, "so keep your shoes on." Foujita showed Roskolenko his work—Paris scenes, prewar Okinawa, Mexican peasants, Peruvians, and large screens with leaping cats, dogs, and foxes. Roskolenko says that Foujita prodded him to take those works he admired back to the United States. When Roskolenko objected, saying he could not afford to purchase even one painting, Foujita was again several steps ahead of him:

> "No, only five dollars [Foujita told Roskolenko]. No one wants these paintings. No one comes. You remember me from Paris so you come. You are a sentimental boy. Please! If you have no money, then you pay when you have—when you get back to New York. If you have a few hundred dollars now, that is enough. I paint very fast. In a month, I will have more than those . . ." and he counted out the fifty paintings in the pile on the left. "But if you buy them, I must ask one thing—will you exhibit them in New York? I would like, Mr. Roskolenko, to have another exhibition. My last one was at the Reinhardt Gallery. Oh, so long ago! *Dozoo!* Maybe 1930? You can arrange it for me, please?"

Roskolenko tells of leaving Foujita's house with his jeep full of paintings and of eventually completing his mission. "I did what Foujita asked of me—an exhibition at the Kennedy Gallery later that year and a visa for him to enter the United States, the first one for a postwar Japanese. I had become a forced collector of fifty Foujita paintings and a dedicated man."

In September 1947, at the Kennedy & Company Galleries in New York City, Roskolenko did arrange to show twenty-eight of the Foujita works he had hauled back from Tokyo. Two years after the end of the Second World War, paintings by Japanese artists were not the most welcome commodity in the United States, and Roskolenko grappled with the realities of the marketplace. He wrote a press release, emphasizing Foujita's Parisian fame and eagerness to return to France, while carefully avoiding mention of any questionable achievements during the war. Roskolenko apparently succeeded in soothing some qualms, since certain U.S. journalists became convinced of Foujita's negligible contribution to Japan's war effort. "The war years," wrote *Time* magazine, "which Foujita spent painting hack combat pictures for the Japanese Government (at $33.76 per month), had turned his grey bangs a snowy white." Among the exhibition's cats, nudes, and landscapes was a portrait of Kimiyo as a mermaid, showing Foujita's lurch toward the land of fantasy, where he found more comfort than in his real circumstances. The reviews were good, welcoming back a well-known artist after a long absence from the art scene. "The ink still seemed to spit, hiss and whisper off the tip of [Foujita's] brush," according to *Time*.

Roskolenko had success with the media, but other elements proved to be beyond his control. When no works sold, Roskolenko blamed Yasuo Kuniyoshi, a Japanese artist who had made his home in the United States since 1906. During the war, Kuniyoshi had endured many hardships. He was proclaimed an enemy alien, was subjected to house arrest, and had his bank funds impounded. To prove his loyalty to his adopted country, he twice gave talks that were transmitted to Japan on U.S. shortwave radio broadcasts, urging the Japanese to stop the war. Although once a friend of Foujita's, Kuniyoshi was not about to let a former friendship get in the way of his opposition to the show at the Kennedy Galleries. "Kuniyoshi, whom Foujita had befriended years before, attacked Foujita," Roskolenko wrote. "He called the old man a fascist. He also called Foujita a Japanese imperialist and an expansionist, who had marched, as a professor of art, with the Emperor's troops into Indochina in 1941."

Roskolenko writes that he was forced to turn to a dealer specializing in real estate and bird feathers, who took the lot of paintings for a song. Surviving sales records do not completely corroborate Roskolenko's account of the transaction.

Foujita, who saw the deal differently, later said that he hadn't received a penny from the exhibition.

THIRTY-EIGHT

BONDS OF FRIENDSHIP

The government notice came to the center that all interned Japanese would move to Jerome Relocation Center in Arkansas. The time had come when we were forced to ride in old, old trains that had been out of use for many years. Fresno to Arkansas was a long way to go.

—*Henry Sugimoto*

Although his show at the Kennedy Galleries ran into some trouble, Foujita was fortunate in other ways. Word of the exhibition reached Henry Sugimoto, who was, like Kuniyoshi, a Japanese artist living in New York City. An old friend, too, Sugimoto was not one to be bothered about Foujita's wartime doings. After Sugimoto tracked down Foujita's Tokyo address, the two Japanese artists resumed a correspondence begun in 1933 and interrupted by the war. Only Foujita's side of the correspondence has been made public, but these letters leave no doubt about his desperate, near hysterical wish to leave Japan. Foujita insisted that he bore no responsibility for the war and had created war art only because of military pressure. In his letters to Sugimoto, he raged about fellow Japanese artists, describing them as monsters jealous of his international reputation. They wanted to put him down, hound him, prevent him from leaving Japan. Trapped in a world that had shrunk suddenly, Foujita felt himself pursued by petty-minded enemies.

"I was surprised," Foujita wrote around 1966, recapturing the mood of those days, *"that those I had been closest to in the past, my friends especially—practically everyone—turned against me and betrayed me. Those I had trusted, all of them, behaved badly."*

Sugimoto also had a lot to complain about. Born in Japan in 1900, he had arrived in the United States at age nineteen and soon set about becoming an artist. After graduation from the California College of Arts and Crafts, Sugimoto went to Paris in 1929, where he seems to have been one of the few artists in the world who did not run into Foujita. Summoned home to help his family during the Depression, Sugimoto had a successful exhibition in San Francisco, and this led to a contract with the Courvoisier Gallery—Foujita had a show at this same San Francisco gallery upon his return from Latin America. It was there that he met Sugimoto for the first time. Sugimoto's work attracted so much notice at his own show that the Museum of Modern Art in New York City contacted him about an exhibition. He turned down the offer because of other shows scheduled in California. To his lasting regret, Sugimoto knew nothing about the New York art world and had never heard of the museum.

Sugimoto's reputation was growing when Japan attacked Pearl Harbor in December 1941. While this put an end to his plans for the future, he was certainly not alone. Along with approximately 120,000 Japanese-Americans sent off to internment camps, Sugimoto and his family were incarcerated for more than three years. He had previously been a painter of landscapes, but vistas of Yosemite did not suit a barracks in Arkansas. During those years and after, Sugimoto filled his canvases with scenes from life in the camps—confused children, the communal washroom, sons going off to war—apparently never getting over what had been done to him and others.

Once Sugimoto was released in 1945, he, along with his wife and daughter, decided to start again in New York City. "I think my father did become melancholy later," Sugimoto's daughter, Madeleine, told me. "He felt that he had made wrong decisions, that he should have done certain things earlier, before the war. 'I missed my opportunity,' he said, with real disappointment. But he never expressed real negativism about what had happened to him. Maybe he kept it inside him, and I didn't hear it or sense it. But he kind of looked ahead and decided to pursue his art in other ways. I can't say that he carried a sense of bitterness. Maybe he did for a short time. But it was more a sadness or a disappointment that my father felt."

"Some Occupation officers went off with my work," Foujita wrote later, remembering his postwar travails, *"eagerly helping themselves to my paintings. Soon another person, acting fast, took it upon himself to hold an exhibition of my works in America. He kept this a secret from me and seems to have made a big profit."*

Beginning in 1948, Foujita sent Sugimoto plaintive, lengthy requests for help, including a barrage of information about what had to be done to get him an exit visa out of Japan. Foujita also told Sugimoto of his continued role in current events in Japan. When, for example, it was announced that Foujita was not on the purge list,* newspapers made that their biggest story of the day. The radio also broadcast the report six or seven times so that everyone in Japan, Foujita noted, knew that he had been cleared of wrongdoing during the war. Foujita writes that from the beginning he had never doubted his innocence, and anyway, the Way of Heaven always knew the truth. The Way of Heaven, however, could not get him a visa, and that's why Sugimoto was essential.

There could have been no better champion than Sugimoto, who dedicated himself to getting the importunate Foujita out of Japan. By then, Sugimoto would have had few illusions about either the American or the Japanese government and so had no firm loyalties to be pulled asunder as he went about this task. It is a combination to be contemplated: the Japan-born American resident Sugimoto, who had been stripped of his civil rights and his livelihood by the American government, and Foujita, who considered himself stripped of his reputation by perfidious former friends. Both men had acquired a grim understanding of the world, and presumably, little could surprise them. In New York, Sugimoto asked Kuniyoshi for help with Foujita, but was refused. Sugimoto next teamed up with Harry Roskolenko, and between

---

*Distinct from the category of those accused of war crimes, people who were believed to have cooperated with the war effort in some capacity were barred from public office—purged by the U.S. occupation.

them, they tried to get Foujita a guarantor and promise of employment, requisites for obtaining a visa to enter the United States. Foujita, in his frenzy of scheming to get out of Japan, was ready to live in New York for a while before going to Paris.

"You also should go to Paris at least once," Foujita advised Iwasaki Taku, a young artist who visited him in Tokyo after the war. *"That's a city that loves and nurtures artists. You really must go . . . Of course, I am going to Paris too. No matter what the difficulties are, I will overcome them . . . The Japanese art world is awful. I am totally shocked at how artists have changed since the end of the war. I did so much for them during the war and now not a single one of them comes to visit me."*

If you think about Japan's chaotic cultural and political atmosphere, with "democracy" and "peace" suddenly getting all the attention, if you next think about an economy in utter disarray, with old currency and old fortunes gone, if you think about the discredited Japanese art establishment and the rise of unruly new voices, and if you add to these the loneliness of a sociable, once-influential artist quickly pushed to the sidelines, then Foujita's volatility is understandable. On the city streets, signs of the war's aftermath were everywhere—the shortages, the skyrocketing black-market prices, the disabled former soldiers in white with their begging bowls. Foujita had more to contend with than just the stigma of his wartime activities.

Those who knew Foujita well could not miss his agitated state. His nephew asked him to create the sets for a Tokyo performance of *Swan Lake*, one of the rare full-scale productions of the ballet outside of Russia in those days. In an unconfirmed tale, Foujita sounds like his old self when he boasts that he will do a better job than Diaghilev's Ballets Russes and the Bolshoi. The brashness did not last long, for when he undertook another stage commission, he was unable to control his temper and often shouted at the others in French.

His art gave more telling proof of the strain. If he had created a work like *My Dream* (1947) during another period in his life, he would have provided a serene background for the sleeping nude so peaceful in repose. But in 1947, Foujita would not allow his subject the gift of restful dreams. Arrayed around the nude in *My Dream* is a rapacious circle of cats, dogs, wolves, rats, and rabbits, all drawn with his usual care as well as with unusual nastiness. Though dressed in human clothes, these animals are Foujita's most beastlike, and with their hungry, wicked faces, they seem to be planning to consume the woman. Foujita probably would have said that he understood her predicament, since recently he had also gained experience at being clawed to pieces.

"*Some of my colleagues,*" he wrote in his later account, "*had failed in their attempts to entrap me as a war criminal and thus consign me to oblivion in the art world, and so they made secret allegations against me at the French consulate and tried to prevent me from getting permission to go abroad.*"

Before appealing to Sugimoto, Foujita had actually made attempts to leave Japan via another route, by applying for a visa to France in February 1946. After many months passed without any action being taken, he learned that his request had been indefinitely shelved at the French consulate. In the years to come, Foujita stuck to the view that his visa had been stalled because enemies in the Japanese art world had spread those slanders about him to French authorities. Others dismiss this kind of thinking as a mark of Foujita's explosive mental state, with too much solitude stoking his anxieties. The French, after all, had reasons of their own to delay his visa, since many in France were not keen to welcome back their former enemy's most prominent war artist.

Whatever the reason for the delay in the application process, the story of Foujita's attempt to leave for France and his eventual failure was reported by Japanese newspapers. With the appearance of such headlines as "Paris Gets Revenge on War Artist Foujita," he became convinced that journalists, too, were pleased to sabotage his departure plans. On top of this, there was gossip about the money he'd made from his New York exhibition. Since all foreign currency transactions were subject to occupation rules, Foujita felt obliged to quash reports of any illegal overseas sales. "If I could go abroad, I would like to, since I have lived there for many years," he told a reporter. "But I'm not thinking of selling my paintings for that purpose. Because of present world conditions, the time is not yet ripe for my departure for France." (In his letters to Sugimoto, Foujita alludes to a possible agreement between himself and Roskolenko whereby Roskolenko retained one thousand American dollars made from the New York exhibition, to be given to Foujita after he left Japan. Whether Foujita ever received any of that money is not known.)

While hostile news items mocked Foujita's hopes, he continued to ready himself for an exit, trading his cash for more easily convertible and transportable diamonds and jewels. In October 1948, Foujita was further demoralized when the artist Ogisu Takanori succeeded in getting a visa for France and thereby became the first Japanese artist to return to Paris after the war.

"I'm disgusted with these artists who are constantly fighting with each other," Foujita complained about his Japanese colleagues to Iwasaki. *"They don't argue about art. They fight over petty things like territory or power. I'm sick and tired of the art world. Why can't they get along with each other? They're not artists, they're all politicians. They want to create a troop of followers, expand their power, and become the king of the mountain, issuing orders."*

Finally, Foujita decided to give up on France for a while and take the detour to the United States. It is more proof of Foujita's charm and fame that he had managed to form close bonds with influential U.S. occupation officials. "It was said that their relationship was, from the start, that of artist to artist, transcending national boundaries and transcending matters of love and hate," wrote Yamada Shin'ichi, a Japanese artist who also worked for the occupation. Because of his American contacts, Foujita claims to have been able to produce a variety of etchings and also Christmas cards for occupation officials that were sent to General MacArthur, President Truman, and the Japanese emperor.

His most useful new friend was Frank E. Sherman, civilian director of an occupation art program and eager Foujita admirer. About thirty years younger than Foujita, Sherman was from Cape Cod, Massachusetts, and had studied art in the United States and Paris. He had not met Foujita in Paris, but he did catch a glimpse of him at the Dôme in 1939. Toward the end of 1945, the star-struck Sherman arrived in Tokyo, where he was in charge of projects like printing the Far East editions of *Newsweek* and *Time*, supervising Christmas decorations, and making posters for football games—all to help Americans entertain themselves in Japan. Arriving in his yellow station wagon and equipped with gifts of Scotch whiskey, cheese, and cigarettes, Sherman finally met Foujita face to face at his Tokyo studio. In a display of exquisite manners, Sherman also brought a letter of introduction from another Japanese artist.

Sherman need not have bothered with such formalities, since Foujita would have recognized a godsend when he saw one, even if it did not come bearing gifts. Soon Sherman was facilitating Foujita's overseas correspondence by letting him send and receive letters through his own military mail. This courteous and accommodating American fan seems to have taken charge of organizing Foujita's application for a visa to the United States.

Sherman also looked out for himself, accumulating an extensive collection of Foujita's works during this period. On one occasion, Foujita heeded Sherman's artistic advice and replaced the bleak, rocky setting for the three nudes in *The Three Graces* (1946–48) with a cheery field of colorful flowers. "Come now, the war's over," Sherman told Foujita. "Life isn't all that bad."

"We had also accumulated a collection of unusual home furnishings," Foujita recalled later. *"We got rid of everything, passing them on to people for a pittance. I still think about how painful this was to my poor wife . . . We didn't leave a single thing in Japan."*

Foujita went into hiding several months before his departure for the United States, fearful that nosy reporters or a vengeful acquaintance would wreck his travel plans again. Once he received his visa for the United States, the French consulate finally got around to also granting him a visa. Since Foujita had by then secured teaching positions at the Brooklyn Museum of Art school and at the New School, he decided to proceed as scheduled to New York City. His wife's visa had been delayed, and so Foujita departed from Tokyo by himself, taking a Pan American flight on March 10, 1949. In a smart checked jacket, he took his leave of his homeland, never to return. His parting shot was not the last Japan heard of his anger: *"Artists create paintings. Artists shouldn't have any work other than paintings . . . I pray that the Japanese art world will come up to world standards . . . I bid farewell to all in Japan. To everyone in the art world, I say, Don't fight with each other and be well."*

THIRTY-NINE

IMPERFECT REFUGE

Since Foujita's arrival in America last spring he has produced an astounding number of highly realized, elaborately delineated compositions that reveal not only amazing dexterity but suggest a new direction for him.

—Art Digest, *November 15, 1949*

feel free. I can enjoy my life so much. Every day I discover many wonderful stimulus." After he reached New York City, Foujita continued to compose letters. This time he wrote to Frank Sherman back in Tokyo, to inform him about his progress in the New World and to urge haste in getting Kimiyo her visa: *"New York is unexplainable great city."* Transplanted to a hotel on West 61st Street in Manhattan, Foujita changed from the pleading, nerve-wracked correspondent of the letters to Sugimoto into a liberated and hopeful tourist on his own in the big city. He had to write to Sherman in English, and his messy syntax adds a helter-skelter zest to his prose. Foujita interspersed his English with delightful illustrations of himself in Manhattan, gamely trying out a General Electric automatic iron for the first time or bungling the fare on the bus: *"To-day was wonderful fine day. I went to fifth av, and the first time I saw Easter's annual parade."*

Roskolenko and Sugimoto had gone to meet Foujita at the airport upon his arrival; Foujita is said to have tearfully told Sugimoto, "I will never forget what you have done for me." Madeleine Sugimoto was fourteen in 1949, and she remembers the visits of her father's new friend from Japan. "Mr. Foujita seemed like such an international person in his behavior," she told me. "And there was something about the way he moved and talked. You know, I have in my mind an image of Japanese men—and this certainly did not seem like Japanese body language. It was just different. He used to hum songs. I don't know, he just did things that you didn't expect a Japanese man to do. He just wasn't that formal.

"Maybe because he was with my father, he felt comfortable. It seemed to me that he was not 'a Japanese man from Japan.' I really only had contact with 'Japanese men from Japan' when I saw them walking on the streets or in restaurants. So I'm just saying that as an observation. Mr. Foujita wasn't that way at all. He wore his clothes in a different way. He wore a tweed jacket and shirts that were open at the collar. He didn't wear a necktie. He was very informal. I suppose those little bits of things lead me to say that he was much more international. He didn't give off that feeling of being a Japanese person even though physically he looked like one—no, really he didn't look that Japanese, either." Judging from the photographs, Foujita's kappa hairstyle had not yet fully grown back. But even so, Madeleine says, "His hairstyle was distinctive."

Madeleine remembers her father and Foujita strolling along Riverside Drive together, near the family's modest fifth-floor walk-up on West 100th Street. She was much impressed by Foujita's continental style, for whenever they met, he kissed her on both cheeks, in the French way. "Mr. Foujita was very, very sweet and gentle. But also very playful. One time, my mother gave him a banana to eat, and he peeled it, and then he ate it. I happened to be in the room. He dropped the peel on the floor. Maybe he was doing this because I was there. To get a rise out of me. I said to my mother, 'Mr. Foujita has terrible manners. He just dropped that banana peel on the floor.' My mother said, 'Oh, no, he's playing with you. Really, he's not that kind of person.' You know, he was that way. He liked to relate to people in different ways."

As the weeks passed, Foujita visited Sugimoto more frequently for emergency consultations. Madeleine, a Japanese-American brought

up in the United States, did not understand the adults' Japanese conversations, but she remembers the recurrence of the word *jama*, "hin-
drance." Of *jama*, there was plenty, and Foujita does not seem to have
been prepared for these problems. According to Foujita, his principal
adversary was Kuniyoshi, who had spread the word about the arrival of
this Japanese "militarist" and "collaborator." Almost immediately, the
Brooklyn Museum of Art school became skittish about its commitment to employ Foujita as a teacher. *"Mr. Peck [director of the Brooklyn
Museum of Art school] is so nice man and very sympathetic for me, but he
afraid around his reputation,"* Foujita wrote to Sherman. Foujita never
did teach there, or anywhere else in New York.

Unable to recognize any genuine principle in Kuniyoshi's attitude,
Foujita told himself and others that Kuniyoshi was only trying to prevent a competing Japanese artist from settling down in his territory. Yet
Kuniyoshi's rebuff rankled to the end. "He disliked and shunned me,"
Foujita wrote some twenty years later. He added, with more satisfaction than accuracy, "Later on, Kuniyoshi's works were no longer shown
at the Museum of Modern Art. I heard he was put on the Communist
blacklist and died soon after, not having had a spectacular career. He
was a very small-minded, cautious person. Many people in New York
also disliked him. A pitiful person."

In May 1949, Kimiyo finally arrived in New York, and this bright-
ened Foujita's spirits. He sent Sherman an illustration of the reunited
couple sitting in front of their new television set watching a wrestling
program. *"The other day we went at the Madison Sq. Garden to look the
Rodeo Cowboy show, it was so wonderful and we find so many nice boys
in the show . . . Every day and night we are now in T.V. at home. Kimiyo
is afraid of Wrestling. I am so exciting."* With Kimiyo serving as his as-
sistant, Foujita worked hard to prepare for a show at the Mathias
Komor Gallery in November. According to the exhibition pamphlet,
Foujita had created the forty paintings and drawings during his eight
months in New York. The works make plain that his mind was already
elsewhere, since he painted scenes from cultures far from Manhattan,
honoring the French fables of La Fontaine or celebrating the beauty of
a Spanish woman in a lace mantilla.

Café, part of the exhibition, has become one of the most ubiquitous
of Foujita images, widely available as a poster. Appealing to lovers of

Paris banished to the outback and to the brokenhearted everywhere, the picture presents a woman in low-cut black brooding in a French café. This café interior, with authentic wine, waiter, and crumpled newspaper rack, has been cobbled together from the artist's memories of such places, then almost ten years old. The years have taken the sting out of those visions, and in his longing to be back on one of those padded café seats in Paris, Foujita surrenders to clichés. The woman at the table is preoccupied with a private thought, as her wine glass, pen, and ink wait beside her. She pauses over an ink-stained letter on the table, and as a sign of her romantic woe, the sheet for her reply waits blank before her. The white used for the woman's skin and elsewhere again revives Foujita's old painting technique, underscoring perhaps his wish to return to the old days in Paris as well as to his need to make money from a tried-and-true style. An attractive work, with much commercial value, *Café* is an example of Foujita sentimentalized, which is not necessarily Foujita improved.

Time generally hailed Foujita's return, calling the exhibition "one of the year's slickest shows," but noted that the artist, more subdued than on previous visits, greeted visitors "with a slight bow, a miniature smile, and a small, limp hand . . . It was not easy to connect the gentle and sedate old Japanese with the Foujita of old." *Time* and the gallery visitors most appreciated Foujita's animals—among them, a roomful of gluttonous foxes and wolves in human clothes. "No living artist could match his rendering of cats in action, or endow them with such a storytelling variety of expressions." Another review also noted Foujita's diminished vigor: "A more recent type of work includes portrait heads of little girls whose anemic, porcelain-like faces stare listlessly out at the world."

Although ravenous animals dismembered fish and grabbed at frogs in Foujita's pictures inside the gallery, the real commotion took place on the sidewalk outside, where Ben Shahn, along with a group of other artists, had organized a demonstration against Foujita. Signed by more than fifty artists, the petition presented to the gallery offered the following assessment of Foujita as

> the fascist artist who lent himself to lying and distortion in his painting to further the ends of the Japanese militarists . . . He was instrumental, as head of the Japanese Patriotic Art Assn.,

and the Japanese Army Art Assn., in the suppression of Japanese artists who refused to submit to the dictates of the Japanese military fascist government.

A newspaper report on the incident went on to describe Foujita's wartime activities, singling out his most anti-American works:

> His most successful and popular painting was "Raid on Pearl Harbor," done from an aerial photograph . . . Other paintings which won him prizes from the government and Japanese art associations included "The Last Day of Singapore" and "Battle in New Guinea," the last a violent scene of Japanese soldiers bayoneting American troops.

Aside from this article in *The Daily Compass*, a small left-wing newspaper that featured a column by the writer I. F. Stone, the protest received no other notice and so was not considered big news in Manhattan. Foujita, however, appears to have taken fright from the uproar and resigned himself to the impossibility of staying in New York. It had become another city where he would always be marked as a war artist. Nothing seemed to go as planned, since most of the diamonds and jewels he had purchased in Japan turned out to have little value. Foujita, at age sixty-three, would still have to depend on his production of artworks to get along. Avoiding others, he worked continuously on paintings to sell in Paris.

His stamina held, and on January 27, 1950, he and Kimiyo left for France.

FORTY

DOORS CLOSED

We Japanese considered Foujita's change to French citizenship splendid proof of his ability to live anywhere in the world, an act possible because of his personality. But wasn't he really just a traveler who didn't belong anywhere? A life that constantly requires the spotlight seems to meet such a fate. His painting Last Stand at Attu *and* Paris *had brought him into the bright light. He hoped that his change of citizenship would bring him the bright lights once again.*

—Nomiyama Gyōji

Although I knew that Foujita had chosen to retire from city life in his last years, when I visited Villiers-le-Bâcle more than thirty years after his death, I found this French village a strange choice for his country home. Villiers-le-Bâcle is picturesque and historic, but at first glance too empty and out of the way for a man who had once required constant companionship. The detailed maps Foujita drew for prospective visitors, accompanied by the lengthy instructions, now made sense to me, as did the reluctance of some friends to trek out to see him. Kajiyama Miyoko, who routinely made the trip from Paris for Sunday dinners, remembers the quiet and Foujita's enjoyment of the birds in the garden. She also remembers being served only Japanese food without any alcoholic beverages. "He had a life with many ups and downs. It wasn't very peaceful."

Foujita and Kimiyo became French citizens in 1955, emphatically severing their ties to Japan, and four years later they both converted to Catholicism in a highly publicized ceremony witnessed by a large crowd in Reims Cathedral. Upon his baptism, Foujita took the name "Léonard," in honor of Leonardo da Vinci. Kimiyo became Marie-Ange-Claire. Once Léonard and Marie-Ange-Claire Foujita moved to Villiers-le-Bâcle in 1961, they worshipped at the sixteenth-century church just down the street from their house, and the neighbors attest to their religious ardor. Until recently, Foujita was buried in the church cemetery.*

"He personally worked on the design for the renovation," the guide told our group as we toured Foujita's country residence. Donated to the region by Foujita's widow, Marie-Ange-Claire/Kimiyo, the home, now "La Maison-Atelier Foujita," was opened to the public in 2000. "This was an eighteenth-century farmhouse. He turned the former wine caves into regular rooms." Foujita retained such traditional features of a French country home as the wooden window shutters, but looked to Spain for the carved doors and some of the furniture. He made the stone reliefs himself.

From the street, the rustic look of the original building has been preserved in the neatly restored cement and stone façade. The third story and the large windows of his studio are visible only from the garden in back, where Foujita fed the birds and admired his flowers. With their exposed ceiling beams, the rooms have a comfortable informal feeling, providing ample space for cherished items from around the world; in the kitchen—quite up-to-date for those days—French cooking pots are stored along with the Japanese bowls and electric rice cooker. The studio contains not only painting materials but also evidence of his many other projects—a sewing machine, handmade picture frames, dollhouses. As Foujita's final retreat from the center of activity, the house gave him an excuse to show off his handiwork, and

---

*After his death, Foujita was buried in Reims. In 1971, Kimiyo decided to have his remains exhumed and transferred to the cemetery in Villiers-le-Bâcle, where she lived. René Lalou, the head of Mumm champagne, lodged a formal protest with legal authorities, stating that Foujita had expressed the wish to be buried in the chapel he designed at Reims. The ruling backed Kimiyo, and Foujita's remains were exhumed with much secrecy, and his zinc coffin transferred to Villiers-le-Bâcle. In 2003, it was announced that Kimiyo had discovered a diary entry written by Foujita indeed expressing his desire to be buried in Reims and so his remains were transferred once more, this time to the chapel in Reims (*Le Monde*, August 21, 1971; *Asahi shinbun*, October 7, 2003).

there are samples everywhere, from the ceramic tiles with his own de-signs to the bold striped curtains. It is almost as if Foujita, fed up with human beings, preferred to turn his attention to interior decoration.

Clearly, Foujita tried to participate in French country life with his rough, worn dining table and a pail—his well-known signature painted across it—to carry fresh milk from a nearby farm. "Oh, Foujita was a warm person," a French neighbor recalled that autumn day of my visit. "He liked to speak to ordinary people. He liked the simplicity of the countryside." Still, the fresh village air did not wholly soothe him, and so the house throbs with the emotions of a Japanese artist longing for home. From the large collection of Japanese paintbrushes and other Japanese objects in the studio to the records of traditional Japanese ballads (which brought tears to his eyes, his wife said) to that Japanese rice cooker in the kitchen, the nostalgia for Japan is more notable than the French decor.

The letters Foujita continued to write to Henry Sugimoto in New York City complete the picture of a man who could not forget the country he had left behind. No longer did Foujita implore Sugimoto to get him out of Tokyo; instead, he wrote about bringing more of Japan into France. Repeatedly, he wrote to ask Sugimoto to send azuki beans, miso, pickled plums, and other Japanese food supplies unavailable in France at that time. He was delighted to have collected the ingredients for a homemade sukiyaki dinner. Foujita also wrote to Sugimoto about his distrust of people in general and Japanese in particular, and about his withdrawal from society. These letters, taken together with his joy-ous receipt of the latest shipment of *hijiki* (a kind of seaweed), leave the impression that Foujita did not become a French country gentle-man in Villiers-le-Bâcle but rather a Japanese artist in exile.

Foujita, whose verve had once had the same impact on Paris as the tango and who had made friends wherever he went, spent the last years of his life avoiding people. After he removed himself from the crowds, his art took unexpected turns, including portraits of children. Notable for their complete lack of innocence or charm, Foujita's chil-dren are peculiarly burdened with extended foreheads like those seen on aliens in fiction. These vapid children, with their swollen heads, have their distinctiveness, for no one else drew such foreheads or expressionless eyes, but his reputation gained little from this type of originality. His line grew thicker, a result of failing eyesight.

Foujita also liked religious subjects, especially after his conversion, and in his canvases and frescoes, he paid attention to the folds of the garments or hovering angels' wings. When he was almost eighty years old, he received funding from René Lalou, the head of the Mumm champagne firm, to construct a chapel in Reims. "I built this chapel to atone for eighty years of sins," Foujita said, and spent three months executing 1,076 square feet of frescoes; he painted himself and his wife in among the witnesses to Christ's crucifixion. He designed the chapel structure, the stained-glass windows, and almost everything else. "It was thanks to God," he said, "that I could devote myself to this work without becoming exhausted."

In 1965, Foujita received a manuscript about his life and work by the Japanese researcher Natsubori Masahiro. He sent back extensive comments on the text, which have been included in the published book and make for sad reading. Foujita had already made similar attempts at self-defense, and so a sense of fatigue mingles with the grievances. He rehearses, yet again, his view of his dastardly Japanese colleagues, their attempt to get him declared a war criminal, and their interference with his attempt to obtain a visa out of Japan.

Foujita also reveals that his troubles over the war did not end when he returned to France in 1950. Again, he should have anticipated the scrutiny he would face, since France had investigated its own wartime collaborators and would have also been sure to investigate him. About fifty journalists met him upon his arrival in Paris, and he was grilled about reports that he was related to major Japanese war criminals. He was obliged to explain that there was a connection through his brother's wife, but no direct relationship. He was next asked about his notorious trip to Indochina just after the Japanese occupation: Was he the same Colonel Fujita who had beheaded several hundred French prisoners? He replied that they'd mistaken him for someone else, saying, "I was just an artist accompanying the military, lowlier than a common soldier, ranking below the military dogs and pigeons." When he grew annoyed at the queries, a journalist friend intervened to help, and a small brawl with the other reporters ensued. So began Foujita's arrival in France, where the debate about his war record continued.

"I'm a person who doesn't care what people say about me, good or bad," he wrote to Natsubori:

I dislike falsehoods. I don't want to distrust people. But increasingly, times have changed for the worse, and I find that I must distrust people. It has become necessary to distinguish between genuine truth and falsehoods. The times are indeed unpleasant. Socializing with people has become fraught with danger. I've increasingly come to think that I can have my time for myself if I live isolated, away from the distractions of the world. This is my real feeling now. And so, I've removed myself from Paris and live in an isolated village with my doors closed. I haven't abandoned the world. I've just distanced myself from it.

To the end, Foujita kept to his industrious habits, producing in quantity. Sales were good, and there were exhibitions in France and other countries. Though he fumed about his treatment by the Japanese, they became excellent customers. A large number of his works were sold through galleries in Japan, and with their increasing affluence, Japanese tourists in Europe eagerly purchased Foujita's paintings.

Before his death, Foujita sought treatment at a Swiss hospital, and Kajiyama Miyoko went to visit him there. She was not aware of the seriousness of his illness, and though he was dying, Foujita did not want to upset her. In his hospital room, he wore a flashy Japanese fisherman's coat covered with images of fish and the sea. "An ordinary person would have worn a hospital robe," Kajiyama remembered, "but not Foujita. He stood up and struck a really funny pose for me, wearing that loud coat. Even when he was dying, he liked to fool around and didn't want to be gloomy."

Foujita died of cancer on January 29, 1968, at age eighty-one. His wife was with him, as was a group of friends, both French and Japanese.

NOTES

ABBREVIATIONS
Foujita memoirs:

Bura ippon	Bura ippon (Tokyo: Kōdansha, 1984)
Chi o oyogu	Chi o oyogu (Tokyo: Kōdansha, 1984)
Pari no yokogao	Pari no yokogao (Tokyo: Jitsugyō no Nihonsha, 1929)
"Zai-Futsu 17 nen"	"Zai-Futsu 17 nen," in Fujita Tsuguharu gashū (Tokyo: Asahi Shinbunsha, 1929)
Ashihara	Ashihara Eiryō, Watakushi no hanjijoden (Tokyo: Shinjuku Shobō, 1983)
Kondō	Kondō Fumito, Fujita Tsuguharu: "Ihōjin" no shōgai (Tokyo: Kōdansha, 2002)
Montparnasse vivant	J.-P. Crespelle, Montparnasse vivant (Paris: Librairie Hachette, 1962)
Sasaki	Sasaki Shigeo, Shiryō shūsei: Fujita Tsuguharu—sono shōgai to jitsuzō (Tokyo: Gendai Bijutsu Shiryō Sentā, 2003) This and the following Sasaki references are chronological collections of materials by and about Foujita. These compendiums are revised often and have no page numbers. Works generally appear in their year of publication.
Sasaki, "Sengo"	Sasaki Shigeo, Gaka Fujita Tsuguharu no chōsen—sengo 1945–1968 (Tokyo: Gendai Bijutsu Shiryō Sentā, 2003)
Tanaka	Tanaka Jō, Hyōden: Fujita Tsuguharu (Tokyo: Shinchōsha, 1969)

PREFACE

x   *These letters:* Foujita's letters to Henry Sugimoto are in the Henry Sugimoto Archives, Hirosaki National Resource Center, Japanese American National Museum, Los Angeles.

CHAPTER 1: BETWEEN EAST AND WEST

4   "She came in slowly and timidly": Kiki's Memoirs, ed. Billy Klüver and Julie Martin (New Jersey: The Ecco Press, 1996), p. 42.

4   "a small handkerchief": Ibid.

4   "She took my place": Ibid.

5   "In the morning": Ibid., p. 44. The year and the painting referred to in this episode are not certain. There is evidence that a Foujita nude dating from 1921 is the one that sold for 8,000 francs.

6   "I suddenly realized": Bura ippon, p. 115.

6   "In the art of Foujita": André Warnod, "Chez Foujita," Conferencia, February 20, 1928, p. 256.

7   "His work seemed very Japanese": Yōko Hayashi-Hibino, "Les années vingt de Léonard-Tsuguharu Foujita" (Master's thesis, Université de Paris I, 1996), p. 80.

9   "I have never driven a guest away": Abe Tetsuo, "Fujita san no atorie o tazunete," Mizue, March 1953, pp. 39–42.

CHAPTER 2: A TOKYO INTERLUDE

11   "amour surréaliste": Desnos, Foujita & Youki: Un Amour Surréaliste (Paris: Éditions des Cendres/Musée du Montparnasse, 2001).

14   A friend who often went: Oka Shikanosuke, "Doranburu jidai no Fujita Tsuguharu," in Furansu no gaka-tachi (Tokyo: Chūō Kōron Bijutsu Shuppan, 1968), p. 119.

CHAPTER 3: RESTLESS FROM THE START

15   "After long days of rain": Paul Morand, Foujita (Paris: Éditions des Chroniques du Jour, 1928), p. xvii.

16   "delicate sensibility": Natsubori Masahiro, Fujita Tsuguharu geijutsu shiron (Tokyo: Miyoshi Kikaku, 2004), p. 25.

16   "not vulgarity": Ibid.

16   "was very knowledgeable": Ibid., p. 26.

16   "A frog in a well": Ashihara, p. 46.

17   "I am very competitive": Bura ippon, p. 3.

17   "I am not Japanese": Ibid., p. 4.

17   "You only have to look": Okamoto Ippei, "Botchan Fujita," Atorie, December 1929, p. 72.

18   "For no real reason": Chi o oyogu, p. 213.

18   "My brother consented grudgingly": Bura ippon, p. 5.

19   "Having my painting exhibited": Kondō, p. 23.

19   "It did not seem like": From a biography of Foujita's father, Fujita Tsuguakira, published by the Army Medical Corps, January 13, 1943. Quoted in Sasaki.

21   "The importation of 'Western-style' painting": Takashina Shūji, "Paris and Japan in the History of Modern Art," in Inshō-ha kara Ekōru do Pari e (Saitama: Saitama Kenritsu Kindai Bijutsukan, 1982), p. 146.

21   "We are in Japan": Mori Ōgai, "Under Reconstruction," trans. Ivan Morris, in Modern Japanese Stories (Rutland, Vermont, and Tokyo: Charles E. Tuttle Company, 1968), p. 43.

21   *"I used to fool around"*: Pari no yokogao, p. 238.

22   *"One teacher, who thought"*: Kondō, p. 30.

22   *"What I learned at art school"*: Bura ippon, p. 57.

CHAPTER 4: AH, FRANCE!

23   *"Chad had been made over"*: Henry James, *The Ambassadors* (Mineola, New York: Dover Publications, 2002), p. 79.

23   *"Paris was a very old city"*: Ernest Hemingway, *A Movable Feast* (London: Arrow Books, 1996), p. 50.

24   *"I feel this river"*: Henry Miller, *Tropic of Cancer* (New York: Modern Library, 1983), p. 321.

24   *The Japanese found themselves*: For more on the Japanese in Paris, see Watanabe Kazutami, *Furansu no yūwaku* (Tokyo: Iwanami Shoten, 1995), pp. 79–112.

24   *"For us, France was"*: Tamagawa Shinmei, *Ekōru do Pari no Nihonjin yarō* (Tokyo: Asahi Shinbunsha, 1989), p. 36.

24   *"I hope that the delicate"*: Quoted in Watanabe, *Furansu no yūwaku*, p. 108. For the full text of the play, see Kishida Kunio, *Furui gangu: Hoka gohen* (Tokyo: Iwanami Shoten, 1993), pp. 7–74.

24   *Perhaps there is no better way*: For more about Académie Julian, see Eiko Imahashi, *Ito shōkei: Nihonjin no Pari* (Tokyo: Heibonsha, 2001), pp. 115–75.

25   *"The school was in"*: George Biddle, *An American Artist's Story* (Boston: Little, Brown and Company, 1939), pp. 125–26.

25   *"La peinture"*: Imahashi, *Ito shōkei*, p. 132.

26   *But The Art Students of Paris*: For an extended study of Iwamura and his book, see ibid., pp.176–256.

26   *"I struggled to learn"*: Asahi Akira, *Saeki Yūzō no Pari* (Tokyo: Dainihon Kaiga, 1997), pp. 102, 115.

27   *"London, Rome, Munich, Antwerp"*: Iwamura Tōru, "Pari no bijutsu gakusei," in *Geien zakkō: Hoka*, ed. Miyagawa Torao (Tokyo: Heibonsha, 1971), pp. 3–4.

27   *"I just wonder"*: Ibid., p. 6.

28   *"When they play"*: Ibid., p. 24.

28   *"With berets on their heads"*: Imahashi, *Ito shōkei*, p. 188.

29   *"With a bright sun"*: Ibid., p. 189.

CHAPTER 5: LET LOOSE IN PARIS

30   *"This was the first edition"*: Montparnasse vivant, p. 146.

31   *"I was surprised because"*: Foujita letter to Tokita Tomi, August 1913, *Fujita Tsuguharu shokan—tsuma Tomi ate* (Chiba: Pari Ryūgaku Shoki no Fujita Tsuguharu Kenkyūkai, 2003–2004), vol. 1, p. 11.

31   *"I was surprised by"*: Bura ippon, p. 8.

31   *"The very day of my arrival"*: Montparnasse vivant, p. 147.

31   *"pleased, satisfied, proud"*: Ibid.

31   *Later he was sitting*: Ibid.

31   *"without a dictionary"*: Ibid.

32   *"The Parisians love"*: Tamagawa, *Nihonjin yarō*, p. 57.

32   *"When I first set foot"*: Satsuma Jirohachi, *Se shi bon: Waga hansei no yume* (Tokyo: Sanbunsha, 1955), p. 94.
33   *"Look, when it comes"*: Tamagawa, *Nihonjin yarō*, p. 58.
33   *"Foujita was taken to"*: Ibid.
33   *"The other guests drank, sang"*: Ibid.
33   *"Foujita suddenly let out"*: Ibid., pp. 58–59.

CHAPTER 6: A CITY FOR ARTISTS

35   *"Picasso already lived"*: *Bura ippon*, p. 52.
36   *"I, who did not even know"*: Ibid., p. 57.
37   *"For the first seven years"*: Tanaka, p. 90.
37   *"I practiced getting a deep sleep"*: "Zai-Futsu 17 nen," p. 18.
37   *If he was interested in eyes*: Tanaka, p. 90.
37   *"If they don't have shoes"*: "Zai-Futsu 17 nen," p. 12.
38   *"I enjoyed socializing"*: Ibid., p. 14.
38   *"In order to understand"*: Ibid.
38   *"I tried not to be"*: Ibid.
38   *"The French, like the Japanese"*: Ibid.
38   *"I wasn't looking to create"*: Ibid., pp. 16–17.
39   *"No matter how important"*: Ibid., p. 18.
39   *"Paris, that flower"*: Imahashi, *Ito shōkei*, pp. 37–38.
39   *"It's good to have relatives"*: *Bura ippon*, pp. 121–22.
39   *"In the spring"*: Ibid., p. 9.
40   *"One day when I was"*: "Zai-Futsu 17 nen," p. 16.

CHAPTER 7: SETTLING DOWN

41   *"replaced by apartments for the rich"*: Matthew Reinders, ed. and dir., "Who was Modigliani?" from the television series *Montparnasse Revisited* (INA/RM Arts, 1991).
42   *"More than a thousand times"*: Kaminagai Yō, introduction to *Kaminagai Tadashi kaiko ten* (Tokyo: Yūrakuchō Gyararī, 1987).
43   *"An enclosed space"*: Hayashi Yōko, "1913 Pari: Sawabe Seigorō to Kawashima Riichirō soshite Fujita Tsuguharu," in *Sawabe Seigorō isaku ten—zuroku* (Kyoto: Hoshino Garō, 2002), p. 10.
43   *"We artists in Paris"*: "Zai-Futsu 17 nen," p. 15.
43   *"The cat is really me"*: Natsubori, *Geijutsu shiron*, p. 85.
44   *"I decided to stay in Paris"*: "Zai-Futsu 17 nen," p. 15.
44   *"If I wake up"*: Ibid., p. 16.
44   *"I saved only fifteen"*: Ibid.
45   *"I'd say, What's the point"*: *Chi o oyogu*, p. 15.
45   *"Meals were fifty centimes"*: Frederick S. Wight, "Recollections of Modigliani by Those Who Knew Him," *Italian Quarterly* 2, spring 1958, p. 49.
46   *"Foujita worked with Modigliani"*: Hayashi-Hibino, "Les années vingt," p. 10.
47   *"I decided that since"*: *Pari no yokogao*, pp. 242–43.
47   *"He recited Dante"*: Wight, "Recollections of Modigliani," p. 49.
47   *"cold and sad"*: Ibid., p. 51.

47 *"In those days Modigliani"*: Pari no yokogao, pp. 240–41.
47 *"There were many bedbugs"*: Ibid., p. 241.
48 *"Why? Because the husband"*: Ibid., p. 195.
48 *"There is no city"*: Ibid., p. 225.
48 *"Very few living quarters"*: Ibid., p. 226.
48 *"I wondered why his place"*: Ibid., p. 227.

CHAPTER 8: EAGER TO LEAVE
50 *"Three months after arriving"*: Kaneko Mitsuharu, Nemure Pari (Tokyo: Chūō Kōron Shinsha, 2003), pp. 80–81.
50 *"During the boat ride over"*: Sakamoto Hanjirō, Watakushi no e, watakushi no kokoro (Tokyo: Nihon Keizai Shinbunsha, 1969), p. 71.
51 *"I returned from seeing my friend"*: Shimazaki Tōson, Etoranze, vol. 8, Tōson zenshū (Tokyo: Chikuma Shobō; 1967), pp. 235–36.
51 *"During the past five months"*: Ibid., p. 243.
51 *"Sometimes I threw off"*: Ibid., pp. 270–71.
52 *"From the time Marseilles"*: Yokomitsu Riichi, Ryoshū, vol. 8, Yokomitsu Riichi zenshū (Tokyo: Kawade Shobō, 1955–56), p. 37.
52 *"He first arrived in Paris"*: Ibid., pp. 47–48.

CHAPTER 9: OVER A LONG DISTANCE
54 *"a short, dark man"*: Tsukamoto Yasushi, "Chiba ken yukari no yōgaka Fujita Tsuguharu no shokan," Kyūryō, (Narutō Kōkō Dōsōkaishi), no. 25, March 1988, p. 4.
54 *"Let me marry her"*: Chi o oyogu, p. 214.
55 *"Of the people who came"*: Foujita letter to Tokita Tomi, June 1913, Fujita Tsuguharu shokan, vol. 1, p. 3.
55 *"I intended to write you"*: Ibid., August 15, 1913, vol. 1, p. 10.
55 *"I'm staying at the Hotel Odessa"*: Ibid., vol. 1, pp. 11–13.
56 *"I can't even begin"*: Ibid., vol. 1, pp.13–14.
56 *"I applied to the Louvre"*: Ibid., February 10, 1914, vol. 1, pp. 116–17.
56 *"I went to visit"*: Ibid., February 10, 1914, vol. 1, pp. 117–18.
57 *"Even if I could go back"*: Ibid., May 10, 1914, vol. 2, p. 34.
57 *"If I die, I would be sorry"*: Ibid., September 5, 1914, vol. 2, pp. 105–6.
57 *"Now that I am by myself"*: Ibid., October 11, 1915, vol. 3, p. 85.
57 *"It would be fine with me"*: Ibid., June 21, 1916, vol. 3, p. 125.
58 *"I find letters to Father"*: Ibid., June 21, 1916, vol. 3, pp. 125–26.
58 *"I am telling you"*: Ibid., July 10, 1915, vol. 3, p. 57.
59 *"When Foujita first went"*: Kikuhata Mokuma, Ekaki to sensō (Fukuoka: Kaichōsha, 1993), pp. 260–61.
60 *"I am of the generation"*: Newsweek, (Japan/Korea edition), September 4, 2000, p. 44.
61 *"Recently, I have been struck"*: "Jijitsu gonin ni yoru shijitsu waikyoku no kanōsei," Aida, July 20, 2001, p. 31.
62 *"At this time"*: Ashihara, p. 32.
62 *"While I was struggling"*: Yomiuri shinbun, July 20, 1938. Quoted in Sasaki.

CHAPTER 10: BACK TO THE GREEKS

63   "*I am now thirty*": *Chi o oyogu*, p. 215.

64   "*vulgar*". . ."*simple*" *but* "*highly spiritual*": Foujita letter to Tokita Tomi, October 26, 1913, *Fujita Tsuguharu shokan*, vol. 1, p. 42.

64   "*The words* gymnastic exercise": Raymond Duncan, "La Danse et la Gymnastique," speech at the Université Hellénique, May 4, 1914. http://www. fezziwigs.org/dance/c2.p1?book=062.

65   "*a diaphanous younger brother*": Adela Spindler Roatcap, *Raymond Duncan* (San Francisco: The Book Club of California, 1991), p. 9.

65   "*Raymond was in his element*": Ibid., p. 13.

65   "*His long hair*": Robert McAlmon, *Being Geniuses Together* (San Francisco: North Point Press, 1984), p. 275.

66   "*In those days*": Tanaka, p. 51.

66   "*I'll definitely join you*": Ibid., p. 52.

66   "*Dance is composed*": Foujita letter to Tokita Tomi, October 26, 1913, *Fujita Tsuguharu shokan*, vol. 1, pp. 42–43.

67   "*Throughout the world*": Ibid., November 10, 1913, vol. 1, p. 53.

67   "*They were a great success*": Nina Hamnett, *Laughing Torso* (New York: Ray Long & Richard R. Smith, Inc., 1932), p. 63.

67   "*What are you doing*": Tōson, *Etoranze*, p. 255.

69   "*Cadmus was a prince*": Kawashima Riichirō, "Shiryō—Kawashima Riichirō no e-nikki (1915)," ed. Yaguchi Kunio, *Tochigi kenritsu bijutsukan kiyō*, no. 4, 1976, p. 23.

69   "*Tonight there was a great revolution*": Ibid.

69   "*When I look back*": Fujita Tsuguharu et al., *Pari no hiru to yoru* (Tokyo: Sekai no Nihonsha, 1948), p. 46.

70   "*We also went*": Tanaka, pp. 52–53.

70   "*I heard that Yasui*": Kawashima Riichirō, "1914 Pari—Sen'unka Fujita to tomo ni," *E*, no. 52, June 1968, p. 10.

70   "*very well-known*": *Montparnasse vivant*, p. 151.

71   "*a Japanese phenomenon*": Quoted in Youki Desnos, *Les confidences de Youki* (Paris: Fayard, 1999), p. 95.

71   "*Foujita is thinking*": Kawashima, "E-nikki," p. 25.

CHAPTER 11: CARP AND CHERRY BLOSSOMS

72   *Toda Kaiteki*: I am grateful to Kondō Fumito for introducing me to the life of Toda Kaiteki in Kondō, pp. 120–24, and during an interview, 2001.

73   "*I don't even bother*": Tamagawa, *Nihonjin yarō*, p. 205.

73   "*a free spirit*": *Pari no yokogao*, p. 128.

74   "*had a wild, primitive*": McAlmon, *Being Geniuses Together*, p. 303.

75   "*I envy the Japanese artists*": http://www.artelino.com/articles/van_gogh_japonisme.asp. This quotation is from one of van Gogh's letters to his brother Theo. For another translation of the same passage, see *Dear Theo: The Autobiography of Vincent van Gogh*, ed. Irving Stone (New York: Plume, 1995), p. 389.

76   "*not forgetting all*": "L'exposition Foujita chez Bernheim Jeune," *Bulletin de la Société franco-japonaise de Paris*, no. 70, 1929, p. 52.

77   *"In Japan"*: "La peinture japonaise contemporaine au Salon d'Automne," *L'amour de l'art*, January 1923, pp. 722–25.

CHAPTER 12: A WOMAN'S ROLE

78   *"I had bangs, a necklace"*: *Montparnasse vivant*, p. 152.

78   *"Unfortunately, I am a man"*: Tanaka, p. 62.

79   *Jean-Paul Crespelle describes her*: *Montparnasse vivant*, p. 152.

79   *"Nice dress"*: Ibid., p. 153.

79   *"He intended to follow her"*: Tanaka, p. 64.

80   *"magical"*: Sylvie and Dominique Buisson, *Léonard-Tsuguharu Foujita* (Paris: ACR Édition, 1987), p. 52.

80   *"In that period"*: Hayashi-Hibino, "Les années vingt," p. 10.

80   *"smelled of urine"*: Satsuma, *Se shi bon,* p. 99.

81   *"If Asians cannot spend"*: Okamoto, "Botchan," p. 73.

81   *"She was French"*: Hamnett, *Laughing Torso*, pp. 140–44.

81   *"Model? I was a street-walker"*: Charles Douglas, *Artist Quarter* (London: Faber and Faber, 1941), p. 257.

81   *"In a Foreign Country"*: Tamagawa, *Nihonjin yarō*, p. 60.

82   *"I liked to have"*: *Montparnasse vivant*, p. 159.

82   *"This rumor"*: Natsubori, *Geijutsu shiron*, p. 161.

83   *"Chéron would get"*: *Montparnasse vivant*, p. 154.

CHAPTER 13: RISING STAR AT CHÉRON'S

85   *"from a samurai family"*: *Le carnet de la semaine*, December 1918.

85   *Kondō Fumito, who has written*: Kondō interview, 2001.

85   *"Son of General Foujita"*: *Exposition du peintre japonais Tsugouharu Foujita*, Paris, Galerie Chéron, June 1917.

85   *"the unfettered art"*: Ibid.

86   *"Picasso did not only"*: Fujita et al., *Pari no hiru to yoru*, p. 15.

86   *"Picasso, when he's in your studio"*: Mark Hutchinson, "Poor, Forked Animal No More," *Times Literary Supplement*, March 18, 2005, p. 16.

87   *This was shown not only*: For more about Foujita's paintings of the outskirts of Paris, see Hayashi Yōko, "Fujita Tsuguharu no 1910 nendai: Pari shūen to iu toposu," *Genesis* (Kyōtō Zōkei Geijutsu Daigaku Kiyō), June 2004, pp. 44–55.

87   *"revelation"*: F. R. Vanderpyl, "Foujita," *L'amour de l'art*, September 1921, p. 274.

87   *"This was not just japonisme"*: Shimizu Toshio, "Reonāru Fujita—sono gagyō no tenkai," *Reonāru Fujita ten* (Tokyo: Tōkyō-to Teien Bijutsukan, 1988), p. 13.

87   *"There are some Japanese"*: *La démocratie nouvelle*, December 8, 1918.

88   *"Most of the art reviewers"*: "Zai-Futsu 17 nen," p. 19.

CHAPTER 14: TO THE SOUTH WITH FRIENDS

89   *"The sun of art shone"*: "Marc Chagall on Paris," http://spaightwoodgalleries.com/Pages/Chagall_Paris2.html

89   *This international community:* Romy Golan, "The 'École Française' vs. the 'École de Paris,'" in *The Circle of Montparnasse: Jewish Artists in Paris, 1905–1945* (New York: The Jewish Museum, 1985), pp. 81–87.

90   *Golan sees long-simmering:* Ibid.

90   *"The Rotonde":* Ibid., p. 82.

91   *"abandoned the metropolis":* Ibid.

91   *"Let's Not Lose Our Confidence":* Les cahiers du mois, no. 9–10, 1925, p. 153.

92   *"I want to get away from Cagnes":* Quoted in Stanley Meisler, "Soutine: The Power and the Fury of an Eccentric Genius," http://www.stanleymeisler.com/smithsonian/smithsonian-1988-11-soutine.html.

92   *"Once at Cagnes":* Pierre Sichel, *Modigliani* (New York: Dutton, 1967), p. 407.

93   *"a boy of seventeen":* Ibid.

93   *"[I] cut a collar out of the tail":* Wight, "Recollections of Modigliani," p. 50.

93   *"[Zborowski's] method was to sit":* Ibid.

93   *"What were we thinking":* Buisson and Buisson, *Léonard-Tsuguharu Foujita,* p. 62.

94   *"Papa Curel did not take":* Ibid., p. 64.

94   *"I can see Renoir now":* Wight, "Recollections of Modigliani," p. 50.

94   *"Paint with joy":* Sichel, *Modigliani,* p. 410.

CHAPTER 15: SALON'S MAN OF THE HOUR

95   *"clad in a Samurai robe":* Douglas, *Artist Quarter,* p. 297.

95   *"On the opening day":* Chi o oyogu, p. 308.

96   *"You couldn't get through":* Ibid., p. 309.

96   *"Some of my colleagues":* "Zai-Futsu 17 nen," p. 20.

98   *"Before I draw a line":* Ibid., pp. 174–75.

98   *The line was undoubtedly dazzling:* Hayashi-Hibino, "Les années vingt," p. 101.

98   "I'll create works": Foujita letter to Tokita Tomi, December 3, 1913, *Fujita Tsuguharu shokan,* vol. 1, p. 73.

98   *"He kept those two paintings":* Hayashi Yōko, "Fujita Tsuguharu no 1920 nendai—nimai no 'Watakushi no Heya' ni komerareta imi," *Tōkyō-to Gendai Bijutsukan kiyō,* no. 4, 1988, p. 14.

101   "In my whole long life": Natsubori, *Geijutsu shiron,* p. 195.

CHAPTER 16: SAEKI YŪZŌ'S PARIS

103   *Saeki's encounter:* For an account of the visit, see Asahi, *Saeki Yūzō no Pari,* pp. 191–220.

104   *"My teachers are van Gogh":* Ibid., p. 288.

105   *"Only Foujita has the fine touch":* Kondō, p. 78.

105   *"No fragment escapes him":* Vanderpyl, "Foujita," p. 274.

105   *"[The grounds in his works]":* Robert Rey, "Foujita," *Sélection,* January 15, 1921, p. 166.

106   *"In Japan, people think":* Hayashi-Hibino, "Les années vingt," p. 77.

106   *"More than having my picture":* From the Army Medical Corps biography of Foujita's father, Tsuguakira. Quoted in Sasaki.

106   "intime": Hayashi, "Nimai no 'Watakushi no Heya,'" p. 21. See this essay for an account of the reaction to Foujita's submissions to the Tokyo salon.

107 *"There was first of all"*: Nōberu Shobō Henshūbu, ed., *Fujita Tsuguharu to Ekōru do Pari* (Tokyo: Nōberu Shobō, 1984), p. 162.

CHAPTER 17: AN AMERICAN HEIRESS
109 *"flashing camellia"*: Margaret Crane-Lillie Gildea, "About Emily Crane Chadbourne and Other Members of the Crane Family" (Chicago: Archives, The Art Institute of Chicago, September 1978), p. 9.
109 *"sat on a staircase"*: Ibid., p. 16.
109 *"two formidable ladies"*: Evelyn Waugh, *Remote People* (New York: The Ecco Press, 1990), p. 34.

CHAPTER 18: SUCCESS AND DOMESTIC WOE
112 *"passed for a nabob"*: Jean-Paul Crespelle, *La vie quotidienne à Montparnasse à la grande époque 1905–1930* (Paris: Librairie Hachette, 1976), p. 36.
112 *"With his brush"*: Vanderpyl, "Foujita," p. 274.
113 *"Since they were always"*: Fujita et al., *Pari no hiru to yoru*, p. 94.
113 *"It's because women and cats"*: Ibid.
114 *"The war was over"*: Jean-Marie Drot, *Les heures chaudes de Montparnasse* (Paris: Éditions Hazan, 1995), p. 106.
114 *"In particular"*: Ibid., p. 109.
114 *"Woman for sale"*: *Montparnasse vivant*, p. 159.
114 *"Cover him with flowers"*: Sichel, *Modigliani*, p. 509.
115 *"I'm the one"*: *Montparnasse vivant*, p. 160.
115 *"vicieuse et sensuelle"*: Wight, *Recollections of Modigliani*, p. 51.
115 *"Don't ever think"*: *Montparnasse vivant*, p. 160.
115 *"I started getting bored"*: Ibid., pp. 159–60.
115 *"even Foujita's mischief"*: Tanaka, p. 89.
116 *"Foujita wouldn't go out"*: Ibid., p. 90.
116 *"In the swooning circles"*: Diane MacIntyre, *The Silents Majority On-Line Journal of Silent Film*, 1997.
116 *"Sessue! Sessue!"*: Tamagawa, *Nihonjin yarō*, p. 155.
116 *"arrived with the baggage"*: Édouard Ramond, "Koyanagui," *Paris-Montparnasse*, May 15, 1929, p. 20.
116 *"Foujita used to gaze up"*: Satsuma, *Se shi bon*, p. 98.

CHAPTER 19: YOUKI, GODDESS OF THE SNOW
121 *"male cousins, female cousins"*: Desnos, *Confidences*, pp. 7–8.
122 *"He was alone"*: Ibid., p. 39.
122 *"I had not considered that"*: Ibid., p. 40.
122 *"flat nose"*: Ibid., p. 43.
122 *"I have fallen in love"*: Hiraoka Genpachirō, "Fujita Tsuguharu-shi no tegami," *Kokumin bijutsu*, December 1923.
122 *"I don't get tired"*: Ibid.
123 *"I am so happy"*: Ibid.
123 *"in the honorable Mr. Foujita"*: Morand, *Foujita*, p. xi.

125   *"In those days, I drew"*: *Montparnasse vivant*, p. 166.
126   *"What does it mean, Foujita?"*: Desnos, *Confidences*, pp. 52–53.
126   *"No, Foujita"*: Ibid., p. 54.
126   *"Already the blazing life"*: "Le temps de vivre," in *Le cœur innombrable* (Paris: Calman-Lévy, 1919), p. 185.

CHAPTER 20: MOST FAMOUS JAPANESE IN PARIS
128   *"Those who think"*: Fujita et al., *Pari no hiru to yoru*, p. 44.
128   *"the rascals among those"*: *Chi o oyogu*, p. 311.
129   *"Foujita, I saw a picture"*: For an account of this event, see *Fujita Tsuguharu to Ekōru do Pari*, pp. 159–62.
129   *"astronomique"*: *Montparnasse vivant*, p. 167.
129   *"eyesight like a lynx"*: Desnos, *Confidences*, p. 63.
129   *"as content as a child"*: Ibid.
129   *"I became his favorite model"*: Jacqueline Goddard, "Jacqueline et Montparnasse," p. 43.
130   *"He quickly stirred"*: Michel Georges-Michel, "Le peintre en pyjama: Fujita," *Vu*, September 12, 1928, p. 586.
130   *"Traditionally, artists in Japan"*: Hayashi-Hibino, "Les années vingt," p. 83.
132   *"without artifice . . . gigolo"*: Satsuma, *Se shi bon*, pp. 98–99.
132   *"To the standard bourgeois"*: Kondō, p. 105.
132   *"scandal-mongering"*: Natsubori, *Geijutsu shiron*, p. 192.
133   *"a huge charming devil"*: Desnos, *Confidences*, p. 143.
133   *"could be made to stand"*: Alexander Calder, *An Autobiography with Pictures* (New York: Pantheon Books, 1966), p. 80.
133   *"A bit of green carpet"*: James Johnson Sweeney, *Alexander Calder* (New York: Museum of Modern Art, 1951), quoted in http://www.calder.org/SETS_SUB/life/texts/life_texts_sweeney51_con1.html.
134   *"Belle brune de Barcelonne"*: Calder, *An Autobiography*, p. 83.
134   *"Sometimes the horseback rider"*: Desnos, *Confidences*, p. 144.
134   *"That shows you"*: Ibid., p. 145.
134   *"Here comes Youki Foujita"*: Ibid.

CHAPTER 21: GREEN SHEET OF THE TAX COLLECTOR
136   *"The attitude toward copyright"*: *Geijutsu shinchō*, May 1975, p. 79.
136   *"I'm not saying"*: *Yomiuri shinbun*, November 26, 1986.
136   *"There must be printed"*: Ibid.
139   *"Once a Russian artists' association"*: Kondō, p. 88.
139   *"According to his wife"*: Ibid., p. 109.
141   *"In spite of the money"*: *Montparnasse vivant*, p. 168.
141   *"I don't know exactly"*: Desnos, *Confidences*, p. 183.
141   *"astronomical sum"*: Ibid., p. 184.
141   *("Don't read books," . . .)*: Ashihara, p. 236.
142   *"Foujita stood on the deck"*: Kondō, p. 140.
142   *"Sign of a typhoon"*: Ibid., p. 142.

143   *"All he wants is money"*: Kumaoka Yoshihiko, "Hyakki yagyō no Pari," part 1, *Bijutsu shinron,* August 1929, p. 88.

143   *"[The teachers tell] students"*: Kumaoka Yoshihiko, "Hyakki yagyō no Pari," part 2, *Bijutsu shinron,* October 1929, p. 94.

143   *"Even in his old age"*: Kondō, p. 143.

143   *"As soon as Foujita sought"*: Hayashi-Hibino, "Les années vingt," p. 98.

144   *"If you think"*: Pari no yokogao, p. 255.

144   *"We must work magic"*: "Zai-Futsu 17 nen," p. 13.

144   *"Seventeen Years in France"*: Ibid.

144   *"The Life of an Artist in Paris"*: "Pari ni okeru gaka no seikatsu" in *Pari no yokogao,* pp. 235–61.

145   *"Once I even painted"*: Ibid., pp. 258–60.

145   *"I decided to do"*: "Zai-Futsu 17 nen," p. 13.

145   *"When we Japanese express"*: Pari no yokogao, p. 248.

146   *"The influence of artists"*: Mainichi shinbun (Osaka), October 5, 1929. Quoted in Sasaki.

146   *"We artists must not think"*: Pari no yokogao, p. 253.

146   *"Slowly he made his way"*: Tanaka, p. 126.

147   *"He connected with"*: Ibid., p. 127.

147   *"You make sure"*: Ibid., p. 126.

147   *"After about five months"*: Ibid., p. 131.

147   *"You really have to go"*: Desnos, *Confidences,* p. 193.

147   *"kissed her on both cheeks"*: Ibid., p. 191.

148   *"And Foujita adores France"*: Ibid.

148   *"visitors to a zoo"*: Ibid., p. 198.

148   *"Foreign visitors [at the hotel]"*: Ibid., p. 197.

148   *"Don't make a scene"*: Ibid., p. 193.

148   *"Tokyo is very lively"*: Ibid., p. 196.

CHAPTER 22: STUFF OF DREAMS

152   *"His poetry was nourished"*: Dominique Desanti, *Robert Desnos, le roman d'une vie* (Paris: Mercure de France, 1999), p. 25.

153   *"I remember vividly"*: Goddard, "Jacqueline et Montparnasse," p. 45.

153   *"In a café"*: Robert Desnos, *Liberty or Love!* trans. Terry Hale (London: Atlas Press, 1993), p. 13.

154   *"Who among us"*: Robert Desnos, *Oeuvres,* ed. Marie-Claire Dumas (Paris: Gallimard, 1999), p. 846.

154   *Not only were the dreams:* Much about this period in Desnos's life is based on Katharine Conley, *Robert Desnos, Surrealism, and the Marvelous in Everyday Life* (Lincoln and London: University of Nebraska Press, 2003), pp. 45–119.

154   *"will see her secret desires"*: Ibid., p. 111.

154   *"Le bon Vermifug' Lune"*: R. Desnos, *Oeuvres,* p. 794.

154   *"For so many long months"*: "The Night of Loveless Nights," ibid., pp. 904–21. Conley, *Robert Desnos,* pp. 77–79.

155   *"I have dreamed so much"*: R. Desnos, *Oeuvres,* p. 539; Conley, *Robert Desnos,* p. 50.

155   *"I was struck"*: Desnos, *Confidences,* p. 128.

156   *"As touching as an inscription"*: R. Desnos, *Oeuvres,* p. 733.

157   *"The night that I painted"*: Fujita et al., *Pari no hiru to yoru,* caption opposite p. 110.

157   *"Au revoir, Vaugirard"*: R. Desnos, *Oeuvres,* pp. 603–4.

158   *"You back off, Miss"*: Ibid., p. 605.

158   *"Foujita wants to visit"*: Ibid., p. 607.

158   (*"the wine was a little stiff . . ."*): Ibid., p. 610.

158   *"Our short pants"*: Ibid., p. 611.

158   *"band of rowdies"*: Ibid., p. 612.

159   *"On nights like that"*: Ibid., p. 616.

159   *"of all shapes"*: Ibid., p. 617.

CHAPTER 23: TRANSITIONS

161   *"Youki, my dear Youki"*: Marie-Claire Dumas, *Robert Desnos ou l'exploration des limites* (Paris: Klincksieck, 1980), p. 101.

161   *"Robert could have hidden"*: Desnos, *Confidences,* p. 295.

161   His terrible journey: For an account of Desnos's arrest and the aftermath, see Conley, *Robert Desnos,* pp. 174–203.

161   *"But don't worry"*: Desnos, *Confidences,* p. 325.

161   *"Our suffering would be intolerable"*: R. Desnos, *Oeuvres,* p. 1277.

162   *"[The cherry blossoms] are"*: *France-Japon,* no. 29, March 1938.

163   *"Fascism and all its bankers"*: R. Desnos, *Oeuvres,* p. 825; Conley, *Robert Desnos,* p. 97.

163   *"His bangs and his large"*: *Le Figaro,* August 21, 1946.

163   These communications: Foujita's letters to Youki are part of the Fonds Desnos in the Bibliothèque littéraire Jacques Doucet, Paris. Hayashi Yōko notes that while the letters in the Fonds Desnos have been catalogued as beginning in 1922, Foujita did not meet Youki until the summer of 1923, and so the letters must date from some time after that.

163   *"Everyone in Paris is free"*: "Fujita Tsuguharu Pari zadankai," *Bungei shunjū,* November 1929, p. 98.

164   *"In Paris, women"*: Ibid., p. 101.

165   *"wowishly"*: Henry McBride, "Foujita's Cats Win New York Acclaim at First Showing," *The New York Sun,* November 15, 1930.

165   *"Foujita, with his cats and his bangs"*: *The New Yorker,* November 22, 1930, p. 60.

166   *"drinking, . . . gaiety, and fun"*: Dumas, *Robert Desnos,* pp. 97–98.

166   *"pretty redhead"*: Desnos, *Confidences,* p. 226.

166   *"When the cycle of life"*: Ibid.

166   *"I only drank a little"*: Tamagawa, *Nihonjin yarō,* p. 160.

167   *"What I resent"*: Ashihara, pp. 253–54.

167   *"Foujita went out to buy"*: Conley, *Robert Desnos,* p. 73.

167   *"Don't go looking for me"*: Dumas, *Robert Desnos,* p. 97.

167   *"My life is finished"*: Ibid.

167   *"Thank you for everything"*: Ibid., p. 98.

CHAPTER 24: ADRIFT IN THE WIDE WORLD

168   *Perhaps he had drawn*: Foujita letter to Youki, December 21, 1930, Fonds Desnos.

168   *"more conflicts than"*: "Foujita en Cuba?" *Social*, March 1931.

169   *"Even if all Europe"*: Alfred Werner, *Pascin* (New York: Harry N. Abrams, 1959), p. 21.

170   *"I want some nice"*: Jules Pascin, *Jules Pascin's Caribbean Sketchbook* (Austin: University of Texas Press, 1964), p. 16.

170   *"beautiful black women"*: R. Desnos, *Oeuvres*, p. 435.

170   *"I will never forget"*: Ibid.

170   *"Among those who have"*: *Chi o oyogu*, p. 220.

172   *"It's the kind of huge"*: *Bura ippon*, pp. 208–9.

172   *"the extreme silence"*: Maria Cecília França Lourenço, "Maioridade do moderno em São Paulo, anos 30 e 40" (Ph.D. thesis, Universidade de São Paulo, 1990); published as *Operários da modernidade* (São Paulo: Hucitec/Edusp, 1995).

172   *"Is this the same"*: Lecture by Aracy Amaral, "Foujita no Brasil (1931–32): Aspectos de uma visita," February 27, 2003 (São Paulo: Espaço Cultural da Fundação Japão), video of lecture.

173   *"It's 4,000 meters above"*: *Chi o oyogu*, p. 147.

174   *Others have written*: See, for example, José Antonio Fernández de Castro, "Sobre Foujita en la Habana," in *Barraca de feria* (Havana: J. Monterro, 1933), pp. 174–81.

174   *"Only one sausage really exists"*: I am grateful to Rosario Hiriart for her interviews of Cubans who recalled this song about the sausage vendor and believe it was probably the song Foujita heard.

174   *"fresh as recently picked"*: Fernández de Castro, "Sobre Foujita en la Habana," p. 175.

174   *"the Japanese artist"*: Ibid., p. 181.

174   *"represents an example"*: *Diario de la Marina*, November 10, 1932.

175   *"Gringolandia"*: Patrick Marnham, *Dreaming with His Eyes Open* (Berkeley: University of California Press, 2000), p. 258.

175   *"Rivera keeps two pistols"*: *Bura ippon*, p. 212.

176   *"overwrought, dried up, dreary"*: Kitagawa Tamiji, *Mekishiko no seishun: jūgonen o indian to tomo ni* (Tokyo: Nihon Tosho Sentā, 2002), p. 171.

176   *"It's not only"*: Ibid., p. 197.

177   *"There wasn't a single"*: Ibid., p. 199.

177   *"Foujita's exhibition"*: Ibid.

177   *"I was in Mexico then"*: Tanaka, p. 141.

178   *"Even though he doesn't"*: Kitagawa, *Mekishiko no seishun*, p. 200.

178   *"Your family life"*: Ibid.

178   *"Paris may be"*: *Los Angeles Times*, July 6, 1933.

CHAPTER 25: NEW START AT HOME

179   *"Freedom"*: "Fujita Tsuguharu Pari zadankai," p. 98.

180   *"[In France] they quickly bury"*: *Bi no kuni*, January 1937. Quoted in Sasaki.

180   *"junk" . . . "Foujita is supposed to be"*: Kaneko, *Nemure Pari*, p. 93.

181 *"If I go back"*: Watanabe, *Furansu no yūwaku*, p. 108.
181 *With sliding paper screens*: J. Thomas Rimer, "Tokyo in Paris/Paris in Tokyo," in Shūji Takashina and J. Thomas Rimer, eds., with Gerald D. Bolas, *Paris in Japan: The Japanese Encounter with European Painting* (Tokyo and St. Louis: The Japan Foundation and Washington University, 1987), pp. 69, 71.
181 *"Just looking at"*: Ibid., p. 180.
181 *"When he was confronted"*: Ibid.
182 *"The scenes featuring"*: Ogisu Takanori, *Watakushi no Pari, Pari no watakushi: Ogisu Takanori no kaisō* (Tokyo: Tōkyō Shinbun Shuppankyoku, 1980), p. 128.
182 *"Just as they say"*: Sakamoto, *Watakushi no e*, p. 79.
183 *"His present wife is not Youki"*: Quoted in Sasaki.
184 *"Three years away"*: *Hōchi shinbun*, February 16, 1935.
185 *"Now I am truly alone"*: *Tōkyō nichi nichi shinbun*, July 1, 1936. Quoted in Sasaki.

CHAPTER 26: ART FOR THE PEOPLE
187 *"The evening of the vernissage"*: Hasegawa Jin, *Yōgashō* (Tokyo: Bijutsu Shuppansha, 1964), p. 15.
187 *"Everyone was looking forward"*: *Mizue*, October 1934. Quoted in Sasaki.
188 *"You're from the countryside"*: Hirano Masakichi, "Kiki-gaki: waga kaisō no Fujita Tsuguharu," *Hanga geijutsu* 12 (winter), 1976, p. 41.
188 *"cheerful, bright, warm"*: "Burajiru kōhī no hekiga ni tsuite," *Sōgō bijutsu*, February 1935, p. 36.
188 *"I did not make any"*: Ibid.
189 *Hayashi Yōko, who has written*: See Hayashi Yōko, "Fujita Tsuguharu no 1930 nendai," in Tsuji Nobuo Sensei Kanreki Kinenkai, ed., *Nihon bijutsushi no suimyaku* (Tokyo: Perikansha, 1993), vol. 2, pp. 621–48.
189 *"If this is supposed to be"*: "Burajiru no Fujita Tsuguharu o kataru," *Jornal do Nikkey*, March 7, 2003, http://www.nikkeyshimbun.com.br/030307-72colonia.html.
190 *"We must get rid of"*: *Kaizō*, March 1936. Quoted in Sasaki.
190 *"I would like to advise"*: Hayashi, "1930 nendai," p. 639.
190 *"In the first place"*: Ibid., p. 637.

CHAPTER 27: JAPAN'S ALLURE
191 *"Since my return to Japan"*: *Chi o oyogu*, p. 273.
192 *"Rather than paint at an easel"*: Ibid., p. 272.
192 *"Every day I wake up"*: Ibid., p. 273.
193 *"I would like people"*: *Tōkyō nichi nichi shinbun*, August 29, 1937. Quoted in Sasaki.
193 *"I don't think that"*: *Mizue*, October 1937. Quoted in Sasaki.
194 *"I'd like it to be"*: *Akita sakigake*, February 7, 1999.
194 *"I take pride in believing"*: Ibid.
195 *"easily buy two or three"*: Tanaka, p. 162.

196 *"Foujita turned pale"*: Ibid., p. 169.
198 *"Up to now"*: "Fujita Tsuguharu ga eiga kantoku ni natte katsuyaku," *Mainichi shinbun* (Osaka), November 29, 1935.
198 *"portraying Japan in a shameful light"*: For a discussion of the controversy, see *Atorie*, May 1937. Quoted in Sasaki.
199 *"I have depicted the simple feelings"*: Kondō, p. 172.

CHAPTER 28: A MATTER OF COMMITMENT
200 *"Every time I go"*: Ashihara, p. 204.
201 *"Japan is really"*: Ibid., p. 205.
202 *"That's why Japan"*: Ibid., p. 206.
202 *"The youngsters here"*: Ibid.
202 *"Foujita always had the ability"*: Ibid., p. 209.
202 *"Look at Picasso and Matisse"*: Ibid.
202 *"Paris is different"*: Ibid.
203 *"An artist has to protect"*: Ibid., p. 210.
203 *"This coffee is delicious, isn't it?"*: Ibid., pp. 210–11.
203 *"I came to believe whatever"*: Ibid., p. 211.
204 *"All the subjects"*: *Rekitei*, November 1938. Quoted in Sasaki.
204 *"I look forward"*: *Miyako shinbun*, October 2, 1938. Quoted in Sasaki.
204 *"There are now about"*: *Fukuoka shinbun*, October 3, 1938. Quoted in Sasaki.
205 *"an army and navy cocktail"*: *Chi o oyogu*, p. 80. For Foujita's account of his trip, see pp. 79–100.
205 *"in case I vanish"*: Ibid., p. 82.
205 *"Is that what"*: Ibid.
206 *"This is my first experience"*: Ibid., p. 89.
206 *"joyfully"*: Ibid., p. 90.
206 *"At least I have developed"*: Ibid., p. 94.
206 *"to show to the youth"*: Ibid., p. 91.
206 *"the heart-wrenching hardships"*: Ibid., p. 98.
206 *natural calamities of earthquake, fire*: Ibid., p. 96.
207 *"Now, three years after"*: *Tōkyō nichi nichi shinbun*, April 5, 1939. Quoted in Sasaki.
208 *"If I continue like this"*: Ashihara, p. 219.

CHAPTER 29: WARTIME CHOICES
211 *"Don't you remember"*: Haruko Taya Cook and Theodore F. Cook, *Japan at War: An Oral History* (New York: The New Press, 1992), p. 256.
211 *"Artists must be aware"*: "Kokubō kokka to bijutsu," *Mizue*, January 1941, p. 130.
211 *"In their intensity and colors"*: "Dai Tōa sensō kirokuga seisaku no tame gaka genchi haken keikaku," 1943. Quoted in Sasaki.
211 *"All I can say is"*: Kazuo Ishiguro, *An Artist of the Floating World* (New York: Vintage International, 1986), pp. 123–24.
213 *"Sometimes I think"*: Ibid., p. 56.

214   *"the most sparkling time"*: *Ihara Usaburō ten,* ed. Tokushima Shinbunsha and Tokushima–ken Kyōdo Bunka Kaikan (Tokushima: Tokushima Shinbunsha, 1984), p. 12.

214   *"which ordinary people find difficult"*: "Gaka genchi haken keikaku." Quoted in Sasaki.

215   *"Following the imperial will"*: Tsukasa Osamu, *Sensō to bijutsu* (Tokyo: Iwanami Shoten, 1992), p. 161.

215   *"When I was transcribing"*: Ibid., p. 162.

215   *"It is inaccurate to say"*: Ibid., p. 166.

216   *While such statements:* See Michael Lucken, *Grenades et amertume: Les peintres japonais à l'épreuve de la guerre, 1935–1952* (Paris: Les Belles Lettres, 2005), pp. 207–11.

CHAPTER 30: FACING REALITY

217   *"Zekkei—zekkei"*: *Chi o oyogu,* p. 21.

219   *"This* monsieur *is a* grand maître*"*: Ibid., p. 33.

219   *"My friends advised me"*: Buisson and Buisson, *Léonard-Tsuguharu Foujita,* p. 189.

219   *"[Kōno] had to close down"*: Ogisu, *Watakushi no Pari,* p. 118.

220   ON 14TH GERMAN FORCES: *Chi o oyogu,* p. 64.

220   *"The memories of my long years"*: Ibid.

220   *"Of course, Foujita had"*: *Fujita Tsuguharu to Ekōru do Pari,* p. 163.

221   *"The reasons for France's defeat"*: *Chi o oyogu,* p. 71.

221   *"land of the gods"*: Ibid., p. 61.

221   *"Let's give up all luxuries"*: Ogisu, *Watakushi no Pari,* p. 126.

222   *"My kappa has seemed strange"*: *Tōkyō nichi nichi shinbun,* August 7, 1940. Quoted in Sasaki.

222   *"He was a man"*: Ogisu, *Watakushi no Pari,* pp. 118–20.

CHAPTER 31: TO TOIL FOR THE NATION

223   *A recent study calculates:* Sasaki Shigeo, correspondence, 2005.

224   *"In the same way"*: Ashihara, p. 232.

224   *"The 'widely believed theory'"*: Monden Hideo, "Fujita Tsuguharu—sono sensōga seisaku made," *Han,* August 1977. Quoted in Sasaki, "Sengo."

225   *Nomiyama, the author:* Nomiyama Gyōji, "Sensōga to sono ato—Fujita Tsuguharu," in *Yonhyakuji no dessan* (Tokyo: Kawade Shobō, 1982), pp. 11–17.

227   *"Foujita did not reject"*: Ashihara, p. 240.

227   *"I am susceptible"*: Ibid., p. 242.

228   *"I have become stronger"*: Ibid., pp. 243–44.

CHAPTER 32: TALENT FOR THE JOB

231   *"Kindly set your mind at ease"*: Alvin D. Coox, *Nomonhan: Japan against Russia, 1939* (Stanford: Stanford University Press, 1985), p. 699.

232   *"the courageous, bold"*: *Tōkyō nichi nichi shinbun,* September 15, 1941. Quoted in Sasaki.

233   *"Listen,"*: Ashihara, pp. 232–33.

233   *"You don't pay the slightest":* Ibid., p. 234.

233   *"I experienced the awfulness":* Kondō, p. 189.

234   *His great passion:* See, for example, Imaizumi Atsuo, "Fujita Tsuguharu no gei-jutsu," *Shinbiijutsu,* March 1943.

234   *According to Mark H. Sandler:* Mark H. Sandler, "A Painter of the 'Holy War': Fujita Tsuguji and the Japanese Military," in *War, Occupation, and Creativity: Japan and East Asia, 1920–1960,* ed. Marlene J. Mayo and J. Thomas Rimer with H. Eleanor Kerkham (Honolulu: University of Hawaii Press, 2001), p. 200.

234   *"This painting depicts":* *Asahi shinbun,* April 22, 1941. Quoted in Sasaki.

235   *"This oil painting":* *Atorie,* August 1941. Quoted in Sasaki.

235   *In a recent television program:* *Kūhaku no jiden: Fujita Tsuguharu* (NHK documentary, September 23, 1999).

235   *"What do you think?":* Tanaka, p. 182.

237   *"At the entrance":* *Kokusai bunka,* February 20, 1942. Quoted in Sasaki.

237   *"Yes, I do paint them":* Ashihara, p. 268.

238   *"As you can see":* "Futsu-In yori kaerite," *Nanga kanshō,* March 1942, p. 4.

238   *"The night before December 8":* *Asahi shinbun,* December 5, 1942. Quoted in Sasaki.

CHAPTER 33: ARTIST AT WAR

240   *"Lieutenant Lookeast":* Ibuse Masuji, *Lieutenant Lookeast and Other Stories,* trans. John Bester (Tokyo and Palo Alto: Kodansha International, 1971), pp. 23–51.

241   *Ibuse begins his essay:* Ibuse Masuji, "Shingapōru de mita Fujita Tsuguharu," *Geijutsu shinchō,* December 1968.

242   *"This work is interesting":* Ibid.

242   *"But Foujita did not":* Ibid.

243   *"We would come back":* "Shingapōru de no Fujita to watakushi," *Sansai,* March 1968.

243   *"We really had a great time":* Ibid.

245   *"All ties with the French art world":* *Tōkyō nichi nichi shinbun,* December 1-2, 1942. Quoted in Sasaki.

245   *"Farewell to the European Art World":* *Kaizō,* February 1943. Quoted in Sasaki.

246   *"Moreover, for many years":* *Asahi shinbun,* January 7-8, 1943. Quoted in Sasaki.

247   *"Years ago I was very proud":* *Garon,* July 1943. Quoted in Sasaki.

248   *"I feel that I now":* "Sensōga ni tsuite," *Shinbijutsu,* February 1943, p. 2.

248   *"I want to paint perfect":* "Sensōga seisaku no yōten, *Bijutsu,* May 1944, p. 23.

249   *"Ah, Paris":* Kikuhata, *Ekaki to sensō,* p. 269.

249   *"Foujita went mad":* Ibid., p. 36.

250   *"They say that":* Ibid., p. 278.

250   *"At age seventy-three":* Ibid., p. 280.

CHAPTER 34: END IN SIGHT

251   *"In those days":* Ashihara Eiryō, "Fujita no shinjō," *Geijutsu shinron,* March 1968. Quoted in Sasaki, "Sengo."

251   *"Around this time":* Ashihara, pp. 270–72.

252 *"I am working on"*: Segi Shin'ichi, *Kakarezaru bijutsushi* (Tokyo: Geijutsu Shinchōsha, 1990), p. 207.
252 *He worked fourteen hours*: Imaizumi, "Fujita Tsuguharu no geijutsu," p. 30.
252 *"The old masters"*: Ibid., p. 209.
252 *"By creating these"*: Ibid., p. 210.
253 *Before the Americans reached*: Ushijima Hidehiko, *Attu-tō gyokusai sen: Ware tōdo no shita ni umore* (Tokyo: Kōjinsha, 1999). Quoted in Sasaki.
253 *"Every Japanese who could"*: *The Capture of Attu: Tales of World War II in Alaska* (Anchorage: Alaska Northwest Publishing Company, 1985), p. 15.
253 *"Follow the example"*: Sasaki (commentary).
254 *"This year I tried"*: Segi, *Kakarezaru*, p. 209.
254 *"I saw old men"*: Natsubori, *Geijutsu shiron*, pp. 322–23.
255 *"She felt bitter"*: Kondō, p. 206.
255 *"Their food was sumptuous"*: Fujita Tsuguharu to Ekōru do Pari, p. 19.
255 *"Miyamoto, this arm of yours "*: Tanaka, pp. 205–6.
256 *"Somehow once in my life"*: Segi, *Kakarezaru*, p. 211.
256 *"Down there, the sea"*: Robert Sherrod, "The Nature of the Enemy," *Time*, August 7, 1944, in *Reporting World War II*, Part 2 (New York: Library of America, 1995), pp. 173–76.
257 *"We were about 200 meters"*: Quoted in Sasaki.
258 *"The faces of the people"*: *Asahi shinbun*, April 13, 1945. Quoted in Sasaki Shigeo, "Fujita no sensōga (1)," *Live & Review*, July 2000, p. 98.
258 *"Foujita's war paintings"*: Nagaoka Teruko, *Oite nao kokoro tanoshiku utsukushiku* (Tokyo: Sōshisha, 2000), p. 177.
258 *"Foujita had a sense"*: Sasaki, "Sengo" (commentary).

CHAPTER 35: THE WRETCHEDNESS OF DEFEAT

259 *More than 2.7 million Japanese*: John W. Dower, *Embracing Defeat* (New York: Norton/The New Press, 1999), p. 45.
259 *"blackened plain"*: Donald Richie, *The Donald Richie Reader* (Berkeley: Stone Bridge Press, 2001), p. 25.
260 *"Up to now"*: Nomiyama, "Sensōga to sono ato," p. 13.
260 *Looking at the situation*: Lucken, *Grenades*, p. 198ff.
261 *"too controversial"*: "Barse Miller's Award Winning Picture Removed from Show," *Art Digest*, May 1, 1932. Quoted in http://www.tfaoi.com/aa/3aa/3aa11.htm
261 *Miller had written*: Barse Miller letter to Margit Varga, April 7, 1942 (Washington, D.C.: Museum Division, Department of the Army, U.S. Army Center of Military History).
262 *"This office has located"*: Kawata Akihisa, "Sorera o dō sureba yoi no ka: Beikoku kōbunsho ni miru 'sensō kirokuga' sesshū no keii," *Kindai gasetsu*, no. 8, 1999, p. 17.
263 *"You don't hear"*: "Fujita yo yomigaere," *Yuriika*, May 2006, p. 51.
263 *"Was I the only person"*: Quoted in Sasaki, "Sengo."
264 *"I refuse to accept"*: Sasaki Shigeo, "Sengo no bijutsukai no sensō sekinin mondai," *Live & Review*, November 1999, pp. 29–30.
265 *"The Americans arrived"*: Dower, *Embracing Defeat*, pp. 23–24.
265 *"Those who just a month"*: Kazama Michitarō, *Yūutsu na fūkei* (Tokyo: Kage Shobō, 1983), p. 137.

265   *"I am the kind"*: *Asahi gurafu*, October 15, 1945. Quoted in Sasaki, "Sengo."

265   *"Not only does Takamura"*: Takamura Kōtarō, vol. 5, *Gendaishi tokuhon* (Tokyo: Shichōsha, 1978), p. 167.

266   *"Once the war ended"*: Sasaki, "Sengo" (commentary).

266   *"The patriotic sentiments"*: Sasaki, "Sengo" (commentary).

266   *"Fujita Tsuguji: In the creation"*: Sasaki, "Sengo no bijutsukai no sensō sekinin mondai," p. 49.

CHAPTER 36: A VISIT IN JUNE

268   *Certain basic facts in this episode*: For an extensive study of this incident and Foujita's postwar situation, see Sasaki Shigeo, "Fujita no Nihon dasshutsu," *Live & Review*, May 2000, pp. 70–82.

268   *"This reminds me"*: Kazama, *Yūutsu na fūkei*, p. 137.

269   *In 1957*: Funado Kōkichi, *Gadan* (Tokyo: Bijutsu Shuppansha, 1957), pp. 70–71.

270   *"Uchida was not"*: Kazama, *Yūutsu na fūkei*, p. 143.

270   *"I didn't start the war"*: NHK, *Kūhaku no jiden: Fujita Tsuguharu*; for Foujita's original statement, see Natsubori, *Geijutsu shiron*, p. 355.

271   *In an essay*: Nagai Kiyoshi, "Ano koro no koto, ima no koto," *Bijutsu undō*, September 2000, pp. 25–31.

272   *"When faced with"*: Natsubori, *Geijutsu shiron*, p. 299.

272   *"persecution"*: Ibid., p. 42.

CHAPTER 37: ENTER A NEW YORKER

273   *"small street insurrection"*: Harry Roskolenko, *When I Was Last on Cherry Street* (New York: Stein and Day, 1965), p. 87.

273   *"It was a hole"*: Ibid., p. 115.

274   *"comely, strident, Bohemian"*: Ibid., p. 57.

274   *Now Roskolenko had a chance*: For Roskolenko's account of the visit, see his *The Terrorized* (Englewood Cliffs, N.J.: Prentice-Hall, 1967), pp. 102–4.

274   *"When we arrived"*: Ibid., p. 102.

274   *"I have sold only"*: Ibid.

274   *"During the war"*: Ibid., p. 103.

274   *"It is very cold"*: Harry Roskolenko, Kennedy and Co. Galleries press release, 1947 (Harry Roskolenko papers, 1928–81, Syracuse University Library).

275   *"No, only five dollars"*: Roskolenko, *The Terrorized*, p. 104.

275   *"I did what Foujita asked"*: Ibid.

275   *"The war years"*: *Time*, September 8, 1947.

276   *"Kuniyoshi, whom Foujita"*: Roskolenko, *The Terrorized*, p. 171.

CHAPTER 38: BONDS OF FRIENDSHIP

277   *Only Foujita's side*: Foujita's letters to Henry Sugimoto are in the Henry Sugimoto Archive, Hirosaki National Resource Center, Japanese American National Museum, Los Angeles.

278   *"I was surprised,"*: Natsubori, *Geijutsu shiron*, p. 375.

278 *Born in Japan in 1900*: For more about Sugimoto's life and works, see Kristine Kim, *Henry Sugimoto: Painting an American Experience* (Los Angeles and Berkeley: Japanese American National Museum and Heyday Books, 2000).

279 *"Some Occupation officers"*: Natsubori, *Geijutsu shiron*, p. 375.

280 *"You also should go"*: Iwasaki Taku, *Gaka: Gakubuchi no nai jigazō* (Tokyo: Jitsugyō no Nihonsha, 1957), pp. 17–19.

281 *"Some of my colleagues"*: Natsubori, *Geijutsu shiron*, p. 373.

281 *"Paris Gets Revenge"*: Kondō, p. 240.

281 *"If I could go abroad"*: *Nishi Nihon shinbun*, October 6, 1947. Quoted in Sasaki, "Sengo."

282 *"I'm disgusted with these artists"*: Iwasaki, *Gaka*, p. 19.

282 *"It was said that their"*: Sasaki Shigeo, "Fujita no Nihon dasshutsu," p. 78.

283 *"Come now, the war's over"*: Barbara Thoren, "The Week in Art," *Japan Times*, January 16, 1977.

283 *"We had also accumulated"*: Natsubori, *Geijutsu shiron*, p. 375.

283 *"Artists, create paintings"*: *Atorie*, August 1949. Quoted in Sasaki, "Sengo."

CHAPTER 39: IMPERFECT REFUGE

284 *"I feel free"*: Foujita letter to Frank Sherman, *Āteisuto no e-tegami ten: Fujita Tsuguharu kara gendai sakka made* (Tokyo: Meguro-ku Bijutsukan, 2000), letter 13.

284 *"New York is unexplainable"*: Ibid., letter 15.

284 *"To-day was wonderful"*: Ibid., letter 26.

284 *"I will never forget"*: Quoted in Sasaki, "Sengo."

286 *"militarist" and "collaborator"*: Natsubori, *Geijutsu shiron*, p. 377.

286 *"Mr. Peck"*: Foujita letter to Frank Sherman, *Āteisuto no e-tegami ten*, letter 28.

286 *"He disliked and shunned me"*: Natsubori, *Geijutsu shiron*, p. 378.

286 *"The other day we went"*: Foujita letter to Frank Sherman, *Āteisuto no e-tegami ten*, letter 40.

287 *"one of the year's slickest shows"*: *Time*, November 21, 1949.

287 *"A more recent type"*: *Art News*, November 1949, p. 51.

287 *"the fascist artist"*: *The Daily Compass*, November 24, 1949. Quoted in Kawashima Kazuho, "The Life and Art of Foujita Tsuguharu, and Ben Shahn's Condemnation," *Journal of Naniwa College*, no. 22, 1998, p. 352.

288 *"His most successful"*: Ibid.

CHAPTER 40: DOORS CLOSED

292 *"I built this chapel"*: *Time*, October 28, 1966.

292 *"It was thanks to God"*: Quoted in Sasaki, "Sengo."

292 *In 1965, Foujita received*: The book is Natsubori Masahiro, *Fujita Tsuguharu geijutsu shiron*.

292 *"I was just an artist"*: Ibid., p. 379.

293 *"I'm a person"*: Ibid., p. 18.

FOR FURTHER READING

For more about Paris in the 1920s and Foujita's role in it, Billy Klüver and Julie Martin's *Kiki's Paris: Artists and Lovers, 1900–1930* (New York: Harry N. Abrams, 2002) is essential. The standard work about Japanese artists in Paris is *Paris in Japan: The Japanese Encounter with European Painting* (Tokyo and St. Louis: The Japan Foundation and Washington University, 1987). A newer catalogue, which expands upon this theme, is *Japan and Paris: Impressionism, Postimpressionism, and the Modern Era* (Honolulu: Honolulu Academy of Arts, 2004).

In the United States, two essays by art historians have focused on Foujita's war paintings. These are "Embodiment/Disembodiment: Japanese Painting During the Fifteen-Year War," by Bert Winther-Tamaki, in *Monumenta Nipponica* (summer, 1997, pp. 145–80). Mark H. Sandler's essay is "A Painter of the 'Holy War': Fujita Tsuguji and the Japanese Military" in *War, Occupation, and Creativity: Japan and East Asia, 1920–1960* (Honolulu: University of Hawaii Press, 2001). Sandler has written another essay about this period, "The Living Artist: Matsumoto Shunsuke's Reply to the State—Japan 1868: Art, Architecture, and National Identity," in *Art Journal*, September 22, 1996. The essay is available online (http://www.findarticles.com/p/articles/mi_m0425/is_n3_v55/ai_18798613).

In France, Michael Lucken has written extensively about Japanese war paintings, including much about Foujita, in *Grenades et amertume: Les peintres japonais à l'épreuve de la guerre, 1935–1952* (Paris: Les Belles Lettres, 2005). Lucken has written a more general survey in *L'art du Japon au vingtième siècle* (Paris: Hermann, 2001). The catalogue *L'École de Paris 1904–1929, la part de l'Autre* (Paris: Musée d'Art Moderne de la Ville de Paris, 2000) provides a general survey of the artists of the School of Paris.

For collections of Foujita's works, see *Léonard-Tsuguharu Foujita* by Sylvie and Dominique Buisson (Paris: ACR Édition, 1987). A second volume by Sylvie Buisson was published in 2002. Much biographical material is included. Sylvie Buisson's *Foujita, le maître japonais de Montparnasse* (Paris: Conseil Municipal de Dinard et Musée du Montparnasse, 2004) contains lesser-known works, many from early in Foujita's career. The collection *Fujita Tsuguharu gashū*, published in Tokyo by Kōdansha in 2002, has beautiful reproductions and photographs of Foujita.

In Japanese, there are several biographies of Foujita for the general reader. Until recently, the most important has been Tanaka Jō's *Hyōden: Fujita Tsuguharu* (Toyko:

Shinchōsha, 1969), a thorough but frequently censorious look at Foujita's life. This has been counterbalanced by Kondō Fumito's *Fujita Tsuguharu: "Ihōjin" no shōgai* (Tokyo: Kōdansha, 2002), which tends to take Foujita's side. The memoir by Foujita's nephew Ashihara Eiryō in *Watakushi no hanjijoden* (Tokyo: Shinjuku Shobō, 1983) is full of strong opinions, too, but Foujita comes alive here as nowhere else. Yuhara Kanoko's *Fujita Tsuguharu: Pari kara no koibumi* (Tokyo: Shinchōsha, 2006) is the newest and most objective biographical study.

A novel by Kiyooka Takayuki, *Maronie no hana ga itta* (Tokyo: Shinchōsha, 1999), became popular in Japan for its fictional depiction of the liberated lives of Japanese in Paris between the two world wars. There are long sections about Foujita.

FOR FURTHER VIEWING

Many of Foujita's works are viewable online, particularly his cats.

In the United States, I could find only one major Foujita work on display at a public museum, *Portrait of Mrs. Emily Crane Chadbourne* at the Art Institute of Chicago. In Boston and elsewhere, I have heard rumors of works in private collections in the United States, but these remain unconfirmed.

Otherwise, Foujita's works are scattered far and wide, though the most important are in France and Japan. In Paris, the best places to see Foujitas are the Musée National d'Art Moderne, Centre Georges Pompidou (which has a Web site with major Foujita works viewable online) and the Musée d'Art Moderne de la Ville de Paris. There's an excellent portrait of the Marquise de Ganay at the Château Courance (the portrait is on the chateau's Web site). The gleaming murals Foujita created for the Maison du Japon at the Cité universitaire have been extensively restored and are worth seeing. Other important Foujitas are owned by the Musée des Beaux-Arts in Lyon, the Musées Royaux des Beaux-Arts in Brussels, and the Petit Palais, Musée d'Art Moderne, Geneva.

In Tokyo, the Bridgestone Museum of Art often exhibits its wonderful Foujitas. The National Museum of Modern Art has the entire collection of Foujita's war paintings (which are infrequently displayed) and other works. The Meguro Museum of Art has works from the Frank E. Sherman collection, including the illustrated letters Foujita wrote to Sherman in English from New York City.

It is worth a trip to the Ōhara Museum of Art in Kurashiki to see *Before the Ball* splendidly displayed among other works by Foujita's contemporaries. Hirano Masakichi was a major collector of Foujita's works, and his collection, including the huge mural *Seasonal Events in Akita*, is at the Hirano Masakichi Museum of Fine Art in Akita City.

ACKNOWLEDGMENTS

I would like to thank Mrs. Foujita Kimiyo for granting me permission to reproduce Foujita's works.

In the course of tracing Foujita's life, I have received assistance from people in assorted countries who have devoted much time to my questions, both large and small. The generous support of the Japan Foundation made this book possible. In Paris, I was part of Columbia University's Institute for Scholars, and Danielle Haase-Dubosc, Mihaela Bacou, and Maneesha Lal were unfailingly helpful during my months in Foujita's adopted home. My colleagues at the Institute, in particular Herman Lebovics and Steve Ungar, showed me the sights and made my stay in Paris memorable.

I simply could not have written this book without the assistance of Foujita specialists Hayashi Yōko and Sasaki Shigeo in Tokyo. They have provided me with materials and answered endless questions at every stage of my research. I am deeply grateful to them for their many insights, and also for their patience.

No less important is my amazing friend Teruko Craig, who checked through my manuscript with speed and care. She has also been my diligent consultant throughout.

J. Thomas Rimer has been important from the very start. I am indebted to him for his research advice, and also for his enthusiasm and kindness.

In Paris, Martine Grout went out of her way to assist me, a total stranger when we first met. She not only gave me detailed instructions about how to use the French libraries—encouraging me when I faced failure—but in many ways made me feel at home in Paris. Jean-Luc Berthommier of the Bibliothèque littéraire Jacques Doucet has given me invaluable assistance, and Claude Bernés allowed me to use his archives.

Kondō Fumito in Tokyo took the time to discuss his views of Foujita and helped me meet Foujita's former friends and associates.

Just up the street from me in Watertown, Massachusetts, Haruko Aoki Iyer has had a number of her days disturbed by my emergency questions. I am grateful to her for the scrupulous attention she gives to my research troubles.

I did much of my research at the library of the Museum of Contemporary Art, Tokyo, where the staff helped me find my way to many research materials. Close to home, the Harvard-Yenching Library is the next best thing to being in Tokyo.

Mary Few carefully read through the manuscript, and her suggestions, as always, made me rethink many issues.

I met Julie Martin and the late Billy Klüver just before I went to Paris, and they supplied me with important names and places. Meeting them was crucial to my research, and I still rely upon Julie's advice.

Josiane Peltier has cheerfully served as my French adviser.

As he has done repeatedly in the past, Asai Kiyoshi went out of his way to help.

For Foujita's journey to Latin America, I have received help from Niurka Elena Benavides, Susannah Joel Glusker, Rosario Hiriart, Ana Maria Leary, Nora Nava Maldonado, and Iris Russo.

In addition to those whose interviews appear in the text, I would like to thank the following people for their cooperation: Emily Anderson, Jacques Boutersky, Claire-Akiko Brisset, Ikuko Burns, Albert Craig, Yves Dodeman, Joe Earle, Allan Guggenheim, Hamao Masako, Ihara Otoaki, Kajiyama Miyoko, Lindsey Kiang, Kristin Kim, Barbara and Lloyd Lillie, Michael Lucken, Sheila Mabry, Fréderique Martingo, Masunaga Seiichi, Margaret Mitsutani, Mori Kazu, Murayama Shizuka, Ogisu Miyoko, Donald Richie, Lynne Riggs, George T. M. Shackelford, Suenaga Taneo, Takahashi Chikako, Takechi Manabu, Takei Masako, Rosabelle Tarnowska, Jean-Jacques Tschudin, Shukuko Voss-Tabe, Yamanashi Emiko.

My special thanks to my editor, Linda Rosenberg.

My agent, Fifi Oscard, died just before I completed this manuscript. She was very enthusiastic about this project, and I hope that she would have been pleased with the finished product.

INDEX

NO 3 0 '06

DATE DUE

FEB 2 1 2007		
MAR 3 0 2007		
APR 1 4 2007		
MAY 2 2 2007		
MAY 1 4 2007		
NOV 1 6 2014		

Demco, Inc. 38-293